Ensuring
Student Success

Ensuring
Student Success

A Handbook of
Evidence-Based Strategies

Myles I. Friedman

EDIE

THE INSTITUTE FOR EVIDENCE-BASED
DECISION-MAKING IN EDUCATION, INC.

Library of Congress Catalog Card Number: 00-107303
ISBN: 0-9666588-1-7

First published in 2000

The Institute for Evidence-Based Decision-Making in Education, Inc.
A South Carolina non-profit corporation
P.O. Box 122, Columbia, SC 29202

Printed in the United States of America

The paper used in this book complies with the
Permanent Paper Standard issued by the National
Information Standards Organization (Z39.48–1984).

10   9   8   7   6   5   4   3   2   1

In memory of Benjamin S. Bloom,
a masterful educational researcher
and progenitor of many able disciples.
In addition to his many cutting-edge
contributions, he taught his students
how to do significant research and
how to derive meaning from the
research of others.

Contents

Acknowledgments

I want to thank Dr. John B. Hawley for contributing to the publication of this book. I am deeply indebted to Dr. John King and Dr. Marvin Efron for guiding and investing in the development and dissemination of the book, and to Drs. Lorin Anderson, Carolyn Evertson, Lawrence Lezotte, Robert Slavin, Martin Solomon, Arthur Stellar, and John Anderson for critiquing and improving the prepublication manuscript. I also want to acknowledge Drs. Carole Flake, Nancy Freeman, James Dreyfuss, and Ron Leslie for providing research necessary for the development of the book, and Betty Friedman and John Donohue for preparing the manuscript. Finally, I am very grateful to Dr. Glenda Sternberg for contributing so much to the chapter "Implementing Corrective Tutoring."

Introduction

The primary purpose of this book is to help educational change agents and educators to ensure student success through high school by implementing educational practices that research shows to be effective. Far too many students fail to achieve high school learning objectives. As you will see in Chapter 1, "Education's Crucial Challenge," the problem is much more severe than is revealed in data reported by educational institutions. Our schools are turning out more undereducated students than America should tolerate, students who become a chronic burden to society and, for the most part, are incapable of fulfilling their own aspirations. While business and industry are crying out for professionals capable of filling high-tech positions, they are laden with the need to teach basic math and language skills to new employees to qualify them for entry-level jobs. The problem is America's problem. It drains America's vitality. The problem will be solved when there is a substantial reduction in the number of student failures who do not receive a valid high school education.

This problem became critical primarily because of our government's heroic initiatives to educate all of our citizens, a feat that has never been achieved in any nation. As a result, our schools were forced to accommodate and educate vast numbers of disadvantaged and handicapped students who were previously educationally neglected and ignored. Although frequently blamed, our schools do not bear major responsibility for the problem. However, they are, for the most part, responsible for achieving a solution. The goal is laudatory. Our Constitution promises equal opportunity for all. The challenge is onerous. Still, much more can and should be done. It's time to accelerate our progress.

To solve the problem, American educational institutions must base many more of their decisions on research findings. Vast sums of money have been spent over the years to fund thousands upon thousands of research studies. There is much more to be gleaned from these studies to improve educational practice than has been put into practice to date. So far the results of research studies have been used mostly to support conclusions in scholarly publications. Otherwise, the results tend to gather dust on library shelves and in data banks. The research results need to be interpreted and translated in easy-to-understand language so that they can be applied by educational practitioners to increase student achievement.

In this book, most prescriptions proffered for ensuring student success in school are based on research evidence. References are cited should you wish to review the research. To begin to reduce the number of student failures, the prescriptions need to be seriously considered for adoption by educational institutions. Care has been taken to support rather than preempt the decision-making prerogatives of the practitioner. Whenever possible options are described for the decision-maker to consider.

Since it is impossible to consider in one book all factors that might affect student achievement, the options described in Part II of this book will focus on prescriptions that research shows improve instruction and the instructional environment. Although school buildings, administration, counseling, equipment, busing, and other factors may be essential to schooling, instruction has the most direct and potent effect on learning. Furthermore, the sole purpose of schools is to instill desired learning. As will become clear in Chapter 2, research shows that student achievement can be substantially increased by improving the instruction that students receive.

The intended audience for the book is activists who work diligently to improve student achievement, including legislators, school board members, educational administrators, teachers, representatives of educational organizations, business organizations, government agencies, and dedicated citizens.

The book is divided into two parts. Part I, "Key Issues," defines and clarifies critical issues and problems that need immediate attention. After the central problem is defined in Chapter 1, it is analyzed in Chapter 2, "Meeting the Challenge," and a fresh approach to a solution is identified that can be pursued within necessary constraints imposed by present educational practices. However, many educational practices that have been regarded as necessary and are not must be changed. Tradition and necessity are two different things. Although we need to be careful not to throw the baby out with the bath water, we must be able to discern the baby from the bath water and to avoid being bloated with bath water that should be flushed down the drain. Educators have a way of convincing policy makers that arbitrary practices cannot be dispensed with.

Once realistic parameters for deriving solutions are established in Chapter 2, the remainder of the chapter deals with types of interventions that are needed to obtain a solution. This provides the foundation for prescribing more specific solutions in Part II, "Prescriptions." Chapter 3, "Implementing Corrective Tutoring," prescribes methods of providing corrective tutoring for students who need it to enable them to progress in school with their classmates. Corrective tutoring is shown by research to be effective in preventing student failure. Chapter 4, "Making Instruction More Effective," describes 15 instructional strategies that research shows to be effective in increasing academic achievement. They can be incorporated readily in ongoing instructional programs. The more the strategies are employed by teachers, the more successful the teachers are likely to be. In Chapter 5, "Promising and Generic Instructional Strategies" are described. The promising strategies are described because they are distinct from and complement the 15 instructional strategies presented in Chapter 4. Although some research confirms their effectiveness, local pilot testing is needed before they are adopted for classroom practice. Generic instructional strategies are described because they are distinctive in their own way. They incorporate a number of instructional strategies and represent an instructional system. Chapter 6, "Empowering Students to Learn on Their Own," describes strategies students can be taught to enable them to learn without instruction. This not only helps them to succeed in school, it is a key to lifelong independent learning. Chapter 7, "Preventing Impediments to Learning," describes school factors that can and do impede learning if allowed to prevail. Chapter 8, "Effective Preschool Instruction," prescribes methods that research shows to be effective in improving the academic achievement of preschoolers. By using these methods, young children can gain a real head start in school.

Chapter 9, "Teaching Students to Innovate," is a departure from the preceding chapters, which primarily focus on ways to reduce student failure. In this chapter students are taught how to create innovations to advance knowledge, consumer products, the standard of living, and the quality of life. To keep a competitive edge America must continue to introduce innovations, like computers, to the rest of the world. Schooling should not only perpetuate the American culture, it should help advance American interests.

Instead of proposing a single structured program as a panacea for meeting the challenge described in Chapters 1 and 2, a sizable number of varied prescriptions are described. This enables educational institutions to plan their own program, incorporating a combination of prescriptions that serve their purpose and accommodate their local constraints. This book is designed to be a resource for making informed decisions to improve instruction and learning. Almost all of the prescriptions in the book are shown by research to enhance academic achievement. They merit your consideration.

Key Issues

To clarify and not oversimplify problems, key issues are specified first and then contextual factors that bear on them are described. Impinging contextual factors need to be taken into account to effectively resolve problems.

In Chapter 1, the key issue addressed is the need for American educational institutions to reduce student deficiencies and failures. The relevant contextual factors considered are the social values and mandates imposed on public schools by our Constitution. They profoundly influence the functioning of our schools.

In Chapter 2, the key issue or question addressed is: How can student deficiencies and failures be reduced? Seminal research in Chapter 2 shows that student deficiencies and failures can be reduced by modifying the instruction students are given. (Modifications are evaluated and prescribed in the remainder of the book.) Relevant contextual issues are considered next. Educational institutions provide the context that determines how instruction is provided. Therefore, institutional factors that intrude upon and affect the instructional process are assessed as significant contextual variables.

1

Education's Crucial Challenge

The purposes of this chapter are to identify, define, clarify, and, to the extent feasible, estimate the magnitude of educational problems that need to be addressed.

American schools have been under attack ever since *A Nation at Risk* was published by the National Commission on Excellence in Education in 1983. In response, large sums of money were appropriated and spent to solve the problem over the succeeding years, with little to show for it. Unfortunately, we have failed to penetrate to the core of the problem and, as a result, efforts to solve it were doomed to fail. A fresh approach is sorely needed. Let us begin by reassessing student deficiency, because if our students were succeeding there would be little reason to be alarmed. Then let's consider some important effects American values have on American education, before solutions are prescribed in subsequent chapters of the book. American values have a potent, yet often subtle and oblique impact on the education of our youth.

STUDENT DEFICIENCY

The greatest educational problem facing America today is the vast number of our youths who do not achieve a valid high school education. As a result, they are ill prepared for (1) gainful employment in any but the most menial jobs, (2) postsecondary education of any kind, (3) parenthood, or (4) to contribute to the welfare of our nation. Many become social wards, criminals, and drug addicts. The magnitude of the problem is far greater than we have realized and we are much too willing to tolerate it, despite its drain on America's vitality.

Assessing the magnitude of the problem is not easy. We can begin with the dropout rate, which seems to be a favorite way of estimating the loss. It is a place to start, but by no means does it, in itself, reveal the size of the problem. The nature of the dropout problem will be discussed in Chapter 2. The size of the problem is of immediate concern but difficult to estimate because there is great variability in dropout rate estimates, depending on the criteria used to define dropouts. A tenable estimate of the national dropout rate is between 10% and 15%. However, for some disadvantaged inner city school districts it is reported to be as high as 50%. Educational institutions that would rather take credit for their successes than admit their contribution to the problem might claim that a 10%–15% dropout rate is proof of their success. They might suggest that the great majority of their students succeed and that some of their students are not educable.

Although dropouts are often considered to be problems of educational institutions, there is no need for the institutions to have lingering concerns about their dropouts. They are not a burden on educational institutions. Once they drop out they are someone else's problem. From society's perspective the outcome is not so rosy, considering the wasted human potential and burden that the dropout rate imposes on society. Furthermore, the dropout rate does not tell the whole or perhaps the real story. The student deficiency problem is more extensive, complex, and elusive than the dropout problem it encompasses.

Kindergarten through high school curricula are designed to enable students to graduate high school before the age of 19. Students who fall behind their age group along the way and do not graduate before 19 frequently become burdens, requiring a sizable investment in remedial and rehabilitative services. While in school academically deficient students and delinquents impose a burden; when they grow up many deficient students often become social wards. Delinquents often become criminals and progenitors of neglected children and impose a heavy burden on police, social workers, and other government agents.

People who do not receive a high school education by the age of 19 are a significant problem, able to contribute so little and in need of so much extra help, guidance, and control. The number of deficient students needs to be ascertained so that we can gauge the magnitude of the burden. Since no estimates could be found, one was devised by comparing the number of 18-year-olds in the nation in a given year to the number of high school graduates for that same year. For the year 1996 the approximate number of people in the United States attaining their eighteenth birthday by July 1, 1996 was estimated to be 3,789,000. For that same year the estimate for the number of high school graduates was 2,623,000. This indicates that for that year as much as 31% of this population of students did not earn their high school diploma when they were 18 years of age (U.S. Census Bureau, 1998). This is a report from only one year, and although adjacent years are similar, it should not be considered conclusive. But compared to a 10%–15% dropout rate, it shows that the burden school failures impose on society is much greater than is indicated by the dropout rate.

The loss deficient students impose on society is even more severe than is revealed by the high percentage of students who do not graduate high school before the age of 19. To attain a high school education it is necessary to achieve the learning objectives required through high school. Unfortunately, because of social promotion many students graduate high school without achieving all of the high school learning objectives and suffer handicapping learning deficiencies. They have not received a high school education. Receiving a high school diploma and a high school education are not the same.

Moreover, a great many social promotions are awarded. In recent years, as we became more and more a litigious society, militancy has grown by leaps and bounds. Teachers have been assailed for giving low grades and challenged to defend them by irate students, parents, and their lawyers. Failing in school is intolerable to many and can leave an indelible blemish on student records. People will go to great lengths to avert failure and often do. Teachers feel particularly vulnerable when asked to defend their grades because most of them have not been taught how to construct accurate achievement tests or conduct accurate evaluations. As a result, they have become reluctant to give failing grades and to defend them. Moreover, under duress school administrators have been known to find ways to circumvent student failure.

When social promotion occurs there is never a record of it, so there is no direct way to determine how rampant it is. So far the best way to estimate its effects is to observe its aftermath in college and the workplace. In 1995, 29% of college freshmen were enrolled in remedial reading, writing, and math courses (U.S. Department of Education, 1998). In the workplace employers report that they spend approximately 14.2% of their training time teaching elementary reading, writing, arithmetic, English language skills, and other fundamentals. Forty-six point nine percent of employees reported receiving such remedial training during their current employment (Bureau of Labor Statistics, 1995).

Since high school curricula are designed to enable students to achieve learning objectives through high school before the age of 19, age 19 is considered as a standard for comparison, recognizing that all standards are arbitrary and subject to criticism. Achieving high school learning objectives by the age of 19 is more a target to aim for than anything else, with the understanding that all students cannot be expected to achieve the target and that it can sometimes be beneficial to hold students back from progressing with their age group. For example, it may be advisable to enroll late-developing children in the first grade when they are 7 instead of with their 6-year-old age mates to facilitate their success in school. Passing scores on an agreed-upon high school equivalency test or battery of tests can serve to indicate when the standard has been minimally achieved. Youths who do not achieve high school learning objectives by age 19 will be referred to as student failures, not meaning to imply that they are hopeless.

It is clear that the number of student failures is significantly greater than the approximate 31% of 18-year-olds who fail to graduate high school. Although records of social promotions are not kept, reports from colleges and the business world make it clear that a large number of high school graduates do not know the fundamentals of reading, writing, and arithmetic. The fact that illiterates and near illiterates graduate high school is not new. The magnitude of the problem is stunning. Business and industry have complained about the problem for a long time and have given impetus and money toward school reform, but still the problem persists. Many reasons have been given to explain why our nation is at risk. A primary and most critical reason is because there are far too many student failures in the United States.

Student failures are debilitated citizens suffering from a learning deficit that incapacitates them. Although student failures do not die from their malady, both they and society are handicapped by it. To better appreciate the size of the problem, consider that the United States has approximately 275,000,000 citizens. Considering a dropout rate of from 10% to 15%, about 27 million to 40 million of our citizens are socially debilitated. Considering a student failure rate of over 30%, over 80 million of our citizens are socially debilitated. Considering the number of students who graduated high school by social promotion, the problem is even more severe. If over 80 million of our citizens were debilitated by a physical disease, we would declare an epidemic and a national emergency. But because student failures have no physical symptoms, they are much easier to ignore.

Some problems can be expected to abate with the passage of time. However, there is a very real threat that the student deficiency problem will exacerbate, or at least become more evident, in the future because of increased accountability legislation. In many states it is necessary to pass tests that measure achievement of competency standards to be promoted and to graduate high school. This effort to raise standards and to curb social promotion as well as the number of education illiterates that graduate high school will expose a greater number of deficient students who need attention. It will also create pressure for more remedial instruction in schools which, as you will see in the next chapter, is critical if the deficient student rate is to be reduced. Furthermore, the raising of achievement standards may well increase the number of deficient students.

Ostensibly on the brighter side, over 60% of our students seem to progress through school without a great deal of difficulty. Most of these students, however, have well-educated parents who encourage them to attend school and help them succeed. One indicator of the strong relationship between parents' education and the academic achievement of their children is the high positive correlation between level of parents' education and their children's SAT scores (*The Future of Education*, 1994). So it is doubtful that our schools are entitled to full credit for the success of those students.

The growth and effectiveness of the home schooling movement leaves little doubt that a great many parents are disappointed with both our parochial and public schools, and many are quite capable of providing their children with a good education. Home-schooled children are required to pass state achievement tests, and recently a few won national academic contests, such as national spelling bees. For the most part, the arguments that home-schooled children are deprived of many benefits available in schools does not in reality hold up. Home schoolers are organized and see to it that their children have ample association with their peers in religious, cultural, and community organizations. Many of their children join scout troops for peer associations. Boy and girl school scout troops have laws that children learn and abide by. Violence and disorder are much less likely in scout troops than in today's schools. In addition, home schoolers employ specialists to teach subject matter that is beyond their capabilities; for example, advanced math and science. In most cases, home-schooled children are given appreciably more individualized instruction.

The fundamental purpose of education is often said to be *to perpetuate society*. Presently this purpose is not being fulfilled; too many of our youth are incompetent in basic language, math, and other social skills. There is much more that American education can do to remedy the problem, as will be shown in subsequent chapters. Furthermore, we need more relevant and comprehensive data to evaluate the extent to which this purpose is being achieved. Data presently available falls far short. Typically, educational institutions do not assess their impact on society. It needs to be done. Only when the impact of public education on society is comprehensively evaluated is it possible to see that there is a profound problem, not a "manufactured crisis." It is not difficult to emphasize the strengths of public education by selectively analyzing public school data in isolation. For instance, all that is necessary is to publicize student academic successes and exclude student failures.

In conclusion, the magnitude and seriousness of the problems facing American education are not immediately evident looking at contributing factors independently, as is so often the case. It is only by probing level by level to uncover pieces of evidence and then relating them to one another that the depth and breath of the problems can be revealed and understood. The dropout problem cannot be solved without solving the student failure problem because, as will be shown in the next chapter, most dropouts are failing before they drop out. The student failure problem cannot be solved without addressing the social promotion problem because students who are socially promoted do not achieve high school learning objectives and are not ready for a college education or for employment in any but the lowest-level jobs. And the burden that is imposed on business and industry to provide instruction in basic language and math to prepare people for employment cannot be alleviated until students are given a valid high school education in school. However, as you will learn in subsequent chapters, the student failure problem can be alleviated.

Now that the primary problem to be addressed in subsequent chapters—student failure—has been defined and explained, there is a need to consider contextual problems that must be taken into account if the primary problem is to be solved. Oftentimes problems are not solved because impinging contextual factors are not dealt with. The following are contextual factors endemic to the American way of life. These factors are rooted in our Constitution and influence the lives of all Americans and American institutions. They add complexity to public education and create serious problems for public schools when they are not carefully managed. To be more effective, American educational institutions must consider more diligently their impact on the American way of life as well as the impact the American way of life has on their mission and operation. Since the purpose of this chapter is to define and explain problems, to alert and orient the reader contextual problems emanating from our Constitution and affecting education and child rearing will be identified and explained in the next section. It is beyond the scope of this book to amass research to confirm assertions about the contextual influences to be discussed. Volumes have been written about each topic covered under the heading "Education and the American Way." Some research was cited to help define the central problem. The majority of the research cited in this book is presented in Part II to verify the efficacy of techniques prescribed to reduce student failure.

EDUCATION AND THE AMERICAN WAY

Democracy has emerged as the government system of preference, and nondemocratic countries are struggling to reap the benefits of our way of life. Our democracy serves as the paragon for most emerging nations, who must build theirs amid the turmoil of conflicting constituencies that have struggled to preserve their cultural heritage over the centuries and against external enemies who would dominate or subjugate them. Today their hope for democracy presses on, confronted with continuing internal strife among factions that think differently, talk differently, and live differently, and threats from their neighbors. They see the United States as a pluralistic society that, despite the many internal eruptions that could have dismantled our government and the constantly changing ethnic makeup of our society, has made democracy work. They see a high standard of living and a world power—a model to emulate with hope for success.

But the world at large is not nearly so impressed with our educational system. It is generally acknowledged that we are largely responsible for English becoming the language of world commerce, and that the preponderance of books published in English enable people everywhere to share in human lore and advancements. They can learn of our know-how as well as the contributions of great thinkers of the world. However, concerned people here and abroad are puzzled. They have difficulty understanding how our nation, with so great a store of knowledge, so much technical ability, and such affluence can have schools that are so dismally ineffective. We are so proud to be Americans and enamored with the American way that we are apt to overlook its shortcomings and the problems it creates for education.

The large number of student failures is not the only evidence of the ineffectiveness of American schools. Our youth do not compare favorably with the youth of other nations in critical academic areas. Our youth score lower on science and math tests than youth of competitive democracies (Rosier & Keeves, 1991), and math and science competency is an essential requirement for high-tech jobs. However, in many of these comparisons the playing field is not level. Test scores of students in nations that only educate and test an elite segment of their population are compared to test scores of a much broader range of the American population, which includes many disadvantaged students who have not done well in school.

To begin to address the problem, let us first consider the American values that provide a foundation for our education system and need to be dealt with.

Free Enterprise and Education

One of the problems endemic to free enterprise is that it produces failures as well as successes, losers as well as winners. We have come to accept failures as an inevitable by-product of free enterprise. We tend to focus on the benefits of free enterprise in raising the standard of living and do very little about preventing and remediating failures. Instead we treat failures as social dependents who are sustained by charitable contributions from the rich and welfare from the government. Failures are thought of as unfortunate, sympathetic, and inferior. Economic failure tends to be equated to inferiority in general, and inferiority is far too often attributed to inherent traits, such as ethnic origin and stupidity. Sometimes ethnic origin and stupidity are equated.

Treating failures as an inevitable and tolerable result of free enterprise generates an economic caste system of haves and have-nots. Everything has a down side, and the benefits of free enterprise make the shortcomings well worth accepting. So failures are accepted as social dependents and there is little impetus to improve them, even if it were possible. The outcome is that social wards tend to remain as social wards and increase in number. They increase in number for many reasons. They produce more children, and in free enterprise as time passes the rich get fewer in number and the poor get greater in number. And the monetary gap between haves and have-nots widens.

Accepting failures as social wards creates a number of problems. There are more diseases, criminals, drug addicts, and neglectful parents among the downtrodden. And as they increase in number the problems are exacerbated. In addition, they place a greater and greater burden on the productive members of society. It costs more and more to maintain them. Not only does money need to be provided for them; money needs to be provided to create and maintain the charitable and government organizations to systematically donate to the needy.

The American penchant to label people as winners and losers and to demean losers makes failing so traumatic that Americans are prone to deny their own failure rather than face it. In American parlance one of the most disparaging names a person can be called is "loser." It suggests that one is pathetic and hopeless. The denial of failure is common on the institutional level as well as the personal level. All American organizations brag about their successes and downplay their failures. This is necessary to maintain esprit de corps. People want to identify with successful groups, not failing groups. This enables them to partake vicariously and glory in the group's success. On the other hand, people as well as rats abandon sinking ships. The attendance at football games rises when a team succeeds and falls when it makes a habit of losing. The allegiance of sports fans is a fascinating study. They support, encourage, cajole, and coach their team. They forgive their mistakes, argue their causes, and vociferously try to demoralize the opposition. Such devotion, investment, and hard work makes them feel that they had a hand in the outcomes of their team's contests. Devout fans are elated when their team wins and grief-stricken when they lose. Continuing victories make them buoyant and strengthen the bond; continuing losses are endured but fray the bond. Extended losing records may eventually cause fans to transfer their affection and attention elsewhere, where they have expectations of being repaid for their devotion.

When people join groups they are expected to support and show allegiance to the group, whether they become employees of an enterprise or members of a fraternal organization. Members who cast aspersions on their group are considered dissidents, even traitors, and may be scolded, ostracized, or discharged depending on the seriousness of the offense. However, when group failures outweigh group successes by a wide margin, the failures become more difficult to tolerate and hide. Group allegiance becomes strained and the organization is more likely to disintegrate.

Formal organizations tend to be regulated by law. Sometimes the laws hold the organization accountable for success and failure, and provide for the monitoring and dissolution of organizations that fail to fulfill their mission for an extended period. For instance, to succeed businesses must make a profit and disclose their profits and losses to government tax agents annually. Profit is tantamount to success and loss is tantamount to failure. When losses cannot be financed by the businesses and there is little hope for profits in the future, businesses file for bankruptcy and discontinue to operate.

Public educational institutions, like all formal organizations, are chauvinistic. They are quick to draw attention to their successes. They publicize the feats of their star students, faculty, and administrators. In routine speeches and news releases their leaders laud their achievements to faculty, staff, students, parents, and alumni, and promise greater success in the future. They admit that their institutions can improve but not that they have failed. And traditionally educational institutions have not been brought to task for their failure because, unlike businesses, there are no legal mandates for their dissolution. Public educational institutions go on and on in perpetuity despite their failures.

Although their only reason for being is to produce desired learning, educational institutions are almost never dissolved because they have failed to produce desired learning. When faced with the low achievement test scores of their students, they are facile in their machinations to deny blame. They may claim that they teach much more than is measured by the achievement tests used; that the achievement test scores were depressed because of the large number of poor students in their school(s); that present school conditions are not conducive to learning; that there are too few teachers to provide for students' needs; that there are too many disruptive students; that parents are not providing the support needed for their children to succeed; or that funding is insufficient. These are a few of many rationalizations offered for student failure. Commensurately, they draw attention to their many successes—students who have achieved awards, teachers who have been honored, extracurricular successes of sports and debate teams, for instance. In addition, they announce their plans for improvement and create expectations of future success.

And parents, local politicians, and alumni who have allegiance to the educational institutions help ward off attacks. So it is quite difficult to hold schools accountable for the failure of their students to learn, and there are seldom legal provisions to dissolve schools because an excessive number of their students fail to learn.

To make failure more difficult to deal with, students, as well as educational institutions, are prone to deny their failures and draw attention to their successes. And parents who closely identify with their progeny make matters worse. Most parents instill in their children the need to succeed, but if the parents do not value formal education they will not influence their children to succeed in school. They will inculcate in their children the need to succeed in some way outside of school. They might advocate success in acquiring welfare subsidies as they do, or to rise to become a leader of a neighborhood gang, or to become a neighborhood drug czar, or to become a successful thief, or they might stress the importance of obtaining a menial job as soon as possible to contribute to the family income, a job that does not require school learning. This, of course, makes it difficult for schools to impress upon children the value of succeeding in school. Disadvantaged youth are as interested in success as anyone, just not school success.

Advantaged parents do stress the importance of earning high grades in school. However, they create problems for their children by not tolerating school failure. They pressure both their children and educators to ensure that their children succeed in school. Their children are afraid to bring home low grades lest they be punished or reprimanded because the parents equate low grades to failure. Even if their children do not receive failing grades, unless they earn "A's" they are often admonished to improve. Many advantaged parents show a greater interest in their children receiving top grades than in what their children are learning. Instead of asking about their children's learning deficits and seeing what might be done to correct them, they rebuff their children for failing to live up to their expectations and pressure them to do better. They do not accept that any child of theirs cannot succeed in school with sufficient effort. They give their children the impression that they can and should succeed on their first attempt by the way they react to low grades. However inadvertent, this sends the wrong message. Constructive parents need to impart to their children that most goals in life are not achieved on the first attempt. There is nothing wrong with making mistakes; it is to be expected. To succeed they must face and correct their mistakes so that by trial and error and perseverance they will eventually succeed.

It does not help that some teachers give students the impression that they have only one chance to succeed. In oral question-and-answer sessions some teachers give students only one chance to provide the right answer and move from student to student until a correct answer is given. On the other hand, there are teachers who keep working with each student until with their prompting and guidance they are able to elicit the correct answer. The Socratic method is designed to elicit the correct answer from a student after the teacher uses successive questions to cue and guide the student to the correct answer.

All failures are prone to defensively deny their failures, whether the failure is personal or a group's failure. However, denial is very self-defeating because it falsifies reality. It shuts out a traumatic incident to maintain a favorable image. Moreover, shutting out reality precludes the opportunity to face failure and to make corrections in order to succeed. To overcome the natural penchant to deny failure, the least we can do for our children is to teach them that everyone fails in one way or another; it is to be expected. It is most important to face and analyze your failures so that you can learn from them and persist to succeed on a subsequent attempt. People are failures only when they think they are and no longer try to succeed.

Free Choice and Education

Free choice is a sacred right of Americans. However, it is not a right that should be given to young children. It overwhelms them. For children to feel secure they must be provided structure. They must be taught that there are limits to what they can do, and what the limits are, and be able to test and confirm the validity of the limits for themselves. Some of the limits children are taught pertain to natural environmental consequences caused by their actions. For instance, they will be burned if they touch a hot stove. Other limits pertain to social rules and laws created, imposed, and enforced by members of social groups such as families, schools, and governments. For children to feel secure social rules must be consistently condoned and enforced by parents and other teachers who must not arbitrarily punish children for displeasing them when the rules are not violated. To feel secure, people must know what to expect. Children want adults to protect them and to teach them how to protect themselves by defining safe limits that they can confirm for themselves.

Learning limits in general is the basis for learning that personal rights end where other people's noses begin, and that there are benefits in learning rules. Later on, when young children learn that their family is part of a larger community, they will be prepared to understand the benefits of obeying the law. Learning limits is an essential part of the socialization process, and if taught properly induces people to understand the need and benefits of laws, thereby creating harmony between society and its citizens as well as teachers and students. In Chapter 7 research is cited showing that classroom disruption is significantly reduced when teachers establish and enforce student rules of conduct.

Parents, other teachers, and nonconformists need to understand that absolute freedom is neither possible nor desirable. Absolute freedom is not possible because the environment always has consequences for people's actions. To survive, adapt, and flourish, people must learn the consequences of their actions. Absolute freedom is not desirable because people cannot tolerate an unpredictable, chaotic world that does not respond to their actions. Rules and laws are necessary for mental health as well as security. In addition to natural laws, people enact governmental rules and laws to make the consequences of their actions and the actions of others more predictable. Commerce of any kind would be impossible if people did not learn and abide by the same rules. Probably the most fundamental rules are rules of language, which enable people to communicate as a basis for sharing, cooperating, and transacting business with one another.

In recent years, child rearing and educational practices have become much more permissive, to the great disadvantage of our children and the people who associate with them. Overpermissiveness tends to make youth more insecure and more diffi-cult to manage and teach. The problem stems from the fact that rules of conduct are established and enforced much less often. Educators are no longer able to issue corporal and other punishment without fearing legal consequences. They are not only reluctant to discipline students, they are afraid to touch them. Restrictions on educators have prevented them from giving the warm personal attention students need—an ingredient that is critical to student development, one that teaching ma-chines and textbooks cannot provide. Overpermissiveness in the classroom courts disaster. Students are given license to act up, and as a result effective teaching is impossible.

Freudianism is partly responsible for the problem. Freudians teach us that trau-mas in early childhood cause neuroses and psychoses in later life. With this in mind, parents and other teachers became much more reluctant to take any punitive actions, lest they traumatize the child. This interferes with the enforcement of rules and with children learning limits. Outwardly children are more unruly; inwardly they are more insecure.

Another contributing factor is adults giving children freedom to make their own decisions long before they are ready. Children are ready to make a decision when they understand and are able to take the consequences of the decision, and not before. Allowing children to make decisions prematurely bewilders them, and at the very least makes them nervous. Upwardly mobile parents who take vicarious pleasure in showing off their children's precocious achievements frequently vic-timize their children by pushing them beyond their capabilities. They not only tend to expect more than their children are able to deliver, they tend to blame the teacher for their children's failures.

Students have free choice in whether they learn; they can ignore the teacher any time they choose. However, they do not have free choice in what they are taught, and it is misleading to give them the impression that in general they do. K–12 curriculum is designed for them. At most, in the lower grades they may be given choices of reading material when they are being taught to read and choices of top-ics when they are being taught to write. Students are given an increasing number of choices or electives as they progress from one grade level to the next. In college they can choose majors to prepare them for the career of their choice and minors and electives to satisfy their interests. School curricula should be and for the most part are designed to gradually, grade level by grade level, allow students greater choice as they become increasingly ready to understand and take the consequences for their choices. It is advantageous to give students a greater number of choices as they develop and learn; it is important not to misrepresent the latitude of their choices.

Equal Opportunity and Education

Equal opportunity under the law is a gift for which we can thank our forefathers. Although equal opportunity is an ideal, impressive progress has been made to ensure equal opportunity for a greater number of Americans. Mainly, in practice, equal opportunity under the law mitigates against unfairness, suppression, and persecution, but it does nothing to help people recover from failure. Although providing welfare is beneficent, it does not justify depriving failures of the assistance they need to succeed in the future and partake of the American dream. Moreover, being born with equal opportunity under the law by no means provides equal opportunity to succeed in America.

Equal opportunity to obtain an education is not good enough. As shown, the number of deficient students in America is too great a burden. There are too many social wards in America and not enough workers to fill the high-tech jobs required to keep America competitive. People who do not have at least a valid high school education do not have an equal opportunity to succeed; they have little or no opportunity. Education is mandatory under the law. Since our youth are required to attend school, we need to ensure that many more of them succeed in school. This requires that schools do more than they are doing now to help failing students overcome their deficits.

In addition, it is the schools' responsibility to teach students about equal opportunity, how it affects them and their relations with others. Students also need to be taught the limits of equal opportunity. For instance, people of different ages are provided different opportunities. They are allowed to drive a car at about 15 or 16, they are allowed to vote when they become adults, and they are allowed to apply for social security when they are elders.

Child development progresses gradually from egocentrism to ethnocentrism as the child's world expands over the years and children become increasingly aware of larger and larger communities of people and their relationships to those people. Young children live in a self-centered world. They are prepossessed with acquiring their wants and have little cognizance of or interest in the rights of others. They have no sense of equality. They think they have a right to everything they want and become very clever in working their parents to get what they want. They have insatiable appetites, and as soon as they get one thing they want they ask for another. Through social experience and education they eventually learn about their limited rights and the rights of others under law.

The first thing children learn about equal rights is to use to their advantage the principle of equal rights their parents have taught them. They often beseech their parents to buy them something because someone else has it, typically a family member or friend. When they are older many bright children from sophisticated families learn to use child psychology on their parents as an added inducement. To get a game a precocious boy of nine was heard saying to his parents, "My friend Johnny just got a video game and I need one too. It is very important for a child my age to have an educational game like that."

Young children should not be given the impression that they have an equal opportunity to get anything they want. To protect children they cannot be allowed to have equal access to the medicine cabinet, kitchen knives and appliances, and other dangerous things. They need to learn to tolerate privileges their parents, other adults, and older siblings have until they are able to deal with them safely. Later on in school, when they are in classes with children their own age, they can begin to learn about equal rights and opportunity. The teacher can establish for the class rules of student conduct and consequences for violating them and stress that all children in the class have the same rights, opportunities, and limitations according to the rules. Joining the Boy Scouts or Girl Scouts affords another opportunity to learn about equality under the rules.

Money, the American Panacea, and Education

Being a rich, capitalistic country, the United States is prone to overemphasize the things money can buy and to be blind to the limitations of purchasing power. Sayings such as "Every man has his price," "Rich or poor, it's good to have money," and "Money cannot buy happiness" are common parlance in America. Most judicial settlements under American civil law are monetary. Dollar amounts are awarded for pain and suffering, punitive damages, loss of body parts, and loss of life. It seems that almost everything can be equated to money in America, which gives the impression that you can have anything, do anything, and solve any problem if you have enough money.

To be elected, politicians need large sums of money for advertising. Wealthy people contribute money to their campaigns for political favors that make money for them. To be elected and reelected politicians please their constituency by arranging for government grants for local projects. The success of politicians is judged as much by the amount of money they appropriate, raise, and spend for good causes as by the actual goals they achieve. The success of businesses and industries is judged by the amount of money they make, and personal success and worth is associated with personal wealth. Government bureaucrats always press for budget increases and are quick to blame their inability to achieve their goals on a shortage of funds.

Educational institutions also attribute their failures to lack of funds and take every opportunity to obtain additional funding. They seek budget increases routinely for equipment, salary raises, buses, staff, faculty, school buildings, and so on. What is unusual about educational institutions is that they are rarely held accountable for achieving their primary mission—producing desired learning.

Politicians are held accountable at election time; businesses are held accountable at year-end, when their profit-and-loss statements are due. Educational institutions almost never issue routine statements revealing the desired learning they produced, nor cost/benefit analyses calculated to show the learning they produce compared to the money they spend. Although some efforts are being made recently to hold schools accountable, they are rarely held objectively accountable for the desired learning they produce.

No one denies the value of money, and the public and politicians alike stress the importance of education and are more willing to raise money to improve education than for almost any other purpose. Taxes are raised, lotteries are justified, community bazaars are conducted, and educational institutions establish charitable foundations, all to raise money for education. People support almost any kind of fund-raising for education to contribute to their children's future and to the welfare of our nation.

Unfortunately, there is precious little to show for the vast amount of money spent on education. And when educational institutions are pressed to show the value received for their expenditures, they rarely show that it has increased desired learning. More likely they will brag about the computers, books, or equipment they were able to buy, the buildings they were able to build, or the staff they were able to hire. We regularly see the value of our contributions to medical foundations when advancements in treatments are announced. Stringent research and development is conducted and applied to advance medicine. Stringent research is infrequently done in education and, most important, educational research and development findings far too seldom are applied to improve classroom practice. In short, insufficient funds are allocated for educational research. Too little of the research money appropriated for education is spent to improve instruction, the primary cause of learning, and available research facts that can be used to improve instruction are seldom used. Instead, in the name of progress, fads that have not been shown to increase learning are introduced into practice. All educational administrators seem to have innovations they want to introduce as proof of their leadership, but they rarely cite research to prove that their innovations are effective. Money is thrown at education haphazardly. Most of the money spent needs to be funneled to increase learning by improving instruction. Poorer nations that spend much less money on education have far fewer student failures than America has. They have greater success in less-modern schools that have fewer computers, inferior equipment, and fewer counselors, school psychologists, and staff. Brick and mortar, equipment, counselors, buses, and secretaries do not have the direct, potent effect on learning that instruction does. Poorer nations can and do provide effective instruction without spending the amount of money on education that we spend. Most of this book is devoted to prescriptions for effective instruction that research shows to be effective, prescriptions that are not costly to implement.

America's preoccupation with money as a panacea keeps us from appreciating the preeminence of education in solving America's problems. The major problem America has been attacking over the past 20 to 30 years is a syndrome of related maladies: (1) disease, (2) poverty, (3) crime, (4) drug addiction, and (5) educational illiteracy. To remedy these maladies we take our usual shotgun approach and spend large sums of money on all of them instead of looking for causal agents to attack, as they do in the medical sciences. However, we spend more money attacking poverty than any other of the maladies because poverty is the lack of money, and regarding money as a cure-all, we invest more money on welfare than anything else, including welfare for the elderly, the recently unemployed, the disabled, and the indigent.

As time passed and the number of people on welfare increased in comparison to the number of gainfully employed people, welfare became less and less affordable and too much of a burden on the productive. As a result, more of an effort has been made to find ways to return poor, disabled, and elderly people to the workforce. The movement is often justified by claiming that returning to the workforce is good for their self-esteem. Ultimately, sufficient productivity is needed to provide welfare.

It has become more evident in recent years that poverty or lack of money could not be the root cause of the maladies in the syndrome. We have found that families that have been given large welfare checks that sustain a standard of living far above the poor in Third World countries do not improve significantly with respect to disease, crime, drug addiction, and illiteracy. Rather, it seems that a welfare culture is created in which welfare customs are perpetuated from generation to generation, teaching children how to work the system for larger welfare checks and to avoid employment to ensure that welfare checks continue. Committing crimes, taking drugs, or contracting disease does not jeopardize receiving welfare checks, and schooling is not needed to work the welfare system. Government "workfare" programs have been introduced to replace welfare programs in order to break the welfare cycle because giving poor people money does not work.

It is equally naive to believe that reducing disease will cause a reduction in illiteracy, crime, drug addiction, and poverty. At most it might reduce the number of student absences. But disease does not appear to be a root cause of drug addiction, crime, illiteracy, or poverty. Nor does it seem feasible that drug addiction or crime are root causes of the syndrome, although drug addiction seems to be a cause of thefts and eventually disease.

On the other hand, there is every reason to believe that reducing educational illiteracy will cause a reduction in crime, poverty, drug addiction, and disease. It is well known that educated people earn more money than uneducated people and, therefore, have less need to commit crimes to subsist. It is quite possible that educated people are more resistant to drug addiction because they learn about the hazards. Education programs are responsible in large measure for the reduction in the number of smokers. In addition, educated people are able to keep themselves informed of disease prevention and cure regimens. They are more apt to learn how to prevent heart attacks and venereal and other diseases, and how to use hygienic routines.

Spending money on education may well substantially reduce the maladies in the syndrome, but only if spent judiciously to increase desired learning. There may be more than enough money spent on education now if much more of it were spent specifically to increase desired learning rather than for more peripheral purposes. Only by increasing learning can we reduce the large number of student failures in the United States.

I have heard the misguided use of money as a panacea aptly referred to as a disease, called "affluenza." Affluenza is particularly virulent when it infects family relations and child-rearing practices. Well-to-do parents who practice conspicuous consumption to elevate their social status and shower their children with money to supposedly give them all the benefits of life suffer from affluenza. However, money does not buy them enduring friends, nor their children's respect and affection. Nor does money buy their children the love, guidance, and familial support they need to flourish. Moreover, giving children excessive amounts of spending money, buying them almost everything they request, and providing lavish accommodations for them at home, in restaurants, and on vacations gives children the impression that money is easier to come by than it really is for most people, removes the need for them to earn money on their own, and overemphasizes the importance of money in life. Furthermore, it provides them with a standard of living difficult to maintain when they become breadwinners. It also gives them the impression that to be successful they must maintain that standard of living. However, being spared the need to work when they were younger, many of them as adults are ill prepared to compete to earn a living. When parents spend most of their time making, spending, donating, and talking about money and immersing themselves and their children in expensive acquisitions, they hardly have the time or inclination to learn about or indulge in good parenting practices.

Education and the Separation of Church and State

In countries that practice a national religion, religion is taught in school without creating conflicts or legal entanglements. In the United States, the separation of church and state gives rise to chronic moral controversy and litigation. Public schools walk a tightrope between two objectionable positions. On the one hand they are forbidden to teach religion in school. Efforts to teach religious edicts in school meet with protests from activists who vehemently guard the separation of church and state, including politicians and the American Civil Liberties Union. Ultimately our Supreme Courts settle legal controversies, and separation of church and state is on their agenda quite often.

On the other hand, schools are expected to enforce high moral standards, many of which have roots in religious teaching. When students report immoral conduct in school, enraged parents are quick to protest to school principals, superintendents, and political leaders. Moreover, public schools are assailed by the religious right when their teachings seemingly violate the sacred moral principles embedded in religion. Sometimes legal action is taken to stop schools from teaching allegedly blasphemous doctrine. For instance, in the Scopes trial (1925), teaching evolution in public school was contested. Many parents who refuse to tolerate the depravity they impute to public schools home school their children or send them to parochial school.

Most Americans belong to a religious sect of one persuasion or another. Many who don't adopt a moral code to live by. Virtually all parents want their children raised in a moral milieu according to some moral code, even if the moral code is limited to government law. Morals as the term is being used are simply defined in the dictionary as specifications of right and wrong conduct.

Not only will parents not tolerate immorality in the schools their children attend, it is impossible to operate a school conducive to learning without the school establishing a moral code to govern the conduct of teachers, school administrators, and students. Schools establish rules governing the conduct of educators, and high moral standards for educators are expected and enforced by parents and the community. It may be easier to discharge a teacher for immoral conduct than for failing to instill learning which teachers are responsible for instilling. Educators also become familiar with government laws to avoid legal vulnerability and prosecution. Touching students, search of students and seizure of their property, taking students off of school premises, and punishing students can subject educators to legal prosecution. Legal vulnerabilities often lead to the establishment of rules of conduct for school personnel, or at least the giving of advice. In addition, there are rules governing right and wrong, and mundane procedures specifying the way school personnel are to park their cars on school grounds, how to order supplies, and acceptable attire.

Although public schools are prohibited from teaching religion, they do teach morality. All schools routinely establish, teach, and enforce student rules of conduct. To enforce the rules they condone and reward compliance and punish violations by imposing penalties, suspension, and expulsion, depending on the frequency and severity of violations. Students soon learn that it is right to come to class on time, pay attention to the teacher, remember what they are taught, and complete class assignments on time. It is wrong to play hooky, to be late to class, to copy answers from another student's test, to disrupt the class, or to have someone else do your homework for you.

To perpetuate the American culture and prepare students for citizenship, our schools are obliged to teach the laws of the land. To perpetuate American core values, schools teach the Constitution and subordinate laws. In addition, students are taught how laws are enacted, executed, and interpreted by the three branches of our government. Citizens' morality is often taught under the title of civics. Students are also taught how their personal freedom is protected under the law, including the right to a trial by a jury of their peers. Students learn on their own that they do not have the same rights in school. Violations of school rules are usually interpreted, judged, and administered by teachers and school administrators. Not yet being able to fathom or cope with the complexities of moral regulations, students frequently doubt the fairness of the treatment they receive.

School curriculum is often under attack for one moral reason or another. Guardians of moral codes challenge the appropriateness of required subjects and reading assignments because of alleged obscenity. Even the American classic *Huckleberry Finn* has been challenged. Moreover, although America is a pluralistic society that teaches coexistence in the face of opposition, literature that denigrates minorities is not considered politically correct and is subject to censorship attempts, even though it is not legally slanderous or libelous. Political correctness and morality have been equated by many. And despite our right to free speech, political incorrectness is subject to censorship. In addition, even though Americans are given the right of freedom of choice, the penchant of adults to protect children and defend morality gives rise to censorship attempts.

One of the most lingering controversies between religion and education emanates from the teaching of science in school. Religious activists openly challenge the teaching of scientific principles that allegedly conflict with sacred religious doctrine they cite and endorse. Scientific principles that explain the nature, origin, and activities of minerals, plants, and infrahumans do not normally incite much controversy. However, scientific explanations of the origin, nature, and activities of humans ignite heated opposition. Religious activists might accept the separation of church and state and agree that religious principles not be taught in school. On the other hand, when scientific principles that conflict with their religious principles are taught in school, they challenge their validity and protest their being taught.

The most prominent challenge by religious activists to scientific teaching has been on the teaching of evolution in public schools. Without taking sides, there is a need to clarify the issue to promote understanding and avoid unnecessary conflict. Basing biology textbooks on the premise of evolution and teaching evolution in school can be justified by scientists. From a scientific perspective, empirical observations can be made of living things evolving, including the human species. For example, it is possible to observe that humans gain greater control over their environment and amass increasing knowledge in libraries and data banks with each passing generation. On the other hand, many scientists do not accept Darwin's theory as a valid explanation of evolution; they claim that there is insufficient confirmation of his theory. And many scientists find no conflict in accepting evolution as a scientific phenomenon and belonging to a religious group. Although there are grounds for controversy between some scientific renditions of evolution and some religious doctrines, there are also grounds for accommodation.

Many controversies between religion and science are based on different views of causality. Religion teaches first, single, and absolute causation. God is the first, only, and absolute cause of everything in the universe. Science studies observable empirical relationships to establish relative rather than absolute causation. Scientific investigation uncovers empirical causal agents that produce empirical effects. Unobservable causation is outside the scope of science. Often multiple causal agents rather than a single cause are revealed in scientific studies, causal agents that must be present in combination to produce an effect. For instance, it takes minimally a combination of fuel, oxygen, and ignition to cause a flame. So it is difficult, if not impossible, to compare on a common basis scientific and religious causes of effects. And it is tenable to contend, as many do, that science and religion provide complementary, rather than mutually exclusive, views of the universe that can increase and enrich human understanding. Religion and science are different ways humans attempt to solve the mysteries of the universe. For the most part, they attempt to solve different mysteries in different ways.

Humans are always seeking to learn more about themselves and the world they live in. Their inherent drive for understanding is so strong that when they cannot find scientific explanations for the phenomena they observe, they gravitate toward supernatural explanations. A hallmark of human progress is the dispelling of superstition with the increasing discovery of scientific facts over time. Still, there seems to be no end to the need for further scientific investigation. Each scientific study that answers a particular question reveals additional questions that need to be answered in order to further increase our fund of knowledge. So when teaching students about science it is important to discuss its limitations as well as its benefits. For one thing, science can study the effects of morals on human life and observable causes of morals; for instance, how they are introduced, codified, and adopted. But science is not intended to prescribe moral conduct for people to live by.

Although separation of church and state does not allow public schools to teach religion or insist that students adopt a particular moral code, it is important for them to understand that the development and adoption of a moral code is beneficial. Valuing particular behaviors and goals helps define people's personal identity and gives purpose and meaning to their lives. People who do not know who they are and what they value are confused and discontented. People who adopt a moral code tend to be more satisfied with their life. However, there is no indication that having one set of values rather than another brings greater satisfaction.

Having a sense of personal identity and a moral code are signs of maturity. It is a developmental task of adolescents to formulate their own personal identity by reevaluating the values advocated by their parents and those they have learned more casually, and then selecting those values they personally endorse and choose to live by. The conflict between sacred and secular values seriously complicates the undertaking. On the one hand, most sacred values they learn from religion advocate charity and being your brother's keeper. In contrast, the secular values of free enterprise incite competition and a dog-eat-dog disposition. Many people practice sacred values in their house of worship on weekends and secular values during the week.

It is interesting to speculate on the limits of the public schools' participation in the teaching of morality. There is little doubt that schools are obliged to enforce the code of conduct they established to foster learning and the morality embedded in the Constitution, even though the Constitution is partly based on Judaic-Christian morality. On the other hand, unadulterated moral codes of Jewish or Christian religion, such as the Ten Commandments, cannot be endorsed by and taught in American schools. So far schools have been allowed to teach "values clarification" as a subject in schools, presumably to help students avail themselves of their legal right to formulate their own moral code to live by within the law. And presumably values clarification courses would not advocate any particular moral code, religion, or philosophy. It also appears to be legal to teach "comparative religion" and "comparative philosophy" as subjects in school, provided particular religions are not endorsed. However, it may be quite legal for a philosophy to be endorsed when teaching comparative philosophy, provided the philosophy does not advocate illegal behavior. Besides, most often teachers manifest their own moral biases when they teach.

There is no doubt that we want students to learn, subscribe to, and live by the moral code promulgated in the Constitution. There also is little doubt that public schools are obliged to teach Constitutional morality in order to fulfill their responsibility to propagate the American culture and promote good citizenship. It may be legal for schools to teach values clarification and comparative morality if they do not try to undermine the separation of church and state or the right of parents to teach their moral code to their children. Still, with the disintegration of the traditional nuclear family and the increase in the number of single-parent families and "latchkey" students who spend a great deal of time without supervision, schools are, in fact, participating in child rearing more than ever before. Schools are responsible for supervising and teaching more students at younger ages in preschool, kindergarten, and extracurricular programs. Since America wants to raise moral youth, instilled with American values, should not schools at least more explicitly, aggressively, and comprehensively teach the morals promulgated in the Constitution and their implications for daily living? Once students have learned constitutional morality, should not schools help adolescent students take advantage of their rights to develop their own personal moral code within the law by teaching the comparative moral codes and helping them define the moral code they want to live by? At present, feeble, obtuse efforts are being made to teach morality in school without violating the separation of church and state in courses with names such as "character education." Many of these courses teach good manners and etiquette more than morality. Most often good manners have more to do with arbitrary convention than the basic morality embedded in the laws of the land or religious doctrine. Still, it would be riskier to teach morals. The promulgators might be accused of teaching religion or possibly incite a religious group that does not subscribe to the moral being taught.

To foster tolerance and peaceful coexistence in our pluralistic culture, American schools also have an opportunity and an obligation to mitigate the natural antagonism between religious and other factions of different beliefs. Each faction not only has the right to practice their own values, they have the right to attempt to convert others to their beliefs. And many factions aggressively launch conversion campaigns. Peaceful coexistence must succeed despite the campaigns of factions to aggressively recruit converts and, when threatened, to destroy their enemies. Far too many people have been killed over the centuries to defend sacred beliefs that advocate love, nurturance, and charity toward others.

To facilitate students' right and need to develop their own personal values, schools need to teach students how to make their own choices, despite the efforts of others to convert them to their way of thinking. Students need to be taught that it is healthy for them to develop their own personal identity and moral code accommodating government laws and the rules of groups they belong to at the time. In addition, students need to be taught how to find and deliberate alternatives as a basis for making decisions. Only in this way can they exercise free choice and establish their own preferences and sense of right and wrong in the face of imposing influences.

There is no doubt that separation of church and state adds complexity to American life and schooling and causes difficulties for American education. Public schools in countries where there is a single national religion certainly are not assailed for teaching religion in school, and they are less likely to need to consider conflicting moral beliefs in their classrooms. However, the right to free choice of a moral code and other alternatives has always been part of the American heritage, and most Americans appreciate their right to free choice, even though it is more difficult to make informed choices than to have choices made for you.

During World War II, American soldiers were acclaimed for being able to think for themselves and act on their own. When the leader of an American military unit was killed, individual soldiers were able to continue their mission. In contrast, soldiers from authoritarian nations where all soldiers were imbued with the same values and taught to submit to leadership without dissent were often lost and ineffective when their leader was killed. Unfortunately, American schools have given more lip service than effort to the teaching of decision-making and problem-solving procedures needed to think and act independently. School tests require students to regurgitate memorized facts much more often than to use higher-order thinking skills. Overemphasis on rote memorization contributes more to success in trivia games than in meeting life's challenges. A decision-making procedure shown by research to increase academic achievement is described in Chapter 4, and a problem-solving procedure with some evidence showing that it enhances academic achievement is described in Chapter 5. Schools need to spend much more time teaching these higher-order thinking skills.

The primary purposes of Chapter 1 were to identify, define, clarify, and estimate the magnitude of educational problems that need to be addressed. As suggested earlier, the data available to estimate the magnitude of problems was sketchy, and so the findings should not be regarded as conclusive. However, the findings served both to indicate the need to amass more conclusive data and to alert those involved in education that there are critical problems being overlooked and neglected that need to be remedied.

This chapter began by attempting to expose the large number of deficient students produced in America and the tremendous loss of human and economic potential deficient students impose on the United States. Then, as background for pursuing a solution in subsequent chapters, the detrimental effects American values can have on education, if not faced and dealt with, were investigated. It is important to know the contextual factors that contribute to the problem in order to derive a workable solution.

After reviewing problems confronting American education and before presenting solution options, it is both fair and heartening to acknowledge that many of our problems arise and are exacerbated because American education has undertaken the responsibility of providing an education for as many Americans as possible—a pioneering initiative that has never been undertaken in any nation in the history of the world. Although other nations may give lip service to educating all of their citizens, they, de facto, are educating only an elite segment of their population, and no visible initiatives have been launched by them to change. Moreover, despite the intentions expressed in our Constitution to provide equal opportunity for all, until recent years only an elite segment of our population actually received an adequate formal education.

The movement to educate as many Americans as possible gained impetus with the initiating of Community Action and Head Start programs, as well as forced school integration. These initiatives provided new educational opportunities for previously neglected, disadvantaged minority groups, which combined represent a large segment of our total population. In addition, the enactment and enforcement of new laws gave the handicapped educational opportunities not afforded them before. All of these initiatives imposed onerous new burdens on American schools, not the least of which is the weighty student deficiency problem. The U.S. government has launched an heroic initiative to educate as many Americans as possible; it will take an heroic effort by American education to meet the challenge. The purpose of the remaining chapters is to clarify problems and describe evidence-based prescription options that educators can use to meet the challenge. It's time to launch new initiatives that research shows can work.

REFERENCES

Bureau of Labor Statistics. (1995). Washington, DC: U.S. Department of Labor.

The future of education: Perspectives on national standards in America (Nina Cobb, Ed.). (1994). New York: College Entrance Examination Board.

National Commission on Excellence in Education, U.S. Department of Education. (1983). *A nation at risk*. Washington, DC: Author.

Rosier, M. J., & Keeves, J. P. (1991). *The IEA study of science 1: Science education and curricula in twenty-three countries*. Vol. 8 of *International Studies in Education Achievement*. New York: Pergamon Press.

Scopes Trial. (1925). Dayton, TN. University of Missouri Scopes trial web page: www.law.educ/faculty/projects/trials/scopes2000.htm. Columbia, MO.

U.S. Census Bureau. (1998). Washington, DC.

U.S. Department of Education. (1998). Washington, DC.

2

Meeting the Challenge

The primary challenge that must be met by American education is to substantially reduce the large number of our youth who do not achieve high school learning objectives before the age of 19. Although a great deal of money has been spent to reform American education over the past two decades, the enormity of the deficient student problem has not been recognized or addressed effectively.

Since student deficiency is the problem, it is suggested that instead of concentrating on promoting academic success, we concentrate on reducing student deficiencies to avert failure. Failure has its own insidious properties that devastate people and can undermine and preclude their chance for success in the future. Although it may be more pleasant to talk about success, we cannot successfully ensure success without dealing with the undertow of failure.

To explain, as psychologists and, for the most part, common experience tell us, failure is a slippery slope—failure breeds failure. If not checked, repeated failure erodes self-confidence and gives rise to fears and expectations of failure in the future. In time people become preoccupied with their fears and expectations of failure. And to avoid the pain of the failure they anticipate, they become increasingly reluctant to make an effort to succeed. This, of course, makes it more likely that they will fail in the future, as we are reminded by the old saying, "Nothing ventured, nothing gained." People who continue to fail come to regard themselves as failures. Eventually they become hostile, sometimes mentally disturbed. Unfortunately, self-branded failures may not be aware that their self-deprecating feelings prevent them from succeeding and that they need psychotherapy to find relief and to revive hope for success. Quite often they have no idea of how they got into their predicament or what they might have done to prevent it.

Failure has important social as well as psychological consequences. When people are branded as failures by the evaluations of institutions they belong to, they become hostile toward the institutions and authority figures in them. Their hostility prompts them to avenge the insult, usually by retaliating in subtle ways to avoid repercussions. They may be late or absent more often, undermine morale, shirk responsibility, and be uncooperative in any way they can. Given the opportunity, some would more openly and forcefully rebel and sabotage the efforts of the institution. Many of those who are more destructive are called juvenile delinquents when they are young and criminals when they are adults. The more passive ones suffer in silence and often turn their hostility inward, doing more harm to themselves then to others.

Failure in learning all too often follows this virulent pattern. Students who continue to fail in school begin to regard themselves as failures and school as an alien, rejecting environment. They are prone to withdraw from school one way or another. When they are not physically absent, they are mentally absent, turning off the lessons that teachers foist upon them. Student failures who suppress their hostility tend to be docile in class; they simply withdraw mentally and are inattentive. They tend to be ignored as they fall further behind the class, while overburdened teachers are engaged by assertive students who provoke their attention. Student failures who turn their hostility outward tend to act out, distracting classmates and disrupting efforts to teach. These are the students who are reported to administrators, often disciplined, and sometimes suspended from school. These students are among those responsible for school violence. And many older juvenile delinquents get so much gratification from peer acclamation for retaliating against the school that demeans them that they are resistant to efforts to help them. If they cannot get satisfaction from success in school, they take what satisfaction they can from undermining the efforts of the school. They find it hard to be persuaded that a school that caused their failure could possibly help them. The school failed them in two ways. It failed to teach them and then dubbed them a failure on report cards and by retaining them in grade. What price failure?

School failure is very difficult to undo. Once students are repeatedly failed in school and regard themselves as failures they need both instructional and psychological treatment to recover, in which case the psychological treatment must be successful before the students are able to unblock and face once more the learning problems they could not solve previously. If learning failures can be prevented or at least remediated before students see themselves as failures, psychological treatment will not be needed and destructive retaliatory outbreaks against schools and society can be avoided.

The plight of the school dropout provides a case in point. The problem is most often addressed as dropout prevention, when the problem should be addressed as learning failure prevention and remediation. Simply put, learning failure must be prevented or remediated early, or the dropout problem cannot be solved. The evidence has shown for some time that before students actually drop out of school they are failing. According to the Office of Research and Improvement, U.S. Department of Education (1987), poor academic performance is the single most important predictor of dropouts. Forty percent of dropouts reported that their grades were mostly "D's," about 18% mostly "C's," 8% mostly "B's," and 3% mostly

"A's" (U.S. Department of Education, Center for Education Statistics, 1983). This suggests, of course, that most dropouts regard themselves as academic failures. With respect to intervention, Rowls and Lackey (1988) concluded after reviewing available dropout research, "Remedial and compensatory program interventions have a long history of being more effective the earlier they are begun. The earlier we identify students who have problems in school, the earlier we 'treat' those problems, the more likely we and they will achieve success." The picture has been clear for a long time—school failure must be prevented or at least remediated early.

The common practice of social promotion tends to hide and exacerbate rather than fix the problem. Issuing a high school diploma by means of social promotion to students who can't read does not help them in the long run or enable them to read. Furthermore, these students know they can't read and can't help feeling embarrassed and inferior. They are reminded of their inferiority every time they try to read a "help wanted" ad or try to fill out a job application. And they are virtually unemployable, except in the most menial jobs. Social promotion also corrupts the educational enterprise. The sole purpose of education is to produce desired learning, and educational institutions certify that desired learning has been achieved by assigning test scores and grades and by promoting students. Certifying that students have achieved desired learning when they have not makes it impossible for an educational institution to fulfill its reason for being. Social promotions may assuage parental wrath, avoid lawsuits and student protests, and save money in the short term. But how can these outcomes justify falsifying the certification of desired learning? The practice of social promotion is a symptom of an educational institution gone awry. Finally, social promotion exacerbates the students' problems. Students who have not achieved the objectives of their present grade are less able to succeed in achieving the objectives of the next grade level. The deficit between their readiness and the more advanced objectives is much greater; thus social promotion makes future failure much more likely.

The absolute deadline for preventing the failure self-image is promotion time. Sufficient remediation must be provided students before promotion time for them to be promoted without learning deficits. When students are not promoted along with their age mates, it is quite likely that they will consider themselves failures. Promotion is a social ritual that certifies the success of students in school. Being held back in school certifies that students are failures, incompetent when compared to students of their age group that are promoted. Students who are not promoted are likely to see themselves as failures because the educational institution has certified them as failures.

The failures' self-image becomes more ingrained the next school term, when students who are not promoted find themselves in classes with younger students who are more immature in many ways and have less in common with them than their established friends who were promoted. Feeling like an outlander, it is difficult for them to muster the motivation to participate with their new classmates socially or educationally. Moreover, they are reluctant to face again the content and learning objectives they failed to master the last term. Many would rather not participate than face the pain of failure again. And their history does not bode well for their success. Rather than continue to face academic failure, they would prefer being in a situation where they can expect to succeed and are prone to leave the school environment so they can. These are the academic conditions in which failure breeds failure, and eventually dropouts. The damage is extremely hard to overcome and very costly in money and human resources in the long run. It is to be prevented by all means possible.

WHAT CAN BE DONE?

To answer the question we must attack the student failure problem in a way that can be excepted to succeed. So far we have established the importance of remedying student failure before promotion time when the school system formally dubs students failures by retaining them in grade. This establishes realistic time constraints for remediation.

The nature of the solution is implied by a research fact. Benjamin S. Bloom, a well-respected educational researcher known to be meticulous in interpreting research findings, found that all but the most psychologically handicapped students are able to achieve all of the learning objectives pursued through high school. The difference among students is the amount of instruction they may require to achieve the objectives (Block & Anderson, 1975; Bloom, 1968).

So the key to ensuring that students achieve all high school objectives is ample instruction. Furthermore, students need to be provided all of the instruction they need to achieve the required learning objectives before promotion periods end. And, since it is the education system's responsibility to provide ample instruction, the burden for ensuring student success is solely on the education system, not the students, students' parents, or any other scapegoat that might be blamed. Although student qualifications and parental support and assistance help, the buck stops with the education system, since the school is obliged to provide ample effective instruction. It is the school's responsibility to provide instruction based on students' readiness at any given time. And although parental support is important, schools should provide sufficient instruction for students to succeed, even if parents do not provide any supplementary instruction at all. Furthermore, the research implies, in general, that students are capable of achieving present learning objectives, so there is no reason to believe that present standards are excessively high and need to be lowered or that the present curriculum needs to be substantially revised to achieve existing objectives, although refinements are always in order. The research also implies that many more students can achieve high school learning objectives and graduate high school without learning deficits than is presently the case. Moreover, establishing age 19 as a target date for graduating high school without deficits is not unrealistically stringent; the vast majority of students can achieve the target. Clearly, what education systems need to do to reduce the number of student failures is to provide all of the instruction that all students need to be promoted without deficits.

The problem is substantive, not formal. The solution requires increasing learning by means of increased instruction. Many other factors such as busing, school buildings, equipment, and counseling may be essential to schooling, but instruction has the greatest and most direct impact on learning. Yes, instruction is the primary cause of desired learning. So to increase the number of students who achieve the learning objectives required in any given promotion period, they must be given all the instruction they need to achieve the objectives during that period. Promotion periods extend over a relatively long span of time, usually a school year, allowing time for a sizable amount of additional instruction.

WHAT KIND OF INSTRUCTION IS NEEDED MOST?

Now that we have established the importance of providing an ample amount of effective instruction during each promotion period, we need to consider the type of instruction that is lacking. We can find the answer by determining the type of instruction that is insufficient in the classroom.

In classroom instruction teachers spend most of their time teaching the class as a whole. At least initial presentations and demonstrations are made to the entire class. Whatever additional time may be left is devoted to the individual instruction students may need. The problem is that classroom teachers generally do not have sufficient time to provide all of the instruction that all students require to succeed in achieving the learning objectives pursued. Individual students are usually vying for the teacher's attention before, during, and after class, and most teachers provide as much individual attention as they can. However, the individual attention students seek may not be relevant to the learning objectives being pursued at the time, and if they are relevant the students seeking assistance may not be failing and in need of assistance.

The individual instruction required to prevent and remediate failure is *corrective instruction*, which is designed to correct students' mistakes so that they can progress toward the achievement of learning objectives and not fall behind their classmates. Corrective instruction should be initiated by teachers to correct students' mistakes and not by awaiting students' or parents' initiative. Of course, teachers do have some opportunity to correct students' mistakes during group instruction; for instance, during group question-and-answer sessions. Teachers also have the opportunity to correct students' mistakes on tests by writing in the test margins or reviewing the right answers with the class. But this is by no means sufficient to prevent the failure of individual students who need additional remedial instruction to succeed.

It is important to remember that although presentations and demonstrations may be made to the class as a whole, to be effective corrective instruction needs to be individualized. Report cards are given to individual students, not the class as a whole, and individual students are retained in grade, not classes. To ensure that students are promoted their personal mistakes must be identified and corrective instruction must be provided to the individuals that need it, whenever they need it, as much as they need of it.

It is especially important to realize that providing students with all the instruction they need to achieve learning objectives does not "dummy down" the curriculum. The curriculum does not need to be simplified or changed in any way. Furthermore, the learning objectives do not need to be lowered or changed in any way. Still, keeping subject matter and objectives up to date is good practice. Nowhere in this book is it advocated or implied that standards be lowered. All of the prescriptions in this book are directed toward increasing the number of students who achieve existing learning objectives through high school.

EVALUATION AND CORRECTIVE INSTRUCTION

To maximize the number of students who earn promotion, it is necessary to coordinate evaluation and corrective instruction. To be effective, prescriptions for corrective instruction must be based on evaluation. In general, the purpose of instructional evaluation is to assess student progress and to diagnose student performance inadequacies that impede progress. So when students are evaluated one of two key decisions is made: (1) student performance is adequate and they are ready to undertake the next more advanced task in a learning sequence, or (2) student performance is inadequate and corrective instruction needs to be prescribed until they are able to progress. The corrective instruction prescription is indicated by the inadequacies revealed in the evaluation *instrument* used. After each corrective instruction prescription is administered, students are evaluated and additional corrective instruction is prescribed until evaluation indicates that students are ready to progress. There are only two marks students need to be given after task performance evaluation: (1) "mastery" and (2) "not yet." Mastery signifies students are ready to progress, and not yet signifies that they are not yet ready to progress. In this way there is as little suggestion of failure as possible. Much more detail on evaluation and corrective instruction is supplied in Chapter 4, "Making Instruction More Effective."

The sooner students are remediated before promotion time the better because, as indicated, earlier remediation reduces the instances of failure and the likelihood that students will consider themselves to be failures. The first opportunity students have for evaluation and corrective instruction is on their performance of assigned tasks. This may occur during oral question-and-answer instruction, when teachers spontaneously evaluate students' answers and guide them to the right answer accordingly, or they may receive remediation after instruction when students complete an evaluation task such as a test, a composition, or other project. Students are then prescribed corrective instruction based upon their task performances. This kind of evaluation–corrective instruction cycle is repeated over and over in each subject area being taught until report card time. Typically, the next opportunity for evaluation and corrective instruction is report card time, when students' cumulative task evaluations result in grade assignments. At this time teachers are obliged to review inadequacies with students and prescribe corrective instruction to elevate low grades.

Report card learning deficits are much more difficult to remediate than inadequate task performance deficits because of remoteness and complexity. When students fail to perform a task adequately, corrective instruction is prescribed to remediate that specific inadequacy in close proximity to the time the mistake was made. Report card grades are given some time after mistakes have been made and cover many mistakes that may have been made in several content areas, which can be overwhelming to students. This makes it much more difficult to prescribe and administer corrective instruction to raise grades. Nevertheless, helpful corrective instruction can be prescribed to improve report card grades before promotion time, when there is still an opportunity to enable students to earn promotion.

It is possible to make report card grades representative of student performance by assigning grades based upon number of task performance inadequacies. Students with fewer inadequacies would be assigned higher grades, and vice versa. When grades are assigned to students in the various content areas they would be given a list of their task performance inadequacies in each content area, along with an inadequacy count or total. For example, students with 10% or fewer inadequacies could be assigned an "A" in a content area, 11% to 20% inadequacies could be assigned a "B," 21% to 30% could be assigned a "C," 31% to 40% could be assigned a "D," and 41% or more inadequacies could be assigned an "F." With ample timely corrective instruction, residual inadequacies at report card time should be quite low, and almost all students should earn an "A" or a "B."

Grading on the normal curve would not work because it requires that a normal distribution of "A," "B," "C," "D," and "F" grades, for instance, be given to the class. Under these conditions a certain number of students would be assigned an "A" even if, for example, the best students had 40% or more inadequacies. Conversely, a certain number of students would be assigned an "F" even if, for example, they had fewer than 20% inadequacies. It is not our purpose to establish a cogent grading system, but rather to show the importance of grades being solely and directly related to the number of performance inadequacies a student may have in pursuit of learning objectives, regardless of how students' performance may compare to that of their classmates.

The longer teachers wait to correct inadequate performance, the less likely it will be that corrective instruction will work. (For further explanation of this fact see "Providing Contiguity" in Chapter 4.) Corrective instruction is most effective when it is provided soon after task performance is found to be inadequate—while the task is fresh in the teachers' and students' minds. At that time corrective instruction should be given and evaluated repeatedly until student performance is adequate and the student is ready to move on to the next more advanced task in the assigned task sequence. When corrective instruction is administered in this way, students have little basis or opportunity to consider themselves to be failures.

All students make mistakes. Many students fail tests and all students learn from their mistakes and failures; and most learning objectives are to some extent achieved by trial and error. Students take great pride in correcting their mistakes when it expedites their success, and they can tolerate failure provided they do not continue to fail for prolonged periods. It is the schools' responsibility to provide sufficient corrective instruction and encouragement to keep students' hopes of achieving assigned learning objectives alive and to ensure student progress.

When student performance is inadequate and teachers are providing feedback to students before administering corrective instruction, able teachers make it clear that the students have made a mistake, as all people do. People are rarely right the first time, even though some parents would prefer that their children were. The important thing is to correct your mistakes regardless of the number of attempts it may take to correct them so that you can learn and profit from your experience. Sometime a great deal of persistence is needed. People become failures only when they do not persist in correcting their mistakes. Among the most valuable lessons people learn are that it takes persistence to succeed and that it may take a great deal of time and effort to learn the most important lessons in life.

There is nothing more essential that teachers do than to provide corrective instruction appropriately. It is often the difference between successful and unsuccessful teaching. To minister corrective instruction properly, teachers should prepare before teaching corrective exercises for all tasks they require their students to perform. In addition, over time they need to test and refine the corrective exercises until they can be assured that they work. Still, teachers do not have a good lesson plan unless it includes effective corrective exercises. Quite often corrective exercises can be adopted that have been perfected by others. However, it should be acknowledged that during oral question-and-answer instruction, teachers often must react spontaneously to correct students' mistakes.

When students require corrective instruction, they need to be assured that if they complete the teacher's corrective exercises they can expect to eventually, with sufficient time and effort, correct their mistakes and move on. Teachers need to be well enough prepared with tried-and-true corrective exercises to give this assurance to students. Repetition is one of the ploys teachers need to be able to use in corrective instruction. Learning is facilitated when to-be-learned information is repeatedly presented to students and to-be-learned behavior is repeatedly practiced by students. The use of repetition in teaching is explicated in Chapter 4 under the heading "Utilizing Repetition Effectively."

In Chapter 1, societal factors emanating from our Constitution were identified and explained under the heading "Education and the American Way" to clarify important contextual factors that affect the efforts of American educational institutions to educate our youth. Just as society provides the context that determines how educational institutions function, educational institutions provide the context that determines how instruction is administered. Since instruction must be improved to solve the student failure problem, it is important to consider how educational institutions need to change to improve instruction. Following is a discussion of institutional factors that impede the delivery of effective instruction to students. The subsequent assertions are proffered to alert and introduce you to institutional impediments to effective instruction that need to be managed in order to reduce student failure. Impediments to effective instruction will be discussed more thoroughly in Chapter 7, where research findings pertaining to the impediments and their prevention will be cited. Since public bureaucratic educational institutions tend to be perpetuated and are likely to endure, it seems advisable to initially attempt to work within the system to reduce institutional impediments to effective instruction.

Working Within the System

It is not necessary to junk the entire educational system to ensure that more students achieve high school objectives before the age of 19. It is quite possible to work within the system to reach the goal, provided that unnecessary encumbrances are faced and removed. We can no longer consider arbitrary policies and procedures that have become ingrained in the system over the years to be treated as necessities. Effective instruction must become the focal concern of school systems, and other factors must be subordinated to instruction and changed if they interfere with effective instruction. In short, much more time, money, and energy must be invested to improve the effectiveness of instruction in increasing academic achievement, and no other factors can be allowed to prevent this from happening. To begin our quest for constructive reform, let us consider how the problem became acute.

As public education evolved, educational institutions transformed from the one-room schoolhouse to enormous government bureaucracies, and form began to interfere with substance. In the one-room schoolhouse the CEO was the teacher, who devoted the majority of his or her time to instilling desired learning. Most of the school personnel budget was spent for teachers. Now state educational institutions have layers upon layers of administrators in the bureaucracies who worry about so many other issues in addition to instruction and learning that they tend to be diminished in importance, discussed less and less with the passage of time, and receive less budgetary investment. Among the competing issues are school violence, lawsuits, busing, building schools, maintenance, support staff, equipment, counseling, textbooks, salaries, schedules, retirement, benefits, truancy, supplies, suspensions, committee meetings, tardiness, leave, school boards, parent dissatisfaction, recess regulations, hall monitors, paperwork, and school visitations, to name a few. And, as with all government bureaucracies as they grow, regulations tend to multiply and increasingly restrict the options of school personnel. Moreover, as educational systems expand they tend to add more curriculum requirements than they delete, until there is no time for additions, no matter how beneficial they may be. As this happens, sound proposals for increasing academic achievement are shot down because they are untenable given present school conditions. To respond to pressure for constructive change and to show they are progressive, some school systems reserve time to try new ideas in the classroom. However, the ideas are seldom scientifically tested and seldom displace present practice. Many educational administrators do not have sufficient training in scientific research to supervise a scientific test. In addition, many are reluctant to oppose colleagues who have a vested interest in and advocate present practice.

Modern cumbersome educational bureaucracies, however inadvertently, create obstacles that thwart both administrators' and teachers' efforts to increase desired learning. Administrators are responsible for acquiring and organizing the resources necessary to maximize learning, but they lack the control they must have to do their job effectively. When teachers refer disruptive students to administrators they are severely limited in what can be done legally to discipline the students and to prevent further disruptions. They are in a double bind. On the one hand, they cannot allow students to disrupt teaching; on the other hand, they need to keep students in school so that they can continue to learn. Still, administrators do not sufficiently profit from what is known about reducing disruptions. (See Chapter 7 for research-based presentations that can be implemented to reduce disruptions.)

Not only are administrators limited in what they can do about disruptive students, they are severely restricted in what they can do about undesirable teachers. It is exceedingly difficult to discharge teachers, unless they exhibit some really bizarre or destructive behaviors. U.S. industry overcame resistance to firing employees because it became evident that only competent employees could be retained if we were to successfully compete with foreign industry. We need to produce high-quality products efficiently, and only competent workers can meet the challenge. It was only plant closings and resulting loss of jobs that generated enough leverage to allow incompetent workers to be culled out. What will it take to create enough pressure to overcome resistance to replace incompetent teachers? (By incompetent teachers I mean teachers who do not engender sufficient learning in their students to achieve assigned learning objectives.)

Teacher competency can be developed through education. Good teachers are not born. Research has failed to establish that particular inherent teacher characteristics are responsible for student achievement. However, there are some obvious characteristics, such as clear speech, that are important to teaching and other occupations that require oral presentations to be made. It has been shown that neither teacher personality characteristics (Getzels & Jackson, 1963) nor teacher knowledge (Shulman, 1986) has a positive impact on student achievement. On the other hand, research does show that particular instructional techniques, described in Chapter 4, do have a positive impact on academic achievement. These teaching techniques can be taught in pre-service and in-service teacher education to develop teacher competency.

Administrators are likely to have their time and energies sapped by bureaucratic red tape. The administrators' dilemma, symptomatically, tends to be an obligation to attend too many meetings. No one doubts the importance of having meetings to keep people informed and to gain consensus or assent on key issues. However, when meetings are held excessively there is too little time for administrators to arrange for the enhancement of learning. In school systems a major reason for excessive and unnecessary meetings is administrators' reluctance to make decisions that might affect and mar their reputation—and these tend to be the important decisions. Instead of biting the bullet and making decisions, they tend to shunt the responsibility to committees. Committees have many important functions, but they are not effective in making administrative decisions. The saying that "a camel is a horse put together by a committee" refers mainly to the times committees assume administrative responsibility. However, it is easy for administrators to "pass the buck" to committees and other groups under the guise of being democratic and keeping faculty and parents informed and involved, when in fact they are ridding themselves of administrative hot potatoes.

An adage that illustrates the importance of control to administration is that to function effectively, administrators' authority must be commensurate with their responsibility. However, all too often educational administrators do not have sufficient authority to carry out their responsibilities should they want to. This is one reason they tend to pass the buck.

Teachers, too, must be given the authority to fulfill their responsibility; their control of classroom instruction must not be undermined. The classroom is not intended to be a democracy. On the other hand, for teachers to fulfill their responsibility they need to be better trained. All teachers construct and administer achievement tests, but very few receive formal training in the technology of achievement test construction. In addition, too little of pre-service teacher training is devoted to developing the technical skills needed to plan and implement instruction and to remediate student inadequacies.

Unfortunately, in many schools the job of teaching has deteriorated to the point that there is precious little intrinsic satisfaction in a day's work. This is because teachers' control of their teaching has been gradually eroded and to some extent has been subverted. For one thing, teachers have lost control of classroom disruptions. Often, administrators are responsible for making the decision to remove a student. Sometimes disruptive students are returned to the classroom shortly after they have been sent to the administrator for disciplinary action (which may or may not have been taken). Almost all teachers learn that they are not to allow one disruptive student to prevent the rest of the class from learning, but they do not have sufficient authority to practice this preachment.

Teachers have also lost control of what they teach; that is, the content of instruction. It is one thing to require teachers to achieve predetermined objectives, but competent teachers are supposed to know how to instruct their students to achieve the objectives. Nevertheless, teachers are not only directed to teach particular subject matter, they are required to teach from particular state-adopted textbooks. Teachers are aware of their frustrations but tend to describe their complaints rather acquiescently as lack of flexibility because they do not fully understand the causes. To make matters worse, teachers much less frequently engage in the warm, personal relations with students that were commonplace in days gone by. They are reminded of their legal vulnerabilities in dealing with students, and their time is more encumbered with tangential assignments.

It is amazing how many peripheral responsibilities are delegated to teachers that take time away from instruction. Responsibilities that displace instructional planning and instruction may include collecting picture, yearbook, lunch, and field trip money; obtaining permission and medical forms from parents; keeping students' permanent records up to date; filling out forms for hearing and vision screening; making xerox copies for their class; ordering supplies; attending staff meetings and parent conferences; planning and participating in extracurricular activities; cafeteria, bus, and recess duty; distributing fund-raiser information; and so on. It is hard to believe that teachers cannot be relieved from some of these petty chores. Teachers not only need more time to teach, they need out-of-class time to plan instruction. Ironically, while the primary means of reducing student failure is increased instruction, teachers have less and less time to provide instruction.

Teachers are also diverted from instruction in some subtler and stranger ways. They are given to believe by administrators, psychologists, counselors, doctors, parents, and others that to be effective teachers they must know and do things that do not directly enhance academic achievement, such as working with parents, participating in community activities, attending to the psychological needs of students, helping students make friends, teaching etiquette and manners, being a role model, learning about students' family lives, and learning business management procedures. Professional development lectures, workshops, and courses may be conducted to develop these skills in teachers. One skill teachers are often urged to learn and are taught is how to motivate students. They are led to believe that in order for students to learn, teachers must motivate them to learn. And part of pre-service and in-service training is devoted to teaching teachers how to use reinforcement and other ploys to presumably motivate students to learn. As you will learn in Chapter 7, reinforcement does not increase academic achievement.

There is a terrible misunderstanding about children's motivation to learn. Children are born with a voracious appetite to learn. At birth humans are the most helpless of creatures, unable to survive on their own for many years. It is through learning that they acquire the adaptive skills that enable them to flourish in society and dominate animals that are much stronger, faster, and more agile than themselves. There is little doubt that children are motivated to learn.

Unfortunately, schools have failed miserably in maintaining children's motivation to learn. Children enter school with avid curiosity. As soon as they are able to abide separation from their parents and can concentrate on their schoolwork, they become interested in what it may offer them. In the early years, they are fascinated. They learn how to communicate and get along with others and begin to master the tools of their society. Learning is "hands-on"—they learn a great deal about mastering the environment by manipulating it, and they can test new ideas to see if they work. As they progress in school, learning becomes more symbolic, abstract, and removed from the practicality of their daily life. They are less often able to test for themselves the validity of the new knowledge they acquire. Instead they are required to memorize and accept more of the facts they are given on faith. Learning becomes less vital, and they lose interest in school. From this point on only the family values inculcated in the students serve to keep them on task in school. When parents are educated and advocate education, their children tend to succeed in school.

Traditionally, when it was mainly the elite who were educated, wealthy parents who sent their children to school impressed on them the privilege of going to school. Completing school was a family tradition, and students were expected to discipline themselves to succeed. Family mores kept students in school, and discipline provided the leverage to learn. If students failed to discipline themselves sufficiently, they were disciplined. Interest in school was seldom a major issue; disciplining the mind was more the order of the day.

The challenge to schools is to maintain children's natural motivation to learn as they progress through school. One way of maintaining students' motivation is to continue to make students aware of how school learning facilitates their adaptation and success in their world. They need no one to make them aware of the adaptive significance of speech; they use it to get what they want from ministering adults. However, the adaptive significance of grammar is not nearly so obvious, nor is the adaptive significance of math or science immediately evident. In Chapter 5, the section "Enlisting the Control Motive" describes one way of making school learning adaptive and motivating to students to learn.

Another way of thwarting students' motivation to learn is by not providing them with all the instruction they need to succeed in school. There is nothing that kills motivation more than continued failure. Students who repeatedly fail to achieve learning objectives in school lose their motivation to attend school, but they do not lose their motivation to learn. They seek ways of continuing to learn outside of school where they can expect to succeed. One of the most frustrating aspects of teaching is not having the time to provide students with the instruction they need to be successful.

Teachers are among the last to benefit from computerization. We seem more inclined to use computers to displace them than to help them. If we want to improve instruction we had better face up to the fact that the classroom is the basic unit of instruction, and that teachers need to be in charge of the classroom. To the extent that we interfere with teacher control of teaching, we are impairing students' opportunity to learn. In this country teachers historically have been underpaid, and they may well continue to be. Many people turn to teaching because of a missionary zeal to help our youth learn and prosper. Stripping teachers of their control of the learning process has dampened their motivation and caused them undue torment. It is sad to hear so many teachers say that the best part of their job is the liberal amount of time off they have.

Most important, given the large student/teacher ratio in most classrooms, teachers simply do not have enough time to provide sufficient individualized, corrective instruction for all their students who need it. The instructional mode designed for classroom teaching is group instruction. As indicated, much of the teachers' time is spent making presentations and demonstrations to the class as a whole, with little time for individualized tutoring. Although the group is taught and tested as a whole, effective corrective instruction must be prescribed for individual students based on evaluations of their personal performance. Groups can be taught, but individuals are graded on their learning and are either promoted or not promoted, as the case may be. Group learning and performance is only an issue when the group is being evaluated as a team. As a result, group learning is and should be the concern of sports coaches much more than school teachers. Still, teachers cannot prepare a lesson appropriate for the readiness levels of all students in their class. Moreover, as you will learn in Chapter 7, although homogeneity in student readiness may make the teacher's job easier, ability grouping does not enhance academic achievement. Many students may require additional corrective instruction to achieve the class learning objectives, and some of them will not receive it. To solve the problem we must begin by admitting that classroom teachers are unable to provide all the corrective instruction their students need during scheduled class time. Additional corrective instruction must be provided in some other way.

Since the class is almost always the instructional unit, however the educational institution is organized, the learning produced at any given time is a result of classroom instruction. Since classrooms are subject to and contained in educational institutions, the policies and procedures imposed on the classroom by the educational institution determine in large measure the extent to which desired learning will or will not occur in the class. Of course, supplementary instruction provided out of class can improve classroom performance, but it is not routinely provided by the traditional educational institution.

The educational institution also affects learning by intruding on the classroom and disrupting instruction, blaring announcements into the classroom or calling teachers or students out of the classroom. So, however many other functions educational institutions perform, it is what they do to help, hinder, and supplement classroom instruction that determines whether the learning objectives being pursued are achieved. And if desired learning is to be increased, these are the issues that count the most, not tangential issues that occupy so much time. In essence, what educational institutions need to concentrate on is increasing the number of students in each class that achieve the class learning objectives. Since so many students do not achieve required learning objectives, they need to focus on the primary cause of their failure—insufficient corrective instruction—so that they can effect a remedy.

Teachers and instruction seem to be victimized by a bureaucratic mind-set. In a bureaucracy the prestige of administrators is judged by the number of subordinates beneath them in the organization, and administrators enhance their prestige by increasing the number of their subordinates. Consequently, they are continually attempting to hire new subordinates. This tends to continually increase the number of administrators and administrative staff in a bureaucracy. Unfortunately, in an educational institution teachers are subordinate to administrators. Work is delegated to teachers and they have no subordinates to delegate work to, except for the few who have teacher aides. This is the case even though teachers, not administrators, are primarily and directly responsible for instilling desired learning, the only reason the educational institution has for being. There must be a better way to organize educational institutions to achieve their mission.

Finally, it is no longer acceptable for educational institutions to claim success by showing a high graduation rate. They need to show that all students who graduate achieved all of the high school learning objectives and were not socially promoted. Actual academic achievement must be the basis for school advancement. Furthermore, a seemingly high advancement rate is nothing to brag about when a much higher percentage of students have the potential to advance, which is presently the sorry state in America. Since the first concern should be to reduce the number of students who fail, in order to curtail the enormous waste of human potential and money, educational institutions should use as their foremost criteria of success an increased reduction of student failures. This criteria of school success is far too often ignored. Educational institutions are more prone to stress the achievement of star students, staff, fund-raising activities, sports teams, and favorable publicity as evidence of their success.

BASING EDUCATIONAL DECISIONS ON EVIDENCE

To improve education it is not only necessary to clarify priorities and make organizational changes to give administrators and teachers the authority they need to fulfill their responsibilities; it is also necessary to change the way educational decisions are made. Educational decision-makers will need to base many more of their decisions on research evidence. Far too many educational decisions are based on political expediency, antiquated regulations, personal bias, and compelling sales pitches rather than on available evidence. And there is much more evidence available for educational decision-making than most decision-makers are aware of. Unfortunately, even if educational decision-makers were aware of research evidence relevant to the decisions that confront them, few of them have been taught how to interpret research and how to use it to make decisions.

Most educational administrators accountable for budgeting and spending money have been taught in finance courses how to use monetary evidence to project and defend their budgets and to account for their expenditures. They are accountable for their financial decisions and can be discharged for gross negligence in appropriating and spending money. On the other hand, they are not taught enough about educational research to use research to select and implement educational practices or to account for the practices they employ, and they are rarely held accountable for choosing ineffective instructional techniques that fail to produce the desired learning they are supposed to effect. Yet producing desired learning is the primary reason for their budgeting and spending money.

In most professional colleges students are taught how to interpret research findings on the undergraduate level. This enables them to read the research in professional journals to keep abreast of advancements in their profession. The first time most educators are exposed to research is on the graduate level, where they are often required to take an introductory course in educational research. Although all educators need to take an introductory educational research course to keep up with educational advancements, educational decision-makers responsible for selecting and implementing educational practices need additional instruction that enables them to find, analyze, and weigh evidence in order to determine educational practices that are most likely to succeed. For educational decision-makers to be effective, they need to be taught as much about using research evidence to account for educational decisions as they are taught about using monetary evidence to account for budgetary decisions and expenditures.

Another factor that prevents research findings from affecting practice is the gap between educational researchers and practitioners. Educational researchers communicate in their own jargon. Instead of reporting their conclusions in plain English, they use research and statistical terms that even educators who have taken an introductory educational research course may not understand. In addition, educational researchers draw conclusions without discussing their implications for practice. Hardly any educational research reports make recommendations for practice. Yet educational researchers have taken enough education courses to be able to discuss the implications of their findings for practice. Since education is a profession, most educational research reports should end with a section on implications or recommendations for educational practice.

Furthermore, to capitalize on the myriad of fragmentary research studies that have been reported, it is necessary for research findings to be synthesized to indicate the implications the preponderance of evidence has for key issues. For instance, the *Handbook on Effective Instructional Strategies* (Friedman & Fisher, 1998) summarizes evidence showing the effectiveness of 15 instructional strategies in increasing academic achievement, as you will see in Chapter 4. Research needs to be funded and summarized to address such key issues. Acknowledging that the primary purpose of education is to produce desired learning, it is not too difficult to distinguish key from peripheral educational issues. Factors that have the potential of increasing desired learning are key factors that need to be studied, and since instruction is a most direct and potent cause of learning it merits foremost attention.

A most fundamental general question for educational researchers to answer is: What kind of instruction produces what kind of desired learning in what kind of students? Of course, this question needs to be cast in specific terms for each particular research study. For example, does phonics instruction increase the reading achievement of adult illiterates?

Educational decision-makers not only need to use research findings much more often to make their decisions, they need to use theory very cautiously. At present, for the most part, an overabundance of theories are taught in colleges of education and used to guide educational practice, including theories of J. Piaget, B. F. Skinner, L. Vygotsky, Gestalt psychologists, A. Maslow, B. Weiner, D. Bandura, U. Neisser, D. Ausebel, S. Freud, E. Tolman, I. Pavlov, E. Thorndike, and R. Gagne, to name only a very few. Educators are required to memorize at least a few of these theories in college courses, depending on the biases of their instructors. Many of the theories are inconsistent and contradictory, and at best only portions of individual theories have been validated conclusively by research findings. Yet theories are often taught as if they are true in general. It is no wonder that educators are often puzzled and frustrated with higher education. They do not know which theories to believe or what to believe about them, and often have difficulty seeing the relevance of theory to daily practices. It is said that there is nothing more practical than a good theory. The problem is that there are too many conflicting theories with far too little scientific verification. Moreover, many of the theories were not constructed to explain educational issues, and the validity of applying them to explain educational issues is often questionable. It's time to use research evidence to cull these theories and separate fact from fiction. In the physical sciences, research evidence was used to refine and reduce the number of speculative theories. Now there are a parsimonious number of complementary theories that have been confirmed by research. Until education has reached that point, the most tenable approach is to base educational practice on research evidence and take educational theories with a grain of salt. Research rather than theory is the basis for prescribing techniques for ensuring student success in this book.

In conclusion, educational practice can be improved substantially if existing research is summarized to answer key educational questions and subsequent research concentrates on testing primary causes of learning, such as instruction.

All subsequent chapters, except for Chapter 9, provide specific resources and prescriptions for minimizing student failure in achieving present high school learning objectives. The last chapter, "Teaching Students to Innovate," is an objective that should be pursued in school to enable the United States to excel in competition with other nations. Prescriptions for teaching students how to innovate are offered in that chapter. Despite our laudable expressed intentions of providing an education for all Americans that will enable them to succeed, America is still a throwaway society, and too many American lives are being thrown away. American schools need to stop neglecting students who have difficulty achieving high school learning objectives and provide them with the education they need to take advantage of available, elevating opportunities. Research-based prescriptions for reducing student failure and improving American education are offered in the coming chapters. Rather than recommending a single structured, packaged solution, many options are described. This enables educational institutions to develop their own plan, incorporating a combination of prescriptions to serve their purposes while accommodating prevailing local constraints.

REFERENCES

Block, J. H., & Anderson, L. W. (1975). *Mastery learning in classroom instruction.* New York: Macmillan.

Bloom, B. S. (1968). Learning for mastery. *Evaluation Comment* (Ed. J. H. Block) 1, 1–11.

Friedman, M. I., & Fisher, S. P. (1998). *Handbook on effective instructional strategies: Evidence for decision-making.* Columbia, SC: The Institute for Evidence-Based Decision-Making in Education.

Getzels, J. W., & Jackson, P. W. (1963). *Handbook of research on teaching* (pp. 506–582). Chicago: Rand McNally.

Rowls, M., & Lackey, G. (1988). *At-risk in South Carolina: The high school dropout.* Columbia, SC: Wil Lou Gray Opportunity School Research and Training Center.

Shulman, L. S. (1986). Paradigms and research programs in the study of teaching: A contemporary perspective. In M. C. Wittrock (Ed.), *Handbook of research on teaching* (3rd ed., pp. 1–36). New York: Macmillan.

U.S. Department of Education. (1987). Washington, DC: Author.

U.S. Department of Education, Center for Education Statistics. (1983). Washington, DC: Author.

II

Prescriptions

The prescriptions for improving student achievement in Part II will focus on ways to improve instruction and the instructional environment. It was logically asserted earlier that of all the factors essential to operating schools, instruction has the most direct and potent effect on learning. In Chapter 2, research evidence was cited showing that student achievement can be increased substantially by improving the instruction that students are given. Student achievement can be increased by incorporating into teaching the instructional techniques that research shows work, despite the many inefficiencies of the bureaucratic educational institutions that house classrooms. It is also important to create an institutional milieu conducive to instruction and learning by controlling factors that subvert the instructional process. For this reason, Part II will describe prescription options for preventing impediments to learning, as well as prescription options for improving instruction. Options are provided so that you can choose those most appropriate for your purpose after considering local conditions and constraints. There is more research evidence supporting the efficacy of some options than others. Some evidence is derived from group experiments; other evidence is derived from clinical studies of individuals; and still other evidence is gleaned from more casual observations or recordings of events, without intervention. Options that do not have as much research support as others may be more suitable for your purpose. Whatever options you may choose, it is advisable to pilot test their effectiveness in your school before adoption. As you read the following prescription options, keep the big picture in mind. Regardless of which prescription options or combination of options you may choose to test, in order to maximally increase student achievement students must be given as much corrective instruction as they need to achieve the learning objectives being pursued. Both quantity and quality of instruction are important.

The scope of this book is as comprehensive as my expertise allows. Yet it encompasses and circumscribes the central mission: improving student achievement by improving instruction and the instructional environment. I will leave it to others more able than I to reform educational bureaucracies and improve political intervention in education. Vice President Alben Barkley was credited with comparing the relationship between scotch and soda with that of politicians and education: just as scotch does more for soda than soda does for scotch, education does more for politicians running for office than politicians do for education.

3

Implementing Corrective Tutoring

In this chapter we begin our quest for prescriptions to reduce the number of student failures. To lay a foundation, we need to highlight the three points that were shown in the last chapter to be important in preventing and remedying student failure.

- Students must be given as much corrective instruction as they may need to progress with their class.
- Corrective instruction must be individualized based on the problems of individual students.
- Classroom teachers do not have sufficient time during class to provide all members of the class with all of the corrective instruction they may need.

Thus, to ensure that all students progress with their class, they must be given all the corrective instruction they need as a supplement to their classroom instruction. It is also implicit that although individualized instruction can be provided during class, actual individualized corrective instruction is best provided one-on-one. And during individualized corrective instruction, the teacher prescribes corrective instruction to remediate the problems of individual students. This is in fact one-on-one individualized corrective tutoring. The disadvantage of individualized corrective tutoring during class is that the teacher can be distracted at any time by other students in the class who may be vying for the teacher's attention.

Key research shows how much more effective one-on-one tutoring is than conventional classroom instruction in producing academic achievement. The research of Anania (1981), Bloom (1984), and Burke (1983) makes it clear that:

- The academic achievement of tutored students is about two standard deviations above students taught in conventional classrooms. Put another way, the average tutored student outperforms 98% of students taught by means of conventional classroom instruction.

- Tutored students do not require nearly as much corrective instruction as students taught in conventional classrooms.

- About 90% of tutored students attain a level of achievement attained by only the highest 20% of students taught in conventional classrooms.

Wasik and Slavin (2000) cite convincing research showing the effectiveness of one-on-one tutoring in preventing and remediating inadequacies of at-risk students in the early grades. There is little doubt that one-on-one tutoring is much more effective than classroom instruction in producing academic achievement and in preventing and remediating inadequate student performance. On-on-one tutoring can be used as a supplement to classroom instruction to appreciably reduce the number of students who fail in school.

It should be very cost effective in the long run to use tax dollars to pay for one-on-one corrective tutoring as a supplement to classroom instruction (Wasik & Slavin, 2000). It can significantly reduce student failure and the dropout rate, and prepare people for postsecondary education and the job market. It also can prevent costly personal and social problems. Moreover, the need for costly special education classes for the learning deficient can be reduced.

The following are prescription options presently used to implement one-on-one corrective tutoring. They are all designed for students with learning difficulties, although there is considerable variation among them. The review of tutoring techniques is intended to be representative, not exhaustive. It is interesting to note that a number of private enterprise companies make a profit using one-on-one tutoring to remediate students who fail in school. At least one of them guarantees to remediate learning deficits.

The Orton-Gillingham Instructional Program

Introduction: The Orton-Gillingham (O-G) approach to language instruction is designed to be structured, sequential, and cumulative, yet flexible. Emphasis is on cognition and multisensory exposure of students to language elements. It is utilized for teaching individuals and groups.

Grade Levels Covered: Primary grades through adults

Subject Areas Covered: Reading, writing, and spelling

Instructional Tactics: Teaching sessions are action oriented and utilize multisensory training. Auditory, visual, and kinetic exposure reinforce one another. This aids students having difficulties with a specific sensory modality. Students learn to read and spell simultaneously, which differs from traditional phonics instruction. In addition, students study the history of language and study the rules that govern its structure.

The Tutor: The Orton-Gillingham Instructional Program is implemented systematically. Students begin by reading and writing sounds in isolation. Then they blend the sounds into syllables and words. They continue to learn elements of language, the composition of language, and the comprehension of language in a structured, sequential, and cumulative manner. As students learn new material, they continue to review old material until it is mastered. Tutoring is diagnostic-prescriptive in nature. The tutor assesses student performance and prescribes instruction accordingly.

Strict control is maintained over tutor training. O-G tutors must have at least a bachelors' degree, 45 hours of course work in the O-G curriculum, and 100 hours of supervised practicum teaching. Additional requirements must be met to achieve a more advanced level of qualification.

Additional Sources to Consult: More information can be obtained from the Language Tutoring Center, 3229 Debbie Drive, Hendersonville, NC 28739. Required teaching materials can be obtained from Educators' Publishing Service, 1-800-225-5750.

The Wilson Reading System

Introduction: First published in 1988, the Wilson Reading System provided a step-by-step method for teachers working with students who require direct, multisensory, structured language teaching. In 1989, the Wilsons began to provide training to educators in its use. By 1991, their focus had shifted from tutoring to training teachers and distributing Wilson Reading System materials through the Wilson Language Training Corporation.

Grade Levels Covered: Elementary grades through adulthood

Subject Areas Covered: Reading and spelling

Instructional Tactics: The Wilson Reading System teaches students the structure of words through a carefully sequenced, 12-step program that helps them master decoding and spelling in English. Unlike other programs that overwhelm the student with rules, the Wilson Reading System allows the student to learn in small graded increments by using language. Emphasis is on multisensory exposure to language. The system is appropriate for students with and without learning difficulties. Students use readers, workbooks, and group sets provided in the Wilson materials.

The Tutor: Tutors need to be trained for two weeks in the appropriate use of the Wilson Reading System. They are to follow the Wilson instructional system faithfully and use the materials supplied by Wilson. Materials provided for teachers include manuals, rules notebooks, test forms, sound cards, and word cards. Tutor training videos are available but are not intended to replace prescribed training by the Wilson staff. Wilson provides everything needed to utilize their system, for both tutors and students.

The following is a list of the materials provided in the Deluxe Set.

Instructor Materials

- Instructor's Manual
- Dictation Book (Steps 1–6)
- Dictation Book (Steps 7–12)
- Rules Notebook
- WADE: Wilson Assessment of Decoding and Encoding
- Sound Cards in Plastic Box
- Word Cards
- Syllable Cards (Steps 3–6)
- Syllable Cards (Steps 7–12)
- Group Sound Cards (Steps 1–6)
- Group Sound Cards (Steps 7–12)

Student and Additional Materials

- Student Readers 1–12 in Slipcase
- Student Workbooks 1–12, Either A or B Level or Both A and B Level

Additional Sources to Consult: This program is available nationwide. However, teacher training is limited, depending on location. Contact Wilson Language Training, 175 West Main Street, Milbury, MA 01527-1441. Phone: 508-865-5699.

TEACH

Introduction: TEACH is a tutoring program developed by Silver and Hagin (1990) in the Learning Disorders Unit of the New York University Medical Center. The purpose of the program is to diagnose deficits in the component skills of reading and to remediate these specific skills. Emphasis is on diagnosing and treating perceptual weaknesses.

Instructional Levels Covered: First and second grades

Subject Area Covered: Reading

Instructional Tactics: TEACH focuses on teaching four skills needed in reading: (1) pre-reading skills, which include the visual discrimination of letters, recognition of symbols in their correct orientation, the ability to organize symbols in groups, and auditory skills; (2) word attack skills, which involve the use of phonics to decipher words, and the identification of whole words using visual cues, such as letter combinations; (3) comprehension, which involves having a rich vocabulary, being able to select the right meaning of a word, and making inferences; and (4) study skills, which are the tools for acquiring information. However, the actual instructional program focuses more on matching, copying, recognizing, and recalling letters and words than on other reading skills. Students come to tutoring for 30 minutes three to five times a week. Student weaknesses are first diagnosed by an assessment technique called SEARCH, and instructional treatments are prescribed and used accordingly to remediate deficits.

The Tutor: Tutors are certified teachers. The tutor's job is to remediate particular reading difficulties that have been diagnosed by SEARCH, using TEACH instructional techniques. Tutors are given instruction on the appropriate use of the TEACH instructional program. However, nothing explicit could be found on the length of tutor training or the training routine.

Additional Sources to Consult: For more information, contact the Prevention of Disabilities Program, Learning Disorders Unit, the New York University Medical School. Also see the following references: Arnold et al. (1977); Hagin, Silver, and Beecher (1978); Mantzicopoulos et al. (1990); Silver and Hagin (1979, 1990).

Programmed Tutorial Reading

Introduction: Doug Ellison of Indiana University developed the instructional program initially for reading with expectations of expanding it to other subject areas. Emphasis is on sight reading, word analysis, phonics, and comprehension. Students learn the components of reading and how to synthesize them systematically.

Grade Levels Covered: Tutoring begins in the first grade and has been extended beyond.

Subject Area Covered: Reading

Instructional Tactics: Students are selected for tutoring because of their poor performance on standardized reading tests. The program is highly structured. Students learn in small, sequential steps and are reinforced for correct responses. Subsequent assignments depend on students' prior responses.

The Tutor: Tutors do not need to be certified teachers. Many are paid paraprofessionals, volunteers, or parents. Tutors are trained to follow the tutorial program explicitly as prescribed. The tight structure of the program does not leave much room for tutor discretion. Specifics could not be found on the length of tutor training or the training routine.

Additional Sources to Consult: For more information, contact Douglas Ellison at Indiana University. See also the following references: Ellison, Harris, and Barber (1968); Ellison et al. (1965); McCleary (1971).

The Wallach Tutoring Program

Introduction: The Wallachs contend that reading is a skill that can be broken down into components. Students should first be taught to master the components, then they should be taught how to integrate the components until they can read proficiently. Students must first become proficient in the recognition and manipulation of sounds, then acquire proficiency in using the alphabetic code and in blending. Finally, they need to be taught to apply those skills in reading printed material.

Grade Level Covered: First grade

Subject Area Covered: Reading

Instructional Tactics: Students are selected for tutoring who score low on standardized reading tests. They are tutored 30 minutes a day for a year. Students are taught in stages. For the first 10 weeks students are taught to recognize initial phonemes in words that are read to them, to recognize letters, and to associate letters with phonemes. In the second stage, students spend two to three weeks learning to sound out and blend words. For the remainder of the year students apply their skills as they learn to read beginning reading materials.

The Tutor: Paraprofessionals have been used in the Wallach Program. No detailed specifications were given for required tutor qualifications or for a tutor training regimen. Although there is some latitude for tutor discretion, the prescribed format and stages are to be followed.

Additional Sources to Consult: The following references provide additional information on the Wallach Program: Dorval, Wallach, and Wallach (1978); Wallach and Wallach (1976); Wallach et al. (1977).

Reading Recovery

Introduction: The Reading Recovery program, developed by Marie Clay (1985) in New Zealand, appears to be fairly noncontroversial in the world of reading instruction, which can be divided into advocates of intensive phonics instruction and advocates of the whole language approach. The program places emphasis on the development of phonics skills as well as the use of contextual information to assist reading. It is designed for students having trouble learning to read. These students have already had one year of formal instruction. The program is intended to be a short-term, one-on-one tutorial program, supplemental to other reading instruction in the classroom setting.

Grade Level Covered: First grade

Subject Areas Covered: Reading and writing

Instructional Tactics: The Reading Recovery program is administered during half-hour sessions for 12 to 16 weeks. During their daily half-hour sessions, children read many small books. Some of these books are written in a style resembling oral language, while other books use language which the child can readily anticipate. Children also read slightly more difficult texts that they have not previously read. At this point the teacher provides the student detailed support. Children also compose and read their own stories. Reading skills are taught as students read and write, occasionally aided by the use of magnetic letters.

The Tutor: Tutor training is an essential part of this program, with a year's training being required. The tutors learn to observe, analyze, and interpret the reading and writing behaviors of students and design and implement an individualized program for each student. They keep a detailed, running record analyzing the students' performance, moment to moment.

During the first year of training, in addition to teaching a class and tutoring four students, the tutors attend weekly seminars during which they receive training in observational, diagnostic, and assessment techniques. The tutors also participate in weekly "behind the glass" demonstration lessons where they observe, critique, and discuss actual tutoring sessions with their trainers. Follow-up training continues after the first year. The tutors are certified teachers.

Additional Sources to Consult: "Reading Recovery" is a registered trademark of the Ohio State University, with development of most of the authorized materials by Marie Clay. However, most of the Reading Recovery programs in the United States differ to a degree as to how they are developed, implemented, and assessed. For additional information contact G. S. Pinnell, C. A. Lyons, D. E. DeFord, A. S. Bryk, or M. Seltzer at the Ohio State University. Relevant references include: Clay (1979); Clay and Cazden (1990); DeFord et al. (1988); Handerhan (1990); Huck and Pinnell (1986); Lyons (1991); Lyons et al. (1989); Pinnell (1985, 1988); Pinnell et al. (1986).

Success for All Language Tutoring

Introduction: There are several components of the Success for All program, including language arts, mathematics, social studies, science, and a beginning language tutoring program. The beginning language tutoring program will be described here. The other programs will be described in Chapter 5.

 The Success for All tutoring program is based on the premise that students need to learn to read in meaningful contexts and at the same time be given a systematic presentation of work attack skills. There is a certain regularity to language, and direct presentation of phonics is viewed as a helpful strategy which children can use to decipher words. Children also need to build a strong sight vocabulary that will help in identifying words that are not decodable. Along with the systematic presentation of phonics, children engage in reading meaningful connected text. The program has been utilized in public schools to teach disadvantaged students.

Grade Levels Covered: First and second grades

Subject Areas Covered: Beginning reading and writing

Instructional Tactics: There are four components to the Success for All tutoring program. First, children learn to read by reading meaningful text. Reading skills are not acquired by children learning isolated, unconnected information about print. Second, phonics needs to be taught systematically as a strategy for deciphering the reading code. Children engage in reading stories that are meaningful and interesting, yet have a phonetically controlled vocabulary. Third, children need to be taught the relationship between reading words and comprehending what they read. The emphasis on comprehension is directly related to the fourth component, the emphasis on children's need to be taught strategies to help them become successful readers.

In Success for All, the tutoring model is completely integrated with the classroom reading program. The tutor's most important responsibility is to make sure that the student is making adequate progress on the specific skills and concepts being taught in the reading class. Students receive tutoring as long as they need it. Although most students receive tutoring for part of a year, some receive it all year and then continue to be tutored into the next grade. Students are initially selected for tutoring on the basis of individually administered, informal reading inventories given in September. After that, students are assessed every eight weeks to determine their progress through the reading curriculum. Students receive tutoring for 20 minutes each day. A typical tutoring session begins with the student reading out loud a familiar story that he or she has read before in tutoring and in the reading class. This is followed by a one-minute drill of letter sounds to give the student the opportunity to practice the letter sounds taught in class. The major portion of the tutoring session is spent on reading aloud "shared stories" that correspond to the beginning reading lessons. The shared stories are interesting, predictable stories that have phonemically controlled vocabulary in large type and other elements of the story in small type. The teacher reads aloud the small type sections to provide a context for the large type portions read by the students. The tutor works with the student to sound out the phonetically regular words, asks comprehension questions about the whole story, and has the students reread passages out loud to gain fluency. Writing activities are incorporated into the reading activities.

The Tutor: The tutors are certified teachers who also teach a reading class in the school. They are fully aware of what the reading program is. In many cases, tutors work with students who are also in their reading class. When scheduling does not allow this, the student's reading teacher fills out a tutor/ teacher communication form that indicates what lesson the student is working on in class and the teacher's assessment of the specific problems the student is having with that lesson. The tutor uses this information to plan the tutoring session. This communication ensures coordination between the classroom instruction and tutoring.

The tutors receive two days of training to learn to teach the Success for All beginning reading program, and then they receive four additional days of training on assessment and on tutoring itself. Tutors are observed weekly by the program facilitator and given direct feedback on the sessions. Tutors are trained to explicitly teach self-questioning (metacognitive) strategies to help students monitor their own comprehension. For example, a tutor will teach a student to stop at the end of each page and ask, "Did I understand what I just read?" The students learn to check their own comprehension and to go back and reread what they did not understand.

Additional Sources to Consult: For more information, contact the Success for All Foundation, 200 W. Towsontown Blvd., Baltimore, MD 21286. Phone: 1-800-548-4998. Relevant references include Madden et al. (1991); Slavin et al. (1990, 1992).

The Language-Experience Approach

Introduction: The Language-Experience Approach is more of a technique than a reading instruction program. It is worth describing because it is intended to be used when conventional reading instruction programs fail to work and students become frustrated by their continuing failed efforts to read and are reluctant to try again. A purpose of the Learning-Experience Approach is to teach students to read well enough and kindle their motivation to read sufficiently to enable them to progress in conventional school reading programs.

Grade Levels Covered: First, second, and third grade

Subject Areas Covered: Reading

Instructional Tactics: The tutor asks students to tell stories about personal experiences they enjoy tasking about. Together they write the stories in the students' own words. After writing a paragraph, the tutor asks students to read the paragraph. Most students are able to read the story with some assistance from the tutor because they created it and are familiar with the content and progression of events. Moreover, they cooperated with the tutor in writing the story and have had an opportunity to see their oral words translated into writing, and to note the correspondence between the spoken and written language. The same instructional technique is used in each subsequent tutoring session. In addition, the tutor asks the students to read a paragraph that was written in an earlier session.

The Tutor: The tutor should be an accomplished reading teacher, familiar with conventional reading instruction techniques that might be used to help students learn to read. The tutor should also have experience providing remedial instruction for frustrated students who have failed to learn to read in the past.

Additional Sources to Consult: Marvin Efron, Ph.D., 1212 Canary Drive, West Columbia, SC 29169. Phone: 803-794-3444.

Lindamood-Bell Clinical Instruction Program

Introduction: Lindamood-Bell reports that instruction is "based on an individual's learning needs and embodies an interactive, balanced approach. Through Socratic questioning, clinicians teach students to integrate sensory information to help them become self-correcting and independent in all tasks." The program is available nationally.

Grade Levels Covered: Five-year-olds through adults

Subject Areas Covered: Reading, spelling, math

Instructional Tactics: Instruction can occur in one of two ways: (1) Regular—one hour a day for four to six months or (2) Intensive—four hours a day for four to six weeks. Follow-up treatment ranges from one consultation per week to daily sessions.
   The following programs are utilized in the instruction:

- *Phonemic Awareness for Reading, Spelling, & Speech* (Lindamood Phoneme Sequencing Program)

- *Concept Imagery for Comprehension & Thinking* (Visualizing and Verbalizing Program)

- *Symbol Imagery for Sight Words, Phonemic Awareness, & Spelling* (Seeing Stars Program)

- *Visual-Motor Skills* (Drawing with Language Program)
- *Math Computation & Reasoning* (On Cloud Nine Math Program)

The Tutor: The tutor is called a clinician. His/her role is to follow the program precisely. Intensive training is available through workshops, conferences, and internships. On-site consulting is offered.

Additional Sources to Consult: For more information, contact Lindamood-Bell Programs, 1-800-233-1819.

Laubach Literacy Program

Introduction: Laubach Literacy International is a nonprofit educational corporation founded by Dr. Frank C. Laubach. Its purpose is to enable adults and older youths to acquire the skills they need to solve the problems encountered in daily life.

Grade Levels Covered: Teenagers and adults

Subject Areas Covered: Listening, speaking, reading, writing, and math

Instructional Tactics: The Laubach instructional programs are highly structured. Teaching, student evaluation, and remediation of student errors occur sequentially. Reporting and illustrative materials are used to augment initial presentations and demonstrations. Diplomas are given to students when they reach levels of mastery.

The Tutor: No defined credentials are required to teach using the Laubach method. However, to use the method teachers need to follow the instructor's manuals and use the prescribed materials systematically. The following are the materials used to teach beginning literacy at their Level 1.

There are four levels that approximate the first through fourth grade reading levels in the public school system. (This is only an approximate comparison.)

Materials available for Level 1 are:

For the Students:

   Skill Book 1—Text-workbook in reading and writing

   In the Valley—Reader that is utilized after Skill Book 1 is well started

   Checkups for Skill Book 1—Evaluation of student's mastery of skills taught in Skill Book 1

   Diploma for Skill Book 1

For the Tutor:

Teacher's Manual for Skill Book 1 (Contains guides for teaching the skills in students' Skill Book 1)

English as a Second Language (ESOL) Teacher's Manual for Skill Book 1 (Contains guide for evaluating achievement of skills in students' Skill Book 1)

ESOL Illustrations supporting ESOL Teacher's Manual for Skill Book 1

Levels 2, 3, and 4

Similar style workbooks, readers, evaluations, and diplomas are available for all levels.

Supplementary Materials:

For the Students:

Focus on Phonics 1—Sounds and names for letters

More Stories 1—Controlled reader with three extra stories for each lesson

Crossword Puzzles for Skill Books 1 and 2

For the Teacher:

Focus on Phonics 1—Teacher's Edition

Various wall charts, audiotapes, videotapes, and photocopy masters are available at the Center

Similar style supplementary materials are available at all levels

The materials listed above are utilized within a typical Laubach lesson, which includes the introduction of new phonic sounds, practice drilling the phonic sound, practice reading the story, and writing the new sounds.

Listed below are the typical parts of a Laubach lesson:

* Language experience activity (optional)
* Introduction and review of a new letter from a keyword and key picture
* Review of keywords and new words in a story
* Story read by learners with help from a tutor as needed
* Questions asked about the story
* Other activities for teaching reading and writing as appropriate
* Review of letters from previous lessons
* New letters and words written to reinforce reading, letter formation, and spelling
* Creative writing

This program is available nationally at no cost.

Additional Sources to Consult: For more information, contact Laubach Literacy, 1320 Jamesville Avenue, Box 131, Syracuse, NY 13210.

Kumon Math and Reading Centers

Introduction: A Kumon Center is not a traditional classroom environment. In a Kumon Center, students work quietly on their own individualized assignments under the supervision of the Kumon Instructor. There is no lecture and little direct teaching involved. Kumon students visit the Center twice a week. Upon arrival, they hand in completed homework assignments. That day's classwork and future homework assignments are prepared in advance and waiting for the student in an easily accessible file or bin. The student can take any seat and begin to work. First, the student writes his/her name on the worksheet and records the starting time. After completing all of the work, the ending time is recorded. The work is then graded by the instructor or an assistant. Students correct all of their mistakes before leaving and take homework assignments for each day until the next class session.

Grade Levels Covered: Preschool to college in math; preschool to high school in reading.

Subject Areas Covered: Reading and math

Instructional Tactics: The Kumon Program does not use textbooks. Consistent with Kumon's belief in learning by doing, Kumon students progress through the program by successfully completing a series of carefully sequenced worksheets. Kumon achieves this through a progression of incremental steps. Each level consists of 20 sets of 10 worksheets. The instructor may assign additional Kumon-produced exercises as needed. Many Centers have available Kumon magnetic number and alphabet boards to help students learn number or letter sequencing and to improve fine motor hand coordination. Both the reading and math programs have flash cards available. The Kumon Reading Program has a Recommended Reading List of award-winning books that correspond to each level in the materials.

In Kumon, whether students are ready to progress to the next skill level is determined by achievement testing. An achievement test is given when students have finished all of the work in a level and the instructor is satisfied with times and scores. Once students have successfully passed the test, the instructor will discuss the results with parents and advance students to the next level.

The Tutor: Kumon Instructors are educators and local professionals who come from a variety of disciplines. Some are Kumon parents who see the program as a necessary part of the educational environment in their communities. It is the job of the trainer to organize and monitor the overall progress of students, ensuring that both students and staff are following the essential procedures.

Kumon is designed to be a long-term program of individual development. Unlike school classrooms, Kumon Centers are open year-round and are located nationally.

Additional Sources to Consult: For more information, e-mail http://www.kumon.com/work-mastery.htm.

Kaplan Learning Centers

Introduction: Kaplan, Inc., a wholly owned subsidiary of The Washington Post Company, is one of the nation's premier providers of educational services for individuals, schools, and businesses. Kaplan reports that they have served 3 million students in the last 60 years.

Kaplan has a subsidiary, SCORE Educational Centers. At these after-school educational centers, students build academic and goal-setting skills in what the centers deem to be a motivating, sports-oriented environment. Cost varies according to the length of the service plan chosen.

Grade Levels Covered: Kindergarten through eighth grade are covered by SCORE. Other Kaplan centers provide additional services through adulthood.

Subject Areas Covered: They provide instruction in English and all high school subjects. They also provide standardized test preparation including the PSAT, SAT, ACT, SAT II, and entrance and licensing exams.

Instructional Tactics: The curriculum is interactive, utilizing technology, including computer hardware and software which continually assesses and adapts to students' academic needs. An additional component available is in-home, one-on-one tutoring to teach high school academic subjects and proficiency in taking standardized tests.

The Tutor: The teacher serves as an "academic coach." The students' curriculum is pre-prepared and computerized. The teachers are generally college graduates.

Additional Sources to Consult: For more information, contact the Kaplan Educational Centers: 1-888-238-3772.

Sylvan Learning Centers

Introduction: Sylvan Learning Centers are located throughout the United States. They advertise that they offer personalized assessments and programs for students. They state that they use unique motivational methods and certified instructors. Costs vary based on the number of hours of tutoring which the student has contracted to receive.

Grade Levels Covered: Kindergarten through adults

Subject Areas Covered: Reading, math, and language arts

Instructional Tactics: A comprehensive skills assessment is administered to the student. Based upon that assessment, a personalized curriculum is designed which addresses academic weaknesses. The use of positive reinforcement is emphasized. Mastery Learning is the instructional technique employed by Sylvan. (Mastery Learning is summarized in Chapter 5.)

Although Sylvan advertises a 3:1 ratio of students to instructors, one-on-one tutoring is also offered. Instructors utilize their patented "u-shaped" table where the instructor sits in the middle of the "u" with the students on the outside. The Sylvan Skills Assessment is a combination of several tests (standardized) covering multiple skill areas. Vision and hearing screening are included.

In their rendition of Mastery Learning, students must prove that they have "mastered" a concept or skill by using it three to five times, with 80–100% accuracy. At that point the student progresses to the next skill. Periodically, students are retested on skills to ensure retention.

The Tutor: Sylvan advertises that its teachers are certified and specially trained. It is difficult to determine who provides the training and how intensive it is for the teacher. Also, it is unclear by whom the teachers are certified. The teacher's role is to design and implement the program which was developed based upon the assessment. The student typically receives two to four hours of instruction per week for a total of 50 to 100 hours of instruction.

Additional Sources to Consult: For more information, contact the Sylvan Learning Centers: 1-800-EDUCATE.

Before commenting on the individual corrective tutoring techniques previously described, it is important to keep the big picture in mind. One-on-one tutoring is much more effective than group instruction; and any students that fail to master classroom assignments taught by means of classroom instruction should be given one-on-one tutoring until they achieve mastery. The second thing to keep in mind is that corrective tutoring, like most other remedial procedures, is clinical in nature. Remediation is intended to follow a diagnosis/treatment format. Diagnostic procedures are administered first to identify problems. Then treatment procedures are prescribed, based on the diagnosis, specifically to remedy the problems that were diagnosed. The third thing to remember is that a shortcoming of many achievement tests, including standardized achievement tests, is that they reveal when students fail to achieve, but they are inadequate in diagnosing the particular cause(s) of the failure. To be effective, any tests used to evaluate student performance should be constructed to indicate both the level of student performance and strengths and inadequacies in performance, because if we do not know why students have failed we have no basis for remedying their failure. Oftentimes teachers' observations of student performance reveal student inadequacies better than marketed achievement tests.

It is often the case that academic achievement tests and teacher observations are insufficient in revealing causes of academic failures. It is often necessary to use other instruments to identify physical and mental causes of inadequate academic performance. For example, student failure to achieve might be due to a sensory or perpetual disorder. So it is frequently necessary for students to be given vision, hearing, perception, psychological, and other diagnostic tests to locate specific causes of academic failures. If there is a physical or mental cause of academic failure, corrective academic tutoring cannot be effective until the ailment is dealt with. When the ailment is cured or compensated for, students may not require much corrective tutoring to catch up, and once they do catch up they may never need corrective tutoring again. However, if the ailment cannot be cured but can be compensated for, it may be necessary to continue to compensate for the ailment so that the student can continue to learn efficiently; for instance, providing students with glasses to enable them to read.

Typically, diagnosis and treatment of student academic failure begins with a teacher observing students' inadequate task performance, either on a written test or in directly observing students' inability to perform an assigned task. Second, the teacher identifies the specific academic inadequacies so that they can be remediated. Third, the teacher uses corrective tutoring until the students' performance is adequate. This usually entails the teacher reteaching the academic material in ways that are different from the original instruction. A more detailed description of corrective tutoring is provided in Chapter 4 under the heading "Providing Corrective Instruction." Fourth, when corrective instruction continues to be ineffective it is time to refer students to clinicians who can administer physical and mental tests in order to identify underlying causes of the students' poor academic performance. Once the physical or mental causes are identified they can be cured or compensated for, as the case may be, so that the students can be successful academically. With this background in mind, we can begin to highlight and compare features of the tutoring techniques briefly described previously in this chapter.

The Orton-Gillingham Program and the Wilson Reading System are multisensory instructional programs designed to teach language fundamentals to students who have a deficit in a particular sensory modality, such as students with dyslexia. The Orton-Gillingham Program teaches reading, writing, and spelling; the Wilson System teaches reading and spelling. The TEACH program appears to be designed to teach students with perceptual/neurological deficits to read. The Programmed Tutorial Reading technique and the Wallach Tutoring Program also focus on the teaching of reading. In both programs students learn component reading skills before synthesizing them in reading print. The Reading Recovery and Success for All programs have both been adopted by public schools and teach writing as well as reading. Success for All tutoring is designed to be integrated with classroom instruction; Reading Recovery is not. In both programs students engage in reading before they have complete mastery of component reading skills. The Lindamood-Bell and Laubach Literacy programs teach math as well as language skills. The Laubach Literacy Program is designed for teenagers and adults. The Language-Experience Approach is intended to be tried when other reading programs fail with beginning readers.

In addition to programs, there are learning centers that provide corrective tutoring. Students with learning difficulties attend the centers on a regularly scheduled basis. The centers provide their own unique environment. The programs discussed previously tend to be designed for more limited age groups. The Kumon Math and Reading Centers focus on teaching math and reading; the Kaplan and Sylvan centers teach a more extensive range of subjects and prepare students to pass tests. The centers charge a fee and usually cater to students across a wider range of grade levels; the fees charged by these centers can be sizable. Many families cannot afford the investment.

So, available one-on-one tutoring methods are quite varied in the grade levels served, subject areas covered, and their approaches. Still, all of the tutoring techniques are designed to remediate students with learning difficulties. They are all highly structured and prescriptive. Tutors are required to follow the prescribed methods using prescribed materials, and little latitude is allowed for teacher innovation. All of the programs deal with reading problems, recognizing how important reading is to independent and lifelong learning as well as learning in all content areas. Tutoring programs are available to treat beginning reading problems in students of all ages. Many programs are designed for beginning readers in the primary grades to nip reading problems in the bud and enable students to read as early as possible. Once students begin to read, the need to read is so prevalent that they are bound to practice and improve their reading skills and scope. Some of the programs focus entirely on reading; some extend to the teaching of other language skills such as speaking, writing, and spelling. The second most popular tutoring programs are those designed to remedy problems in the learning of math. Some more academically oriented tutoring methods are designed to remediate student inadequacies by reteaching in new ways assignments students failed to master during classroom instruction. Other more clinical programs are designed to diagnose and treat underlying causes when academic reteaching is insufficient in overcoming learning difficulties.

In addition to the compelling research evidence proving that one-on-one tutoring is more effective than group instruction in increasing academic achievement, there is evidence showing the effectiveness of particular tutoring programs. Wasik and Slavin (2000) provide evidence of the effectiveness of the Reading Recovery,

Success for All, TEACH, and Programmed Tutorial Reading programs. Many of the research studies include control group comparisons and show gains in achievement. There is more evidence supporting the efficacy of some programs than others. Although other tutorial programs are not supported by objective research, there is often some clinical evidence that they work gleaned from the treatment of individuals. For example, the Orton-Gillingham Program and the Wilson Reading System have been shown in clinical trials to be effective in teaching dyslexic students to read. Private enterprise learning centers provide evidence to encourage potential customers to pay for their services. Many adopt instructional techniques that have been shown to be effective, including one-on-one tutoring. And in lieu of objective research, they probably can provide supportive testimonials from satisfied parents and other customers.

OTHER TUTORING OPTIONS

In addition to the tutoring programs and centers described previously, there are other tutoring options to consider.

Peer Tutoring

Peer tutoring is a viable, inexpensive option for schools that want to develop and tailor a one-on-one tutoring program as a supplement to their regular classroom instruction. Peer tutoring can be very successful in preventing and remediating student failure, depending on how it is designed and implemented. When peer tutoring is coordinated with classroom instruction there is no need to purchase commercially available packaged programs for the peer tutors to use. Textbooks and teaching aids have already been selected and are available to use for corrective instruction. The classroom teacher can point out for peer tutors the particular concepts to-be-tutored students are having problems with the textbook the class is using and perhaps make suggestions for correcting the problems. The primary task of the peer tutor will be to reteach the material the tutee failed to grasp through previous instruction. Peer tutors can be very successful if they are assigned to correct tutee inadequacies in learning specific class assignments and are given the material and guidance they need to reteach it. On the other hand, peer tutors can be made to fail if they are assigned to remediate gross pronounced learning deficits that have exacerbated over the years. Students with such pronounced learning deficits need long-term remediation and are the types of students that find their way to remedial learning centers or are referred to counselors and special education classes. It is also quite possible that they may continue to be neglected and fall farther and farther behind their age mates. Finally, peer tutors should be provided any diagnostic information they may need.

Peer tutors do not require extended training if all they are asked to do is help student tutees with specific well-defined, immediate problems. One-on-one tutoring is so effective that unhurried, personalized instruction focused on correcting the inadequate performance of a current assigned task may be all that is needed. However, peer tutors can profit from some training in uncomplicated effective instructional strategies, such as how to use repetition effectively in teaching. (A thorough explanation of how to use repetition and other instructional strategies research has shown to be effective in increasing academic achievement can be found in Chapter 4.) At the very least, peer tutors should be given some advice on how to reteach inadequately learned assignments. It is most important that peer tutors have competent supervision from teachers adept at corrective instruction whenever they need it. Not only do the supervisors need to provide guidance to the peer tutors, they should be available to provide tutoring to help with difficult cases.

Before considering a peer tutoring program for your particular needs, it would be advisable to consult the literature on peer tutoring. For reviews of research on peer tutoring see Cloward (1967); Devlin-Sheehan, Feldman, and Allen (1976); Greenwood, Delquardi, and Hall (1989); Scruggs and Richter (1985); Von Harrison and Gottfredson (1986). Important references include Clay (1979); Clay and Cozden (1990); DeFord et al. (1988); Goodman, Watson, and Burke (1987); Handerhan (1990); Huck and Pinnell (1986); Lyons (1991); Lyons et al. (1989); Pinnell (1985, 1989); Pinnell et al. (1986). Both cross-age and same-age peer tutoring are covered in the literature. Although it may be more advantageous to have older students tutor younger students, same-age tutors can be effective. As you will see in Chapter 7, in general, ability grouping does not work. One reason heterogeneous grouping is more effective may be that more advanced students can tutor students in their class who are having problems. When designing your own tutoring program, it is well to keep in mind that no single peer tutoring system has emerged as the most effective for all circumstances. While designing a peer tutoring program to meet your needs, it is well to consider different peer tutoring formats and adopt those components that suit your purpose and local conditions and constraints. For instance, "Success for All" utilizes an articulation and coordination format between classroom teachers and tutors that may be advantageous.

On-Line Tutoring

One of the latest tutoring modes is on-line tutoring. A great many would-be tutors are presently offering their services on the Internet for those willing to hire them. One problem with on-line tutoring is that it is often difficult to ascertain the qualifications of the tutors offering their services. They may not be qualified teachers and/or they may not be competent in providing instruction in the particular subject area needed to remediate the particular problem a student may be having. In addition, they may not be competent in following the clinical diagnosis/prescription format necessary to provide effective corrective instruction. Before engaging an on-line tutor, it is also well to keep in mind that one-on-one tutoring that has proven to be effective requires face-to-face contact.

Effective tutors have the opportunity of benefiting from nonverbal communication and monitoring a student's performance of assigned tasks as they are performing them. Personally observing student performance enables the tutor to prompt and cue students to the correct outcome, preventing them from making mistakes they may have otherwise made. It is important to remember that tutored students do not require much remedial work because they can be guided to correct solutions, thereby preventing failure. Face-to-face tutors, like all teachers, use teaching aids as appropriate, such as computers and other teaching machines, and they may give students unsupervised homework assignments. However, these are given as supplements to provide students practice in perfecting task performance. Teaching machines are not used instead of tutors, and good tutors make certain that students are able to perform tasks without supervision before giving them independent assignments. To be effective, tutors need to provide the personal attention and observation of student performance needed to remediate student performance. On-line tutoring may be a wave of the future, but it falls short of providing the face-to-face guidance and corrective tutoring many students need.

Other tutoring options that need to be considered include location of tutoring sites, potential tutors, and student eligibility for tutoring. Tutoring can be made available on the school premises after school or during school hours when study periods are assigned. Tutoring can also be provided after school on church and temple premises or in community facilities. It is also possible to provide tutoring in students' homes.

Many different types of people have been engaged to serve as tutors throughout our nation. Tutoring can be implemented on a part-time basis. However, most formal tutoring programs can benefit from the services of a full-time director to manage the hiring of tutors, tutor training, coordination, scheduling of tutoring, and the acquisition of tutoring materials. The director needs to be a tutoring expert familiar with clinical diagnostic/prescriptive procedures as well as referral resources for students with special needs, such as students with hearing problems.

Other tutors can be engaged part-time. Some of the possibilities for implementing part-time tutoring can be by qualified students, retirees, employed professionals interested in moonlighting, and parents and teachers. Some retirees who are unwilling or unable to work full-time are eager to tutor children part-time; it makes them feel useful and productive. Retirees are available in every community, everywhere in the country. Many civil servants, such as policemen, firemen, and other government employees, tutor children in addition to their full-time job. Professionals employed full-time in the private sector volunteer to tutor our youth part-time. Some corporations encourage and reward their employees for tutoring children part-time. There are corporations that undertake to provide tutoring services for one or more schools in their community. Many parents engaged primarily in child rearing and homemaking serve routinely as tutors. And many of our underpaid teachers supplement their income by tutoring part-time. There is no shortage of potential part-time tutors, many of whom can be engaged inexpensively, even for free.

Student eligibility for tutoring is another issue that needs to be considered. School-sponsored tutoring can be made available only to students who are referred by their classroom teacher or counselors. As a matter of policy, such referrals might be restricted only to students who have failing grades or it might be extended to students with less pronounced learning difficulties. On the other hand, tutoring might be extended to include all students in school. Students who are not referred for tutoring but who may want to clarify misunderstandings that are troubling them might be permitted to avail themselves of tutoring. Making tutoring available to all students serves to prevent as well as remediate student learning inadequacies to a much greater extent. And because any student can obtain tutoring services, more students are apt to use it. Moreover, tutoring is much less likely to stigmatize students as inferior. All students are provided the opportunity to find out what they don't know, which philosophically emphasizes the importance of satisfying students' interests and curiosity as well as achieving assigned learning objectives. To make tutoring totally informal and to manifest an "open door" policy, a tutoring room or center could be designated where students could drop in any time to be tutored or, if need be, to schedule an appointment for tutoring.

DESIGNING A SCHOOL TUTORING SYSTEM

We have not begun to develop the kinds of effective school tutoring systems possible utilizing available tutoring options. Once it is understood that the most effective means of preventing and remediating student failure is providing one-on-one tutoring as a supplement to classroom instruction, many resources can be considered in designing a tutoring program tailored to meet the needs, constraints, and prevailing conditions in a particular school. The tutoring options described previously should not be considered as mutually exclusive choices. Many of them can be utilized in combination, and particular components of packaged tutoring programs can be used in designing a custom-made tutoring system. There are, however, certain features that all effective tutoring systems need to incorporate:

1. One-on-one, face-to-face tutoring needs to be maximized so that tutors can personally observe and oversee students' task performance. Teaching aids and machines can be used to supplement personal supervision but not to replace it. Computers need to be used more to relieve tutors from nitty-gritty tasks such as record keeping and less for tutoring.

2. Tutoring needs to follow a diagnostic/prescriptive format in which all tutoring prescriptions are based on the diagnoses of student inadequacies. Paper-and-pencil tests can be used to identify students' inadequacies and, to the extent possible, the causes of the inadequacies. Personal observation

of student performance needs to be used to confirm causes of student inadequacies and to reveal causes that cannot be identified using paper-and-pencil tests. Second opinions are desirable to confirm questionable diagnoses and in selecting appropriate prescriptions. Computer data banks can be used as available to cue and suggest possible prescription options.

3. A quiet atmosphere devoid of distractions needs to be provided to maximize the benefits of one-on-one tutoring.

4. A tutoring director needs to be employed to supervise tutoring and tutor training. Novice tutors can be allowed to begin tutoring without extensive training. Initial training might involve as little as showing novice tutors how to reteach subject matter they are familiar with to students who did not learn it adequately during classroom instruction. Additional tutor training can be provided as needed. The director must be aware of available academic diagnostic and prescriptive procedures and be able to use them. In addition, the director must be able to make referrals to professionals better able to diagnose and treat underlying, nonacademic problems.

5. An inventory of academic testing instruments needs to be available to pinpoint academic inadequacies and, as much as possible, causes of inadequacies in learning the subject matter taught in the particular school. An inventory of alternative teaching methods and materials also needs to be available for reteaching topics that students fail to learn from regular classroom instruction of the school curriculum.

6. Minimal services that need to be provided include the diagnosis of academic inadequacies of all subject matter taught in the school and the reteaching in new ways of all subject matter taught in the school. In addition, simple screening instruments need to be used to identify underlying physical and psychological problems of students who fail to benefit from the reteaching of subject matter they fail to grasp; for example, an eye chart. The screening devices are to be used to determine the type of clinician a student is to be referred to, not for diagnostic purposes.

Other decisions that need to be made in designing a school tutoring system include: (1) which students are eligible for tutoring, (2) where tutoring services are to be provided, (3) the times tutoring is to be made available, (4) tutor qualifications, (5) amount of tutor training to be required, and (6) available packaged tutoring programs to be utilized in the system. These and other decisions will need to be made depending on the policies, curriculum, resources, and goals of the school system.

In conclusion, recognizing the effectiveness of one-on-one tutoring in remediating learning difficulties, it is important to note that, in general, one-on-one tutoring seems to work:

- Using trained tutors who may or may not be certified teachers.

- To prevent student failure as well as to remediate student failure.

- In all subject areas.

- With almost all types of students.

- At all grade levels.

- And can be cost-effective in the long run.

- Best if it begins in the primary grades.

- Whether or not it is closely integrated with classroom instruction.

- When tutoring prescriptions are based on effective diagnosis of learning difficulties.

- As a supplement to classroom instruction.

- Whether components of the reading process are taught before students are allowed to read print, or while they are learning to read print.

  Teaching parts and not wholes, or wholes and not parts, does not appear to be effective. In the *Handbook on Effective Instructional Strategies* (Friedman & Fisher, 1998), 50 research studies are cited in Chapter 9, "Providing Subject Matter Unifiers," which indicate that understanding parts/whole relationships increases academic achievement (p. 114). The evidence also shows that whole language instruction is ineffective (p. 239).

Last, but not least, timely, early one-on-one tutoring markedly reduces grade retention and special education referrals. It also tends to be more effective than reducing class size or adding teacher aids (Wasik & Slavin, 2000; see also Chapter 8). Most relevant, it can be used to appreciably reduce the number of student failures.

One-on-one is undoubtedly the most effective student/teacher ratio for increasing student achievement. However, as you will learn in Chapter 7 when student/teacher ratio is discussed, the more student/teacher ratio is reduced below 15:1, the more student achievement tends to increase. So one-on-one tutoring is the most effective means of providing corrective instruction. If one-on-one tutoring is not feasible, the smaller the student/teacher ratio is below 15:1 when implementing corrective instruction, the more effective instruction is likely to be. It should also be noted that generic instructional programs that research shows increase academic achievement provide corrective instruction in groups of five or less when the students in the group need corrective instruction for the same learning deficiencies—for example, "Direct Instruction." (See Chapter 5 for an introduction to "Direct Instruction" and for references that provide more detail on this generic program.)

Following are additional references.

REFERENCES

Anania, J. (1981). *The effects of quality of instruction on the cognitive and affective learning of students.* Unpublished doctoral dissertation, University of Chicago.

Arnold, L. E., Barnebey, N., McManus, J., Smeltzer, D. J., Conrad, A., & Descranges, L. (1977). Prevention of specific perceptual remediation for vulnerable first-graders. *Archives of General Psychiatry*, 34, 1279–1294.

Bloom, B. S. (1984, May). The search for methods of group instruction as effective as one-to-one tutoring. *Educational Leadership*, 4–17.

Burke, A. J. (1983). *Students' potential for learning contrasted under tutorial and group approaches to instruction.* Unpublished doctoral dissertation, University of Chicago.

Clay, M. M. (1979). *Reading: The patterning of reading difficulties.* Exeter, NH: Heinemann.

Clay, M. M., & Cazden, C. B. (1990). A Vygotskian interpretation of Reading Recovery. In L. Moll (Ed.), *Vygotsky and education* (pp. 206–222). New York: Cambridge University Press.

Cloward, R. D. (1967). Studies in tutoring. *Journal of Experimental Education*, 36, 14–25.

Deford, D., Pinnell, G. S., Lyons, C., & Young, P. (1988). *Reading Recovery. Volume IX, Report of the follow-up studies.* Columbus, OH: Ohio State University.

Devlin-Sheehan, L., Feldman, R. S., & Allen, V. L. (1976). Research on children tutoring children: A critical review. *Review of Educational Research*, 46, 355–385.

Dorval, B., Wallach, L., & Wallach, M. A. (1978). Field evaluation of a tutorial reading program emphasizing phoneme identification skills. *The Reading Teacher*, 31, 748–790.

Ellison, D. G., Barber, L., Encle, T. L., & Kampwerth, L. (1965). Programmed tutoring: A teaching aid and a research tool. *Reading Research Quarterly*, 1, 77–127.

Ellison, D. G., Harris, P., & Barber, L. (1968). A field test of programmed and directed tutoring. *Reading Research Quarterly*, 3, 307–367.

Goodman, K., Watson, B., & Burke, C. (1987). *Reading miscue inventory* (2nd ed.). New York: Richard C. Owen.

Green, J., & Weade, R. (1985). Reading between the words. *Theory into Practice*, 24, 14–21.

Greenwood, C. R., Delquardi, J. C., & Hall, R. V. (1989). Longitudinal effects of classwide peer tutoring. *Journal of Educational Psychology*, 81, 371–383.

Hagin, R. A., Silver, A. A., & Beecher, R. (1978). Scanning, diagnosis, and intervention in the prevention of learning disabilities: II. TEACH: Learning tasks for the prevention of learning disabilities. *Journal of Learning Disabilities*, 11(7), 54–57.

Handerhan, E. (1990). Reading instruction as defined "successful" teachers and their first grade students within an early intervention program. *Education Abstracts International*, No. AAC910512.

Huck, C. S., & Pinnell, G. S. (1986). *The Reading Recovery Project in Columbus, Ohio. Pilot Year, 1984–1985.* Columbus, OH: Ohio State University.

Lyons, C., Pinnell, G. S., Deford, D., McCarrier, A., & Schnug, J. (1989). *The Reading Recovery Project in Columbus, Ohio. Year 3: 1988–1989.* Columbus, OH: Ohio State University.

Lyons, C. A. (1991). A comparative study of the teaching effectiveness of teachers participating in a year-long or 2-week inservice program. In the 40th Yearbook of the National Reading Conference, *Learner factors/teacher factors: Issues in literacy research and instruction.* Chicago: National Reading Conference.

Madden, N. A., Slavin, R. E., Karweit, N. L., Dolan, L. J., Wasik, B. A., Shaw, A., Leighton, M., & Mainzer, K. L. (1991, April). *Success for All third-year results.* Paper presented at the annual convention of the American Educational Research Association, Chicago.

Mantzicopoulos, P., Morrison, D., Stone, E., & Setrakain, W. (1990, April). *Academic effects of perceptually and phonetically based intervention for vulnerable readers.* Paper presented at the annual convention of the American Educational Research Association, Boston.

McCleary, E. (1971). Report of results of Tutorial Reading Project. *The Reading Teacher,* 24, 556–559.

Pinnell, G. S. (1985). Helping teachers help children at risk: Insights for the Reading Recovery program. *Peabody Journal of Education,* 62(3), 70–85.

Pinnell, G. S. (1988, April). *Sustained effects of a strategy-centered early intervention program in reading.* Paper presented at the annual convention of the American Educational Research Association, New Orleans.

Pinnell, G. S., Short, A. G., Lyons, C. A., & Yolng, P. (1986). *The Reading Recovery Project in Columbus, Ohio. Year 1: 1985–1986.* Columbus, OH: Ohio State University.

Scruggs, T. E., & Richter, L. (1985). Tutoring learning disabled students: A critical review. *Learning Disability Quarterly,* 8, 274–286.

Silver, A. A., & Hagin, R. A. (1979). *Prevention of learning disabilities.* Submission to Joint Dissemination Review Panel. Washington, DC: U.S. Department of Education.

Silver, A. A., & Hagin, R. A. (1990). *Disorders of learning in childhood.* New York: John Wiley & Sons.

Slavin, R. E., Madden, N. A., Karweit, N. L., Dolan, L., & Wasik, B. A. (1990, April). *Success for All: Effects of variations in duration and resources of a schoolwide elementary restructuring program.* Paper presented at the annual convention of the American Educational Research Association, Boston.

Slavin, R. E., Madden, N. A., Karweit, N. L., Dolan, L., & Wasik, B. A. (1992). *Success for All: A relentless approach to prevention and early intervention in elementary schools.* Arlington, VA: Educational Research Service.

Von Harrison, G., & Gottfredson, C. (1986, Spring). Peer tutoring: A viable alternative to cross-age tutoring. *Contemporary Issues in Reading,* 125–131.

Wallach, L., Wallach, M. A., Dozier, M. G., & Kaplan, N. E. (1977). Poor children learning to read do not have trouble with auditory education but do have trouble with phoneme recognition. *Journal of Educational Psychology,* 69, 36–39.

Wallach, M. A., & Wallach, L. (1976). *Teaching all children to read.* Chicago: University of Chicago Press.

Wasik, B. A., & Slavin, R. E. (2000). *Preventing early reading failure with one-to-one tutoring: A review of five programs.* Center for Research on Effective Schooling for Disadvantaged Students. Baltimore, MD: The Johns Hopkins University.

4

Making Instruction More Effective

To provide context for the descriptions of the effective instructional strategies that follow, this chapter will first offer a rendition of the instructional process and decisions that pertain to it. This will clarify the definition of key instructional terms and their relationship. There are so many terms associated with instruction and so many complicated versions of the instructional process that there is a need to clarify one's orientation at the outset. Although there is no need for the reader to subscribe to this rendition, there is a need to understand it.

POLICY OBJECTIVES

Although educational policy objectives are not a part of instruction, they serve to initiate and guide the formulation of instruction. Policy objectives are desired student outcomes to be achieved by means of instruction. Policy objectives are established by policy makers, such as legislatures and school boards. They are typically expressed in lay, abstract language. The setting of policy objectives is prerequisite to instructional decision-making, but it is not a part of it.

INSTRUCTIONAL PLANNING

Five major decision-making points in instructional planning are: (1) deriving learning objectives, (2) planning instructional tasks, (3) planning evaluation, (4) planning task assignments, and (5) planning teaching.

Deriving Learning Objectives

Abstract policy objectives must be translated into concrete learning objectives so that student achievement can be evaluated and demonstrated. For this reason, learning objectives are defined as terminal tasks that students are to be able to perform, with the following proviso: The outcome of task performance must be observable. For student achievement to be evaluated and demonstrated, it is necessary that the outcome of student performance be observed. It would be more advantageous if student performance could be observed as well. This would reveal inadequate aspects of student performance responsible for inadequate achievement. A number of learning objectives may need to be achieved to manifest the achievement of a policy objective. It behooves those responsible for deriving learning objectives to work with policy makers to ensure that the intent of policy objectives is captured in the learning objectives.

Planning Instructional Tasks

Tasks are student/subject matter interactions formulated for students to perform to enable them to achieve a specified outcome. Task planning is the organizing of a sequence of tasks students are to perform, leading progressively from minimal entry-level tasks that are designed for students with particular readiness characteristics to tasks that represent achievement of a learning objective. Task planning includes the planning of *corrective tasks* for students who fail to perform *progressive tasks* in the sequence. Thus, task planning involves the planning of both progressive tasks and corrective tasks.

The above prescription results in the planning of an instructional unit. A number of instructional units are organized to achieve a policy objective. Complexity in the organization of instructional units to achieve a policy objective is most often necessary. Excessive complexity within an instructional unit can impair learning and is to be avoided.

Planning Evaluation

Evaluation is defined as the comparison of actual task performance to criteria specifying competent task performance and the diagnosis of insufficiencies in a task performance. Planning evaluation consists of:

1. Developing a procedure to identify and record actual task performance.
2. Establishing criteria of competent task performance.
3. Specifying a procedure for comparing actual and competent task performance.
4. Developing a procedure for diagnosing insufficiencies in task performance. It is beneficial, if not necessary, to diagnose causes of insufficiencies in order to correct them.

Planning Task Assignments

Tasks are assigned to students based on their performance on evaluation instruments.

Planning placement assignments entails specifying the readiness characteristics that students are to possess to be assigned to a particular task sequence leading to the achievement of a learning objective. Placements are made when students' readiness characteristics match the entry-level requirements of the first task in a sequence. When a match is made it may be said that students are ready to perform a task. Thus, *readiness* is defined as possessing the knowledge, skill, and disposition necessary to perform the assigned tasks being considered.

Achievement task assignments are planned so that students who perform a task in a sequence correctly are assigned to perform *progressive tasks*, that is, more advanced tasks in the sequence. Students who do not perform tasks in a sequence correctly are assigned to perform *corrective tasks* until they are able to perform the failed tasks correctly.

Planning Teaching

Teaching is defined as guiding and facilitating students' task performance in order to achieve a learning objective. Thus, planning teaching entails planning strategies that will enhance student task performance. Among other things, strategies that enhance communication, transfer of learning, recall, understanding, problem solving, and student attentiveness need to be considered and incorporated in teaching plans.

Instruction

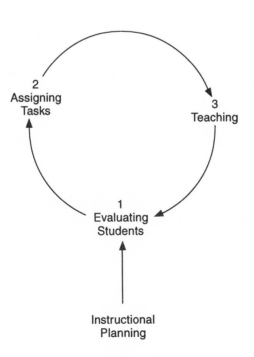

As the above cycle shows, instruction begins after instructional planning, which is in preparation for instruction. First, students are evaluated to determine their readiness to perform tasks in a sequence leading to the achievement of the learning objective. Second, they are assigned either progressive or corrective tasks based on the evaluation. Third, teaching ensues, that is, student task performance is guided and facilitated. The cycle is repeated over and over until the learning objective being pursued is achieved.

As can be seen, the process defines a feedback loop which can be used as the basic unit for analyzing instruction.

INSTRUCTIONAL STRATEGIES THAT IMPROVE ACADEMIC ACHIEVEMENT

The following descriptions of effective instructional strategies are elaborations and extrapolations of those described in the *Handbook on Effective Instructional Strategies: Evidence for Decision-Making* (Friedman & Fischer, 1998). The descriptions in the *Handbook* purposefully do not stray far from the research. From 50 to over 200 research studies are cited in the *Handbook* to support the effectiveness of each of the strategies described in increasing academic achievement. The purpose of the *Handbook* is to present in brief the unvarnished facts and the data that validates them. Using the data as a foundation, teachers and instructional planners can construct curricula and instruction in accordance with their own orientation to meet their local needs.

The presentations of the effective instructional strategies here represent cogent conceptualizations of the data, although admittedly there may be others. The purpose of these conceptualizations is to provide additional suggestions to help teachers, instructional planners, and administrators formulate effective instructional programs to increase academic achievement and to reduce student failure.

The presentation of each of the effective instructional strategies will follow the same format. First, a brief orientation to the strategy will be given. Second, the number of studies that support the effectiveness of the strategy in enhancing academic achievement will be given. Third, the instructional tactics for administering the instructional strategies are described. Fourth, illustrations of applications of the strategy are provided to elaborate the use of the strategy. As you will see, applications include everyday applications, instructional applications, and subject area applications. The number of studies that support each strategy and the instructional tactics for administering an instructional strategy are extracted and cited from the *Handbook on Effective Instructional Strategies*. More can be learned about each instructional strategy by consulting the *Handbook*. Cautions as well as extensive references are provided.

Defining Instructional Expectations

ORIENTATION

After instructional planning is completed and teaching begins, the first effective instructional strategy that should be employed to achieve any learning objective is defining instructional expectations. That is, (1) the learning objective, (2) the procedures for achieving the learning objective, and (3) the criteria used to determine the successful achievement of the learning objective are clearly defined for the students. When students do not know what the learning objective they are to achieve is, the procedures they are to employ to achieve it and the criteria for determining successful achievement of the objective learning will be impaired. Students may become confused or frustrated, and may flounder in their efforts to achieve the learning objective.

Number of Supportive Studies: 169

INSTRUCTIONAL TACTICS

The following tactics are shown to increase academic achievement.

- The learning objective must be defined. Before pursuing any learning objective, it is important to let students know what they are expected to achieve in simple words the students can understand.

- Procedures for achieving the learning objective must be defined. Once the learning objective is specified, students are to be told how they are expected to achieve the objective. This is a matter of giving them an overview of the tasks they are expected to perform to achieve the objective. There is often more than one way to achieve an objective, and often there is a preferred way.

- Performance criteria must be defined. Students must be given a clear idea of the criteria that will be used to determine successful achievement of the learning objective—the performance criteria they are expected to meet. Whereas the initial defining of the learning objective is more general for the purpose of orientation, performance criteria are to be specific in order to reduce ambiguity.

ILLUSTRATIONS OF APPLICATIONS

Everyday Applications

Defining Objectives

If the parents' objective is to improve the way a child keeps her room, they must define the objective for the child. For example, "You need to keep your room cleaner and neater."

Defining Procedures to Be Used

To facilitate the achievement of the objective, the parents must define the procedures their child is to use to achieve the objectives. For example, "You need to mop your floor, vacuum your carpet, put your belongings away, dust your furniture, and smooth the wrinkles out of the blanket and sheets when you make your bed."

Defining Criteria for Success

To make certain the child knows when he/she has successfully kept his/her room neat and clean, parents must define the criteria for success. For example, "Your room will be considered neat and clean when there is no dirt on the floor or rug, your belongings are stored in their appropriate place when you are through with them, there are no wrinkles in your bed linens and blanket, and there is no dust on your furniture."

Instructional Applications

Defining the Learning Objective

In general, students have to be informed beforehand exactly what the learning objective is so they know what they are expected to achieve before making an attempt.

Defining Procedures to Be Used

Procedures to be employed by the students must be specifically identified beforehand so that the students know how they are expected to achieve the objective and do not deviate or flounder in their attempts. For instance, if the learning objective is to be able to add fractions, addition of fractions should be specifically identified as the procedure to employ in order to reduce the likelihood that the student will employ the procedure of conversion of fractions to decimals and thus fail to adequately perform the assigned task.

Defining Criteria for Success

Students must be informed beforehand the criteria for successful accomplishment of the learning objective. Failure to do so may result in the students thinking they have successfully accomplished the assigned task when they have only partially accomplished the assigned task or they have failed to complete the assigned task. In either case the students may think they have achieved the learning objective when they have not.

Subject Area Applications

Science

Defining Objectives

For a unit on deciduous trees in the north central area of the United States, a possible learning objective that should be defined for the students before instruction is that the students will be able to identify the leaves of white oak, red oak, elm, white birch, and red maple trees.

Defining Procedures

Procedures to be employed that should be identified beforehand might include studying labeled samples of the leaves, pictures, and/or specimens.

Defining Criteria for Success

Criteria for successful accomplishment of the learning objective that should be defined for the students beforehand might be that they will be able to correctly identify at least four of the five leaf types.

Math

Defining Objectives

For a unit on converting fractions, a possible learning objective that should be defined for the students before instruction might be that the students will be able to convert simple fractions to decimal equivalents.

Defining Procedures

Procedures to be employed that should be identified beforehand might include employing division of the numerator by the denominator.

Defining Criteria for Success

Criteria for successful accomplishment of the learning objective that should be defined for the students beforehand might be that they will be able to convert correctly 80% of the fractions to decimals on an end-of-unit test.

Language Arts

Defining Objectives

For a unit identifying the main ideas in a text, a possible learning objective that might be defined for the students before instruction is: Students will be able to identify the main ideas in a prose selection.

Defining Procedures

Procedures to be employed that should be identified beforehand might include outlining the selection.

Defining Criteria for Success

Criteria for successful accomplishment of the learning objective that should be defined for the students beforehand might be that they will be able to identify correctly 80% of the main ideas in a specified prose selection.

Social Studies

Defining Objectives

For a unit on the location of the 50 states of the United States, a possible learning objective that might be defined for the students before instruction is: Students will be able to identify the location of each of the 50 states on a map.

Defining Procedures

Procedures to be employed that should be identified beforehand might include employing the use of a map of the United States to memorize the location of each state.

Defining Criteria for Success

Criteria for successful accomplishment of the learning objective that should be defined for the students beforehand might be that they will be able to label correctly the location of 80% of the states on a blank map of the United States.

REFERENCE

Anderson, S. A. (1994). *Synthesis of research on Mastery Learning* (Information analysis). ERIC Document Reproduction Service No. ED 382 567.

Taking Student Readiness into Account

ORIENTATION

Student readiness is defined as student knowledge, skills, and dispositions necessary to perform a task. The preeminence of readiness in determining student success in achieving learning objectives cannot be overemphasized. Students must possess the particular readiness characteristics necessary to perform a particular task for them to successfully achieve the learning objective being pursued. When students do not possess the readiness characteristics necessary to perform the tasks that enable achievement of the learning objectives they are not likely to achieve the objectives, even if other effective strategies are employed in teaching the students.

Number of Supportive Studies: 171

INSTRUCTIONAL TACTICS

The evidence well supports the need to consider student readiness when planning teaching, assigning tasks, and evaluating performance of tasks. The following tactics are derived from studies that demonstrate the benefits of considering student readiness when planning, teaching, assigning, and evaluating performance of tasks. Discretion has been used to interpret and reduce overlap in tactics used in different studies and to elaborate tactics.

Tactics employed are:

Planning: Tasks leading to the achievement of a learning objective should be sequenced so that earlier tasks in the sequence provide students with the skills and knowledge they need to perform subsequent tasks. The number of tasks planned in a sequence should be based on the difficulty level of the learning objective to be achieved. A greater number of tasks should be planned to achieve a more difficult learning objective.

Evaluation: Accurately evaluating the students' current knowledge, skills, and disposition should be a basis for assigning tasks to students.

Assigning Tasks: In assigning tasks, the knowledge and skills of the students must be sufficient to meet the demands of the tasks.

Teaching: A mastery level of performance should be attained for each task so that students who learn to perform a task are ready to perform the next task in the sequence.

ILLUSTRATIONS OF APPLICATIONS

Everyday Applications

When a person first learns to drive an automobile there are certain prerequisite knowledge, skills, and dispositions one must possess in order to properly operate the vehicle. There are also prerequisite knowledge, skills, and dispositions one must possess in order to pass examinations and obtain a driver's license.

Instructional Applications

Planning for Placement

Instructional planners must know how to analyze and use information in students' files to assess students' readiness characteristics. They must be able to determine whether students' (1) knowledge, (2) skills, and (3) disposition enable them to perform entry-level tasks in planned sequences, and they must be able to place students correctly by matching student readiness characteristics with entry-level requirements of planned task sequences.

Plans must be made in classroom instruction to teach the students' readiness requirements to begin an assigned task sequence beforehand to ensure that students are ready to begin. Such "refresher" instruction remediates student readiness deficiencies that are most often present in classes of students.

Planning Task Sequences

Instructional planners must be able to plan task sequences for students with particular entry-level readiness characteristics. In addition, they must be able to sequence tasks so that earlier tasks in the sequence provide students with the knowledge, skills, and dispositions required to perform subsequent tasks.

Instruction

Evaluation

Prior to teaching students to perform a new task sequence, teachers must inspect students' previous evaluation records to assess their readiness to begin the sequence.

During instruction, teachers must evaluate task performance of each task in the sequence to determine students' readiness for the next task.

Task Assignment

Based on evaluation, teachers must determine whether students are ready to undertake a new task or need corrective instruction to enable them to perform the new task.

Teaching

Teachers must make sure that students master the performance of a prerequisite task to ensure that they are ready to perform the next assigned task. In classroom instruction, when deficiencies in readiness are evident or suspect, it is advisable to provide refresher instruction to reteach readiness requirements before proceeding.

Subject Area Examples

Science

Instructional Planning

In order to assign students to task sequences, the instructional planner should check the individual student records for information on the students' prior performance in science classes. Additionally, any information available on students' science achievement or ability scores on standardized tests should be taken into account.

To teach the dissection of a frog, the instructional planner might plan to begin with a task on the proper use of the required tools, such as the scalpel, followed by a task on using the scalpel to make an incision in the frog.

Instruction

Evaluation. The teacher would need to evaluate students' ability to use the scalpel properly to determine the students' readiness for the next task.

Task Assignment. Based on the evaluation, the teacher must determine whether a student is ready to progress to using the scalpel to make an incision in the frog or needs remediation on the proper use of the scalpel to enable the student to progress to dissecting the frog.

Teaching. The teacher needs to make certain that the students master the proper use of the scalpel to ensure that students are ready to perform the next task in the sequence.

Math

Instructional Planning

In order to assign students to task sequences, the instructional planner should check the individual student records for information on the students' prior performance in math classes. Additionally, any information available on students' math achievement or ability scores on standardized tests should be taken into account.

For a class on the addition of fractions, the instructional planner might want to develop a sequence of tasks beginning with the addition of fractions with like denominators, such as 1/2 + 1/2, then follow with the addition of fractions with unlike denominators, such as 1/2 + 3/4, and perhaps next the addition of complex fractions, such as 1 1/4 + 5 3/4, and so forth.

Instruction

Evaluation. The teacher needs to evaluate the students' task performance of each task in the sequence to determine the students' readiness for the next task. For instance, the teacher would want to ensure that when a student adds 1/2 + 1/2 that the answer the student arrives at is 1 before allowing the student to progress to the next task of adding fractions with unlike denominators.

Task Assignment. Based on the evaluation, the teacher needs to determine whether a student is ready to progress to the next task of adding fractions with unlike denominators, or if there is a need to provide the student with remediation on the adding of fractions with like denominators to enable the student to proceed to the next task of adding fractions with unlike denominators.

Teaching. The teacher needs to make certain that students master the performance of adding the fractions in a particular task in the sequence before allowing them to proceed to the next task to ensure that the students are ready to perform the next task in the sequence.

Social Studies

Instructional Planning

In order to assign students to task sequences, the instructional planner should check the individual student records for information on the students' prior performance in social studies classes. Additionally, any information available on students' social studies achievement scores on standardized tests should be taken into account.

For a class on the states of the United States and their capitals, the instructional planner might wish to sequence the tasks so that the students first learn the names of all of the states and then the name of the capital for each state.

Instruction

Evaluation. The teacher needs to evaluate the students' knowledge of the names of the states before allowing them to progress to the task of naming the capital of each state.

Task Assignment. Based on the teacher's evaluation of the students' knowledge of the names of the states, the teacher needs to determine whether each student is ready to progress to learning the names of the state capitals or whether corrective instruction is required on the names of the states.

Teaching. The teacher needs to make sure that the students master the names of the states to ensure that the students are ready to learn the name of the capital of each state.

REFERENCES

Anderson, S. A. (1994). *Synthesis of research on Mastery Learning* (Information analysis). ERIC Document Reproduction Service No. ED 382 567.

Obando, L. T., & Hymel, G. M. (1991, March). *The effect of Mastery Learning instruction on the entry level Spanish proficiency of secondary school students*. Paper presented at the annual meeting of the American Educational Research Association, New Orleans. ERIC Document Reproduction Service No. ED 359 253.

Rosenshine, B., & Stevens, R. (1986). Teaching functions. In M. C. Wittrock (Ed.), *Handbook of research on teaching* (3rd ed., pp. 376–391). New York: Macmillan.

Providing Effective Instructional Evaluation

ORIENTATION

Most often when research studies on instructional evaluation are reviewed they include findings on remediation or corrective instruction as well as evaluation. This is because they are so intermeshed. A primary function of evaluation is to diagnose the need for corrective instruction, and corrective instruction is based on diagnostic evaluation. For this reason, when research is the focus of inquiry, usually evaluation and remediation or corrective instruction are discussed together (for example, in the *Handbook on Effective Instructional Strategies*).

On the other hand, when the instructional process is the focus of inquiry, a clearer and more precise understanding can be achieved when evaluation and corrective instruction are analyzed as distinct instructional functions. Therefore, instructional evaluation will be discussed first, and then corrective instruction.

Number of Supportive Studies: 219

INSTRUCTIONAL TACTICS

The following tactics are derived from studies that demonstrate their benefit on student achievement. Discretion has been used interpreting, elaborating, and reducing overlap in tactics used in different studies.

Tactics employed are:

Planning: Procedures for evaluating student performance must be planned beforehand. Tasks must be sufficiently short to enable frequent evaluation of student performance and to avoid excessive task complexity so that it is possible for students to perform tasks correctly on their first attempt.

Evaluation: Frequent quizzes, tests, and other forms of performance evaluation should be employed. Evaluation procedures should enable the diagnosis of student inadequacies as well as the assessment of student progress.

Feedback: Students are to be informed of the correctness of their performance on assigned tasks. Their achievements and/or efforts are to be acknowledged, as appropriate, and they are to be encouraged to undertake their next challenge with expectations of success.

By far the most difficult aspect of evaluation is the construction of achievement tests to assess student achievement and diagnose inadequacies in achievement. All teachers construct achievement tests, but few are given adequate instruction in achievement test construction. The following conceptual guidelines are offered to make the construction of rudimentary achievement tests easier and achievement testing more accurate. If the guidelines cannot be applied, more instruction in the fundamentals of achievement test construction is indicated.

GUIDELINES FOR CONSTRUCTING ACHIEVEMENT TESTS

Achievement tests developed to assess student task performance must yield valid, objective, and reliable assessments of student task performance.

Validity

Achievement tests are valid to the extent that they assess the task performance they are intended to assess. To develop valid achievement tests the task performance being tested must correspond to the tasks and learning objectives of the particular instructional units one intends to teach.

Objectivity

Achievement tests are objective to the extent that different scorers are consistent in scoring the same task performance. Objectivity is facilitated when scoring keys or scoring criteria are developed and used to score test results.

Reliability

Achievement tests are reliable to the extent that there is consistency in the scoring of repeated attempts to perform the same task. Reliability is facilitated when scorers have more than one opportunity to score a student's performance of the same task.

Developing achievement tests is less complex if educators develop a test to assess the achievement of one learning objective (pertaining to one instructional unit) at a time. After this is accomplished, achievement tests can be combined to assess achievement of more than one learning objective.

DIAGNOSING INADEQUACIES IN TASK PERFORMANCE

To ensure that achievement tests enable the diagnosis of inadequacies, student performance of each task in the sequence enabling the achievement of the learning objective being pursued must be assessed. In this way inadequacies in performing particular tasks in a sequence can be isolated and remediated.

Educators must be able to develop two types of achievement tests: (1) Scoring-Key Achievement Tests and (2) Scoring-Criteria Achievement Tests.

Scoring-Key Achievement Tests

For this type of test, multiple test items are constructed for which there is one correct or best answer. For each test item, students select the answer they think is correct from among at least four alternatives to reduce the chance of guessing a correct answer. A scoring key is developed that designates the correct answer for each test item. Typically, scoring key achievement tests are paper-and-pencil tests that are completed by the students and can be scored either by hand or by machine.

Validity, objectivity, and reliability are facilitated for scoring-key tests as follows:

Validity: Validity is facilitated by ensuring that the test items pertain to and cover the task sequence and learning objective being taught.

Objectivity: The use of a scoring key ensures that there will be consistency in the way different test scorers score the test.

Reliability: To facilitate reliability:

1. Construct more than one test item for each task in the sequence, enabling the achievement of the learning objective being pursued.

2. After giving the test, check the responses to see if students responded consistently to the two or more test items constructed for each task. If so, reliability has been attained. If not, the test items need to be refined until the responses are consistent.

Scoring-Criteria Achievement Tests

For this type of test, scorers observe and compare student performance to criteria designated as adequate performance. Scoring criteria are used to score term papers, essay exams, student projects and products, oral exams, and other student performances for which a scoring key is not feasible or appropriate.

Validity, objectivity, and reliability are facilitated for scoring-criteria achievement tests as follows:

Validity: Validity is facilitated by ensuring that scorers are actually scoring student task performance of intended tasks in the sequence that enable the achievement of the learning objective being pursued.

Objectivity: The use of scoring criteria ensures that there will be consistency in the way different test scorers score the same observations. When scoring criteria are complex, training may be needed to ensure that scorers use the criteria accurately.

Reliability:

1. To facilitate reliability, scorers must observe more than one student attempt at performing a task before scoring the student's task performance.

2. If there is consistency in scoring the different observations, reliability has been achieved. If not, additional observations must be made until inconsistencies can be reconciled.

COMPARING TEST RESULTS TO STANDARDS OF ADEQUATE PERFORMANCE

Once observations of student performance are made they are compared to pre-established standards of adequate performance so that adequate performance can be acknowledged and inadequate performance can be remediated.

Instructors who are qualified to teach students how to perform a particular task are also qualified to judge the adequacy of students' performance of the task. When achievement tests are constructed to assess the performance of multiple tasks (for instance, a diverse multiple choice test), 80% or more correct is often used as a criterion of adequate performance.

ILLUSTRATIONS OF APPLICATIONS

Subject Area Examples

Science

Scoring-Key Achievement Test: An example for a chemistry lesson on the periodic table might be for the teacher to develop matching items for which the student is to match the names of elements with the symbol for that element. The student's responses are then compared to a scoring key of the correct response required. Or perhaps multiple-choice items are developed for which the student must select the correct response containing the correct symbol for a stipulated element and the student's responses are compared to a scoring key of the correct response required.

Scoring-Criteria Achievement Test: An example for a science laboratory project might be to have the students write a report of the procedure(s) they used and their final results. The teacher would then use previously developed step-by-step scoring criteria to assess the adequacy of each student's report.

Math

Scoring-Key Achievement Test: An example for a math lesson on solving algebra problems might be for the teacher to develop multiple-choice items for which the student must select the correct response containing the answer for a stipulated algebra problem. The student's responses are then compared to a scoring key of the correct response required.

Scoring-Criteria Achievement: An example for a math lesson on solving algebra word problems might be to have the students set up the problem, displaying the step-by-step procedures they used and their final answer. The teacher would then use previously developed step-by-step scoring criteria to assess the adequacy of each student's performance.

Social Studies

Scoring-Key Achievement Test: An example for a lesson on the dates for major events of the Revolutionary War might be for the teacher to develop multiple-choice items for which the student must select the correct response containing the correct date for a stipulated event. The student's responses are then compared to a scoring key of the correct responses required.

Scoring-Criteria Achievement Test: An example for a social studies lesson might be to have the students write an essay on a major event that happened during the Revolutionary War. The teacher would then use previously developed step-by-step scoring criteria to assess the adequacy of each student's report.

Language Arts

Scoring-Key Achievement Test: An example for a vocabulary lesson might be for the teacher to develop multiple-choice items for which the student must select the correct response containing the correct definition for a stipulated word. The student's responses are then compared to a scoring key of the correct response required.

Scoring-Criteria Achievement Test: An example for a reading lesson might be to have the students write a book report. The teacher would then use a previously developed step-by-step scoring criteria to assess the adequacy of each student's report.

REFERENCES

Anderson, S. A. (1994). *Synthesis of research on Mastery Learning* (Information analysis). ERIC Document Reproduction Service No. ED 382 567.

Brophy, J., & Good, T. (1986). Teaching behavior and student achievement. In M. C. Wittrock (Ed.), *Handbook of research on teaching* (3rd ed., pp. 328–375). New York: Macmillan.

Obando, L. T., & Hymel, G. M. (1991, March). *The effect of Mastery Learning instruction on the entry level Spanish proficiency of secondary school students.* Paper presented at the annual meeting of the American Educational Research Association, New Orleans. ERIC Document Reproduction Service No. ED 359 253.

Rosenshine, B., & Stevens, R. (1986). Teaching functions. In M. C. Wittrock (Ed.), *Handbook of research on teaching* (3rd ed., pp. 376–391). New York: Macmillan.

Providing Corrective Instruction

ORIENTATION

The importance of remediation on student success in achieving learning objectives cannot be overemphasized. Remediation of failing students may be the greatest challenge to instruction. The research shows that dropouts fall farther and farther behind before they drop out of school. So far we have been ineffective in remediating failing students to enable them to progress in school. Educators could be more successful if remedial tactics, which research shows to be effective, were employed.

Number of Supportive Studies: 219

INSTRUCTIONAL TACTICS

The following tactics are derived from studies that demonstrate their benefit to student achievement. Discretion has been used in interpreting, elaborating, and reducing overlap in tactics used in different studies.

Tactics employed are:

Planning: Procedures for correcting student performance must be planned beforehand. Corrective tasks, like other tasks, must be sufficiently short to enable frequent evaluation of student performance and to avoid excessive complexity so that it is possible for students to perform tasks correctly on their first attempt.

Assignment: Corrective tasks are to be assigned when students perform tasks incorrectly. Students who need remediation are to be assured that they will receive all the help they need and that their concerted efforts will ultimately result in success. Their success, however, depends on their receiving task assignments they have the readiness ability to perform and that they are given the help they need to be successful.

ILLUSTRATIONS OF APPLICATIONS

Everyday Applications

When a child is learning to hit a baseball, a coach will likely show the child the proper stance, show the proper swing of the bat, and instruct the child to "keep your eye on the ball." The child will then step up to the plate and attempt to hit a pitched ball. If the child is not successful, the coach will evaluate what the child has done wrong, tell him/her what was done wrong, show how it should have been done, and then have the child practice doing it correctly until he/she is able to hit the ball.

Instructional Applications

Remediation can be seen as taking two forms: (1) spontaneous remediation during teaching and (2) remediation of inadequate test performance. It may be worthy to note that the word "test" is intended to include quizzes, exams, homework assignments, and student projects.

Spontaneous Correction During Teaching

The research indicates that the following should be used to correct inadequate student performance during teaching:

- During oral question-and-answer teaching:
    1. Correct responses are to be acknowledged as correct.
    2. Incorrect responses can be remediated as follows, depending on the teacher's diagnosis of the response.
        a. Teachers can provide and explain the correct response if they think a careless mistake has been made.
        b. If the teacher thinks students lack understanding the teacher can (1) provide prompts and hints to lead students to the correct response. or (2) re-teach the material.
- While monitoring seatwork, group projects, etc.:
    1. Acknowledge and discuss correct performance.
    2. Point out and discuss incorrect performance.
    3. Show students how to correct their mistakes.

Correction of Inadequate Test Performance

The research supports the preparation, prior to instruction, of corrective tasks for students who fail to perform each progressive task in a sequence enabling the achievement of the learning objective. It should be emphasized that prior to instruction, remedial tasks should be prepared for *each* progressive task in a sequence of tasks.

Remediation of students' inadequate test performance should adhere to a general format as follows:

- Assure students that they will receive the help they need and that their continuing efforts will ultimately bring success.
- Point out and discuss with students their test performance inadequacies.
- Show students how to correct their test performance inadequacies.
- Have them correct their mistakes.
- Prescribe practice exercises that provide correct responses.
- Retest student performance.

Subject Area Examples

Science

For a lesson on fluid mechanics in which students are to learn to determine flow rates under a variety of conditions:

Spontaneous Correction During Teaching

While teaching the knowledge and skills necessary for the students to perform the task assignment, the teacher might:

- Ask a series of questions designed to evaluate student understanding, acknowledging correct responses and diagnosing the cause of incorrect responses. After diagnosing the cause of the incorrect response, the teacher determines and provides the type of remediation needed.
- Assign a series of practice problems for the students to work on in class. The teacher should circulate among the students as they practice, perhaps commenting in the presence of correct performance, "Yes, you are doing that right" or perhaps in the case of incorrect performance, "No, that is not quite right because. . . . Here is what you should have done."

Correction of Inadequate Test Performance

For a lesson on fluid mechanics, a teacher might give a homework assignment consisting of problems for which the student is to determine flow rates under a variety of conditions. After collecting and grading the assignment, the teacher should follow the general format for remediation of inadequate test performance for students who made mistakes in the assignment.

Math

For a math lesson in which students are to learn the procedures they need to use to solve basic algebra problems:

Spontaneous Correction During Teaching

While teaching the knowledge and skills necessary for the students to perform the task assignment, the teacher might:

- Ask a series of questions designed to evaluate student understanding of the algebraic procedures to be used. The teacher should acknowledge correct responses and diagnose the cause of incorrect responses. After diagnosing the cause of the incorrect response, the teacher determines and provides the type of remediation needed.

- Assign a series of algebraic problems for the students to practice in class. The teacher should circulate among the students as they practice, perhaps commenting in the presence of correct performance, "Yes, you are doing that right" or perhaps in the case of incorrect performance, "No, that is not quite right because. . . . Here is what you should have done."

Correction of Inadequate Test Performance

For a lesson on the procedures to be used to solve basic algebra problems, a teacher might give a homework assignment consisting of problems for which the student has to use the procedures to solve a variety of basic algebra problems. After collecting and grading the assignment, the teacher should follow the general format for remediation of inadequate test performance for students who made mistakes in the assignment.

Social Studies

For a lesson on U.S. history in which students are to learn the dates of major events that occurred in the nineteenth century:

Spontaneous Correction During Teaching

While teaching the knowledge and skills necessary for the students to perform the task assignment, the teacher might:

- Ask a series of questions designed to evaluate student knowledge of the dates for the major events, acknowledging correct responses and diagnosing the cause of incorrect responses. After diagnosing the cause of the incorrect response, the teacher determines and provides the type of remediation needed.

- Have the students construct an outline of the major events while they are in class. The teacher should circulate among the students as they practice, perhaps commenting in the presence of correct performance, "Yes, that is correct" or perhaps in the case of incorrect performance, "No, that is not quite right because. . . . Here is what you have put there."

Correction of Inadequate Test Performance

For the lesson on the dates of major events in nineteenth-century U.S. history, a teacher might give a homework assignment for which the student is to construct a hierarchical tree diagram of major events for that period. After collecting and grading the assignment, the teacher should follow the general format for remediation of inadequate test performance for students who made mistakes in the assignment.

Language Arts

For an English composition lesson in which students are to learn the difference between a verb and an adverb:

Spontaneous Correction During Teaching

While teaching the knowledge and skills necessary for the students to perform the task assignment, the teacher might:

- Ask a series of questions designed to evaluate student understanding of the difference between verbs and adverbs, acknowledging correct responses and diagnosing the cause of incorrect responses. After diagnosing the cause of the incorrect response, the teacher determines and provides the type of remediation needed.

- Assign an in-class practice in which students are to construct lists of as many verbs and adverbs as they can think of. The teacher should circulate among the students as they practice, perhaps commenting in the presence of correct performance, "Yes, that is right" or perhaps in the case of incorrect performance, "No, that is not right because. . . . This is the list that word should be on."

Correction of Inadequate Test Performance

For the lesson on the difference between a verb and an adverb, a teacher might give a homework assignment for which the student is to write a short essay containing descriptive examples that highlight the difference between verbs and adverbs. After collecting and grading the assignment, the teacher should follow the general format for remediation of inadequate test performance for students who made mistakes in the assignment.

REFERENCES

Anderson, S. A. (1994). *Synthesis of research on Mastery Learning* (Information analysis). ERIC Document Reproduction Service No. ED 382 567.

Brophy, J., & Good, T. (1986). Teacher behavior and student achievement. In M. C. Wittrock (Ed.), *Handbook of research on teaching* (3rd ed., pp. 328–375). New York: Macmillan.

Obando, L. T., & Hymel, G. M. (1991, March). *The effect of Mastery Learning instruction on the entry-level Spanish proficiency of secondary school students.* Paper presented at the annual meeting of the American Educational Research Association, New Orleans. ERIC Document Reproduction Service No. ED 359 253.

Rosenshine, B., & Stevens, R. (1986). Teaching functions. In W. C. Wittrock (Ed.), *Handbook of research on teaching* (3rd ed., pp. 376–391). New York: Macmillan.

Providing Contiguity

ORIENTATION

When relationships are being taught, which is very often the case, the to-be-related events must be presented to students close together in time and space (that is, contiguously) so that the students are able to perceive the relationships. Otherwise, students will not be able to learn the relationships. In teaching relationships, effective instruction requires that to-be-related events be presented or shown to students contiguously.

The jigsaw puzzle illustrates the importance of contiguity. When a puzzle is solved and the pieces are appropriately and contiguously intermeshed, the relationships among the pieces are revealed in a complete picture. Before beginning, when the pieces are strewn haphazardly on the table, the relationships among them cannot be perceived.

Number of Supportive Studies: 178

INSTRUCTIONAL TACTICS

The evidence supports the need to make events contiguous when teaching, assigning tasks, evaluating, and remediating performance of tasks. The following tactics are derived from studies that demonstrate the benefits of contiguity when teaching, assigning, evaluating, and remediating performance of tasks. Discretion has been used to interpret and reduce overlap in tactics used in different studies and to elaborate tactics.

Tactics employed are:

- *Instructional Planning*: The tasks students are to perform to achieve the learning objective should be broken down into small increments so that they will be performed as close together as possible.

- *Teaching*: To-be-associated events should be presented to students as close together as possible. This applies to the association of to-be-associated subject matter and to consequences that are to be associated with student behavior. Teaching devices that can be used to promote contiguity among to-be-associated events include focusing attention on and highlighting relationships.

- *During the Instructional Process*: Student task performance should follow instruction as soon as possible; evaluation of student task performance should occur during or immediately after student task performance; feedback to students on the correctness of their task performance should occur immediately, or very soon, after evaluation; and remediation should occur immediately following feedback.

ILLUSTRATIONS OF APPLICATIONS

Everyday Applications

A person planning a lengthy tour can more readily relate one part of the tour with another if an itinerary is prepared to facilitate association among parts.

Names and costs of products are placed on or near the products they identify to facilitate their association with the products.

Musicians of an orchestra must play in close proximity to one another for the relationship among sounds they make to be perceived by an audience as the intended composition.

Instructional Applications

- *Highlighting the contiguity among events*. In astronomy, students can be taught about constellations by directing their attention to the contiguous patterned relationship of the stars in constellations such as the Big Dipper.

- *Providing for contiguity in behavior–consequence relationships*. Disciplining students soon after an infraction will help them understand that the discipline is a consequence of the infraction, and thereby increase the effectiveness of the discipline.

- *Arranging time and/or space to provide contiguity*.

Condensed time: Using time-lapse photography to condense time in order to demonstrate relationships.

Condensed space: Drawing a map to condense space in order to demonstrate the relationships among distant places.

- *Providing contiguity in the instructional process*. Learning is facilitated when evaluation occurs during and soon after instruction, and remediation is administered soon after mistakes in task performance are detected.

Subject Matter Examples

Science: Using time-lapse photography to show the relationship between planting a bulb and the blooming of the flower.

Social Studies: Using maps to show relationships among continents, nations, and major cities of the world.

Math: The steps of procedures used to solve an algebra problem should be demonstrated contiguously.

Language Arts: There must be sufficient contiguity among parts of a story to provide for continuity. Without sufficient contiguity, those seeing, hearing, or reading the story could not follow the story line.

Reading: (1) Letters of words must be printed contiguously for the words to be readily recognized. (2) Pages of publications are bound contiguously to facilitate the decoding of the message. (3) The table of contents of publications provides contiguity among sections of the book to enable readers to see relationships among parts and chapters.

Writing: (1) Writers must learn not to leave gaps between parts of the message they are attempting to convey so that their message will be understood. (2) Words conveying a message must be presented contiguously for the message to be understood. (3) Particulars supporting conclusions authors wish readers to draw must be presented contiguously to the conclusions so that readers can see that the particulars warrant the conclusions.

REFERENCES

Anderson, S. A. (1994). *Synthesis of research on Mastery Learning* (Information analysis). ERIC Document Reproduction Service No. ED 382 567.

Rosenshine, B., & Stevens, R. (1986). Teaching functions. In M. C. Wittrock (Ed.), *Handbook of research on teaching* (3rd ed., pp. 376–391). New York: Macmillan.

Utilizing Repetition Effectively

ORIENTATION

Most people are at least vaguely familiar with the benefits of repetition to learning. They have heard that "practice makes perfect" and have memorized a poem or a part in a play by repeating the lines.

Two modes of repetition are known to improve learning.

1. *Repeated presentations*: the repeated presentation of to-be-learned information to students enhances their learning of the information.
2. *Practice*: student repetition of assigned tasks or practice perfects their learning or performance of the tasks. The challenge to educators is to include repetition in instruction without engendering boredom.

Number of Supportive Studies: 68

INSTRUCTIONAL TACTICS

The studies analyzed indicate that repetition will enhance learning if the following tactics are employed:

- To-be-learned information is repeatedly presented to students.
- To-be-learned tasks are repeated or practiced by students.
- Repetition is frequent. In general, frequent repetition enhances learning more than infrequent repetition.
- There is variation with repetitions to avoid boredom. Presentations of the same information can be varied with respect to the media used: for example, oral, written, and pictorial presentations of the same information can be made. Also, examples, applications, and demonstrations can vary from one presentation to the next, and repeated performance of the same task can be varied. For instance, in learning to write, students might write in different contexts, such as "My Favorite Pastime," a newspaper article, or a letter.
- Repeatedly testing students on to-be-learned information enhances their learning of the information.

ILLUSTRATIONS OF APPLICATIONS

Everyday Applications

Repeated Presentations

- Telling your children repeatedly not to take other people's property.
- Writing a policy statement and then summarizing the important points.

Practice

- Baseball players practicing their hitting to improve their batting average.
- Reciting the lines of a poem over and over until they are memorized.

Instructional Applications

In general, frequent repetition is advantageous, provided the repetitions do not become exhausting and/or boring. Students need respite from repetition and variation from one repetition to another. Moreover, students need to progress to new challenges as soon as the achievement of a learning objective has been mastered.

Repeated Presentations

Arranging for the repeated presentation of to-be-learned information to the student, varying the form and context of the presentations to avert boredom.

Presentations can be made to varying senses: smell, taste, sight, hearing, touch, and combinations of them. Students can learn the characteristics of peaches by seeing, smelling, touching, and tasting peaches, and by hearing the sound that is made when a peach is bitten into.

Presentations can be made to the same sense in a variety of ways. Peaches might be presented visually in different contexts, such as on a tree, in a box, on the dinner table, in an ornamental fruit arrangement, or in a bin at a supermarket. The meaning of a word can be taught visually by having the student read its definition and then having the student read the word in different appropriate contexts that clarify its meaning. Also, a teacher can lecture on a subject and at the end summarize the main points of the lecture, or in a lecture a teacher may give several different examples and illustrations of a major point.

Practice

- Practicing on a computer to become more proficient.
- On the first day of class teachers might recite their students' names repeatedly until the teachers memorize the names.
- Rehearsing an oral presentation until it can be proficiently delivered.

Combining Repeated Presentations with Practice

- Practice augments repeated presentations when students are assigned homework and take quizzes on the content of a lecture.
- Teachers demonstrate a skill and then guide students as they practice it. Then they have students practice the skill on their own.

The following format illustrates how repetition can be used to enhance learning in consecutive instructional periods.

Instructional Period 1

- Present to-be-learned information
- Assign additional work on the information
- Quiz the students on the information

Instructional Period 2

- Review the to-be-learned information presented during Period 1
- Present new to-be-learned information
- Assign additional work on the new information
- Quiz students on the information presented in Periods 1 and 2

Instructional Period 3

- Review the to-be-learned information presented during Periods 1 and 2
- Present new to-be-learned information
- Assign additional work on the new information
- Quiz students on the information presented during Periods 1, 2, and 3

And so on. Progress is made in this way to take advantage of the benefits of repetition in teaching and testing while progressing toward the achievement of the learning objectives being pursued. Progress must be planned in addition to repetition to avoid boredom.

Subject Area Examples

Science: (1) Providing instructions for a lab experiment, quizzing the students on the instructions, and then guiding the students as they conduct the experiment. (2) Repeatedly writing down the parts of the human anatomy until they are memorized.

Math: Reciting the multiplication tables over and over until they can be recited with no mistakes.

Social Studies: (1) Repeating the names of the 50 states until they are memorized. (2) Listing in order the steps for enacting legislation over and over until they can be listed without error.

Language Arts: (1) Reciting the alphabet again and again until it is learned. (2) Teachers giving a number of examples of irony in literature.

REFERENCES

Hines, C. V., Cruckshank, D. R., & Kennedy, J. J. (1985). Teacher clarity and its relationship to achievement and satisfaction. *American Educational Research Journal*, 22(1), 87–99.

Kulik, J. A., Kulik, C. C., & Bangert, R. L. (1984). Effects of practice on aptitude and achievement test scores. *American Educational Research Journal*, 2(2), 434–447.

Peterson, H. A., Ellis, M., Toohill, N., & Kloess, P. (1985). Some measurements of the effects of reviews. *The Journal of Educational Psychology*, 26(2), 65–72.

Petros, T., & Hoving, J. (1980). The effects of review on young children's memory for prose. *Journal of Educational Psychology*, 30, 33–43.

Watkins, M. J., & Kerkar, S. P. (1985). Recall of twice presented items without recall of
    either presentation: Generic memory for events. *Journal of Memory and Language*,
    24, 666–678.

Clarifying Communication

ORIENTATION

An essential aspect of instruction is the clear communication of information to
students to facilitate their understanding of (1) the learning objectives they are
assigned to pursue, (2) the tasks they are assigned to perform to enhance their
achievement of the learning objectives, and (3) the means of evaluating their performance. Although educators may appreciate the importance of clear communication in conversation and in professions such as "newscaster" and "trial lawyer," the
following explicates the relevance of clear communication to instruction, elements
of clear communication, and tactics for achieving clear communication. Clarity of
communication has a distinct application to instruction and learning.

Number of Supportive Studies: 111

INSTRUCTIONAL TACTICS

The benefits of clear communication to students are well supported by the evidence. However, there is a need for instructional planners and teachers to know the
particular tactics that can be used to ensure clear communication in the classroom.
The following tactics are derived from the studies that demonstrate the benefits of
clear communication. Discretion has been used to interpret and reduce overlap in
tactics used in different studies and to elaborate tactics.

Tactics that ensure clear communication are:

- Providing examples and illustrations of concepts being taught.

- When speaking, avoiding the use of "er," "um," "uh," "ah," "you know,"
  and other halts in the flow of speech.

- Avoiding irrelevant interjections of subject matter and relevant interjections at inappropriate times.

- Being precise in statements, including sufficient detail in presentations to
  avoid vagueness.

- Using transitional terms such as "next," "the last item is," "this concludes,"
  "tomorrow we will," "these were the four causes of . . . 1, 2, 3, 4," "first we
  will . . . ," "second we will . . . ," third we will. . . ."

- Providing explanations to clarify cause–effect relations. This is necessary
  in answering the question "why."

- Describing the tasks students are to perform, explaining and demonstrating
  how to perform tasks, and defining performance standards.

- Showing the relevancy of concepts being taught to students' lives.

- Using multiple and diverse approaches to clarify a concept: for instance, using a number of different illustrations or using media that involve a number of senses, such as sight and hearing.

- Providing for question-and-answer instruction. Questioning students and correcting their answers, as well as answering student-initiated questions, sharpens their understanding and corrects misconceptions. Question-and-answer instruction may be incorporated in textbooks and in lesson plans, or teachers can encourage students to ask questions at any time.

- Using simple language. Rarely used and excessively complex terminology are to be avoided.

ILLUSTRATIONS OF APPLICATIONS

Everyday Applications

Clear communication is important in all walks of life. People who are aspiring to leadership and management positions need to communicate their instructions clearly so that their subordinates can succeed in carrying them out. Clear communication is also important in resolving differences and facilitating agreement among people. In commerce clear communication is necessary to please consumers and to negotiate contracts.

Instructional Applications

Clear communication to students is necessary at all grade levels, in all content areas, and with all types of students. In general, clear communication is beneficial in education, as it is in most professions. In education, it is beneficial for teachers to be able to speak and write clearly and use nonverbal communication so that they can convey their messages to students and help their students communicate clearly.

Educators as well as other professionals receive training in the fundamentals of clear communication in their public school and college courses. In contrast to most other professionals, teachers must be proficient in question-and-answer instruction, and they do not normally learn this in their basic education. Educators can learn how to conduct question-and-answer instruction that enhances academic achievement by learning the techniques explicated in the tactics presented under "Providing Corrective Instruction" and elsewhere in this chapter.

Subject Area Examples

Science: Teachers must communicate clearly instructions for lab experiments.

Math: Teachers must communicate clearly the procedures that math symbols denote.

Social Studies: Teachers must explain clearly the branches of our government and their functions in contrast to the workings of other forms of government.

Language Arts: Much of language arts instruction is concerned with teaching students to communicate clearly. Toward this end, for example, teachers must communicate clearly rules of grammar.

REFERENCES

Brophy, J., & Good, T. L. (1986). Teacher behavior and student achievement. In M. C. Wittrock (Ed.), *Handbook of research on teaching* (3rd ed., pp. 328–375). New York: Macmillan.

Hines, C. V., Cruckshank, D. R., & Kennedy, J. J. (1985). Teacher clarity and its relationship to student achievement and satisfaction. *American Educational Research Journal*, 22(1), 87–99.

Land, M. L. (1985). Vagueness and clarity in the classroom. In T. Husen & T. N. Postlethwaite (Eds.), *The International Encyclopedia of Education Research and Studies* (Vol. 9, pp. 5404–5410). Oxford, England: Pergamon Press.

Providing Subject Matter Unifiers

ORIENTATION

Subject matter, whatever form it may take, is easier to understand and manage when inherent relationships are conveyed. Research has shown that highlighting parts/whole relationships within the subject matter students are assigned to learn appreciably enhances student learning of the subject matter. Unfortunately, many textbooks used in instruction do an inadequate job of highlighting parts/whole relationships within the subject matter. It is not unusual for a teacher to have to move from one part of a text to another in order to present the subject matter units in an organized manner. Additionally, organization within the individual units is often inadequate in the highlighting of the relationships within the subject matter. There is a need for instructional planners and teachers to consider incorporating unifying schemes into instruction in order to assist students in the identification of the important parts/whole relationships they are to learn.

Number of Supportive Studies: 50

INSTRUCTIONAL TACTICS

Either the teacher or instructional planner provides a unifying scheme that highlights the parts/whole relationships within the subject matter. The evidence indicates this may be accomplished prior to, during, or after instruction. The evidence is not conclusive on which is best.

ILLUSTRATIONS OF APPLICATIONS

Everyday Applications

When people use a cookbook, the table of contents provides an outline of the sections of the cookbook, highlighting the parts/whole relationships. A map of a state highlights the parts/whole relationships in terms of the state, the counties, and the cities.

Instructional Applications

Outlines, textual summaries, hierarchical tree diagrams, matrices, and graphic representations that highlight the relationships among important concepts within a lesson can be provided to help students identify and remember the important concepts.

The following unifying schemes were used to highlight the relationships in a fictional text on types of fish. One unifier is a matrix presentation of the relationships within the subject matter, and the other unifier employed is an outline of the relationships within the subject matter (Robinson & Schraw, 1994).

Matrix

Depth:	200 ft		400 ft		600 ft	
Fish:	Hat	Lup	Arch	Bone	Tin	Scale
Social group:	Solitary	Small	Solitary	School	Small	School
Color:	Black	Brown	Blue	Orange	Yellow	White
Size:	30 cm		45 cm		70 cm	
Diet:	Shrimp		Krill		Prawn	

Outline

Depth	*Fish*	*Characteristics*
200 ft	Hat	Social Group—Solitary Color—Black Size—30 cm Diet—Shrimp
	Lup	Social Group—Small Color—Brown Size—30 cm Diet—Shrimp
400 ft	Arch	Social Group—Solitary Color—Blue

		Size—45 cm
		Diet—Krill
	Bone	Social Group—School
		Color—Orange
		Size—45 cm
		Diet—Krill
600 ft	Tin	Social Group—Small
		Color—Yellow
		Size—70 cm
		Diet—Prawn
	Scale	Social Group—School
		Color—White
		Size—70 cm
		Diet—Prawn

Illustrations of other unifying schemes can be found in the *Handbook on Effective Instructional Strategies* (Friedman & Fischer, 1998).

Subject Matter Examples

Science: A graphic display of a molecule could be used to highlight the relationships among the molecule, the atoms that make up the molecule, and the electrons the atoms share.

Math: An outline of the common steps a student is to follow in solving algebra problems could serve to highlight the relationships associated with solving an algebra problem.

Social Studies: A hierarchical tree diagram of the branches of the federal government could serve to highlight the relationships both within and among the different branches.

Language Arts: A textual summary of the main ideas within a prose selection could serve to highlight the relationships within the prose example.

REFERENCES

Alverman, E. E. (1982). Restructuring text facilitates written recall of main ideas. *Journal of Reading*, 25(8), 754–758.

Bower, G. H., Clark, M. C., Lesgold, A. M., & Winzenz, D. (1969). Hierarchical retrieval schemes in recall of categorized word lists. *Journal of Verbal Learning and Verbal Behavior*, 8, 323–343.

Corkill, A. J., Bruning, R. H., & Glover, J. A. (1988). Advance organizers: Concrete versus abstract. *Journal of Educational Research*, 82(2), 76–81.

Corkill, A. J., Bruning, R. H., Glover, J. A., & Krug, D. (1988). Advance organizers: Retrieval context hypotheses. *Journal of Educational Psychology, 80*(3), 304–311.

Dean, R. S., & Kulhavy, R. W. (1981). Influence of spatial organization of prose learning. *Journal of Educational Psychology, 73*(1), 57–64.

Fisher, S. (1997). *Subject matter unifiers: Synthesis of a body of research.* Unpublished manuscript, University of South Carolina.

Friedman, M. I., & Fisher, S. P. (1998). *Handbook on effective instructional strategies: Evidence for decision-making.* Columbia, SC: The Institute for Evidence-Based Decision-Making in Education.

Horton, P. B., McConney, A. A., Gallo, M., Woods, A. L., Senn, G. J., & Hamlin, D. (1993). An investigation of the effects of concept mapping as an instructional tool. *Science Education, 77*(1), 95–111.

Selinger, B. M. (1995). Summarizing text: Developmental students demonstrate a successful method. *Journal of Developmental Education, 19*(2), 14–19.

Tompkins, R. S. (1991, April). *The use of a spatial learning strategy to enhance reading comprehension of secondary subject area text.* Paper presented at the Annual Indiana Reading Conference, Indianapolis, IN.

Keeping Students on Task

ORIENTATION

If students are to achieve learning objectives, they must stay focused on the tasks they are assigned to perform that enable the achievement of the learning objectives. To keep students on task there is a need for instructional planners and teachers to understand and apply the tactics that ensure that students will focus on the tasks they are assigned to perform.

Number of Supportive Studies: 64

INSTRUCTIONAL TACTICS

The following tactics are derived from the studies that demonstrate the benefits of students focusing more time on performance of assigned tasks. Discretion has been used to interpret and reduce overlap in tactics used in different studies and to elaborate tactics.

Tactics that ensure that students spend more time focused on performance of assigned tasks that enable achievement of the learning objectives are:

- Assign only learning tasks that are relevant to achievement of the learning objective.

- Assign only learning tasks that students possess the readiness capabilities to perform. If this is not adhered to, students will be unable to perform assigned tasks, time will be wasted, and students may be dissuaded from learning.

- Make sure that instruction is well planned and organized.
- Spend more time on demonstration and guided practice (as opposed to independent student practice).
- Make sure the students are ready to work alone before assigning independent learning tasks.
- Make sure that independent learning tasks are directly relevant to prior demonstration and guided practice.
- Assign independent learning tasks to immediately follow guided practice activities.
- Provide detailed instructions on how to perform learning tasks.
- Use question-and-answer instruction to ensure that students understand instructions for performance of assigned tasks.
- Supervise independent activity.
- Minimize disruptions, distractions, and interruptions.

ILLUSTRATIONS OF APPLICATIONS

Everyday Applications

Whatever objective people need to achieve, they can achieve it more readily if they concentrate on the tasks they need to perform to achieve the objective—whether the objective be balancing their checkbook, becoming proficient in a sport, or avoiding automobile accidents.

Instructional Applications

Keeping students on task is a strategy that needs to be applied to achieve learning objectives regardless of the grade level, content area, or types of students being taught. However, it should be acknowledged that it is more difficult to keep some students on task than others. For example, it is more difficult to get young children and students with attention deficit disorders to concentrate on the task at hand for extended periods of time. Teachers of young children need to become familiar with methods of attracting and holding their students' attention, and teachers of students with attention deficit disorders need to recognize their own limitations in providing the help the students need. Although teachers can make a special effort to keep errant students on task, they may need to recommend referral of such students for further evaluation, special education, or counseling in accordance with appropriate guidelines.

Subject Area Examples

Science: Students conducting a lab experiment must be attended to by the teacher lest they become thwarted by a procedure they cannot master by themselves.

Math: Students doing math seatwork can be told to raise their hands when they need the teacher's assistance so that they are on task as much as possible.

Social Studies: When on a guided field trip through a government building, teachers must control unruly behavior so that students can focus on what the guide is saying.

Language Arts: To elicit student interest in a reading assignment, teachers can allow students to choose a short story that interests them.

REFERENCES

Brophy, J., & Good, T. (1986). Teacher behavior and student achievement. In M. C. Wittrock (Ed.), *Handbook of research on teaching* (3rd ed., pp. 328–375). New York: Macmillan.
Rosenshine, B., & Stevens, R. (1986). Teaching functions. In M. C. Wittrock (Ed.), *Handbook of research on teaching* (3rd ed., pp. 376–391). New York: Macmillan.

Providing Ample Teaching Time

ORIENTATION

Academic achievement is maximized when teachers spend class time preparing students to perform assigned tasks and monitoring them during their attempts to perform the tasks to detect and correct inadequacies rather than assigning students to independent activities. Moreover, class time needs to be spent primarily on tasks relevant to the academic objectives being pursued.

Number of Supportive Studies: 63

INSTRUCTIONAL TACTICS

The benefits of increasing the amount of time teachers engage in teaching activities is well supported by the evidence. There is a need for instructional planners and teachers to know the particular tactics that can be used to maximize teaching time. The following tactics are derived from the studies that demonstrate the benefits of increasing teaching time. Discretion has been used to interpret and reduce overlap in tactics used in different studies and to elaborate tactics.

Academic achievement is enhanced when teachers:

- Operate their classroom as a learning environment and spend most of their time on teacher-directed academic activities. In addition to providing the information necessary for students to accomplish tasks they are assigned to perform, the teacher should monitor students as they perform their assigned tasks.

- Minimize or avoid assigning students to independent activities, such as silent reading, written assignments, and other independent tasks. Students are more likely to daydream, doodle, or socialize with other students during independent activities than if they are guided by the teacher during the task performance.

- Avoid assigning students to "busy work" or other activities designed to "kill time."

- Devote time available for teaching to teaching and not to getting organized. Be well prepared and plan daily activities productively. Use available teacher planning time wisely to this end.

- Avoid nonacademic student activities, such as group sharing, socializing, arts and crafts, music, and dance during the teaching of academic subjects. Such activities reduce the amount of time available to teach the academic subjects. Increasing the amount of time students are engaged in these activities has been shown to be negatively associated with student academic achievement. Although important, nonacademic activities should be scheduled in nonacademic settings and should not reduce the time needed for academic instruction.

- Except in the case of an emergency, administrative intrusions into scheduled teaching time, whether in person or over a loudspeaker, should be restricted to normally scheduled break times.

ILLUSTRATIONS OF APPLICATIONS

Everyday Applications

It is most often the case that people pursuing an objective they have not achieved before will achieve the objective more readily if they are given the instruction they need, rather than attempting to achieve the objective on their own.

Instructional Applications

This strategy needs to be applied to pursue any learning objective that students cannot be expected to achieve on their own. Typically, younger students need more guidance than older students. Older students tend to be more self-reliant and are more likely to have acquired skills, such as study skills, that enable them to learn on their own. It is also true that more complex tasks require more teaching time than simpler ones.

Although the focus in this section is on ensuring that teachers provide sufficient teaching time, it is important to recognize that time constraints are imposed on teachers. It is difficult, if not impossible, for teachers to provide ample teaching time when the time scheduled for achieving particular objectives by administrators and instructional planners is insufficient. It is quite common for additional responsibilities to be heaped on teachers, curtailing the time they have to pursue essential academic objectives.

Subject Area Examples

Science: The teacher provides oral, then written instructions on how to build an ant colony, and demonstrates the construction of an ant colony. Students are then given the resources to build an ant colony, and the teacher guides the students as they build their own ant colony.

Math: The teacher explains the need for multiplication and the procedure for solving multiplication problems. Then the teacher monitors and corrects student efforts to solve multiplication problems in class before assigning multiplication problems for homework.

Social Studies: The teacher shows the students a hierarchical chart displaying the relationships among branches of our federal government, explains the functions of checks and balances among the branches, and conducts a class discussion on democratic governments before assigning students to write an essay on the advantages of democratic republics.

Language Arts: The teacher teaches students to outline the ideas presented in an essay, defines the term "main idea," and demonstrates how to find the main ideas in an outline before assigning the students to find the main ideas in a reading assignment.

REFERENCES

Anderson, L. W. (1995). Time allocated and instructional time. In L. W. Anderson (Ed.), *International encyclopedia of teaching and teacher education* (2nd ed., pp. 204–207). Oxford, England: Pergamon Press.

Brophy, J., & Good, T. (1986). Teacher behavior and student achievement. In M. C. Wittrock (Ed.), *Handbook of research on teaching* (3rd ed., pp. 328–375). New York: Macmillan.

Providing Ample Learning Time

ORIENTATION

To prevent unnecessary failure, it is essential that students be given sufficient time to perform the tasks they are assigned to perform. And if students do not adequately perform a task when it is assigned initially, students should be given additional time to master the task with appropriate guidance. Planning is necessary to determine the amount of time that needs to be allocated for a particular task, and there is a wide variety of types of tasks that need to be considered. Students who otherwise could succeed can be made to fail or perform below their potential if given insufficient time to complete an assigned task.

Number of Supportive Studies: 168

INSTRUCTIONAL TACTICS

The evidence well supports the need to allow students ample time for the performance of tasks. The following tactics are derived from studies that demonstrate the need to allow students ample time for the performance of tasks. Discretion has been used to interpret and reduce overlap in tactics used in different studies and to elaborate tactics.

Tactics employed are:

- Sufficient time should be allocated to permit students to perform assigned tasks correctly on an initial attempt.

- In the event a student does not perform a task correctly during the original allocated time, the student should be allowed additional time to correctly perform the task.

- Ample time for students to perform assigned tasks needs to be planned for all assigned tasks, such as in-class learning activities, homework, library projects, and laboratory activities.

ILLUSTRATIONS OF APPLICATIONS

Everyday Applications

Parents can cause their children to fail at an assigned task or feel like a failure if they do not allow a sufficient amount of time for the completion of a task. For instance, parents might tell their child to mow the lawn in 1 1/2 hours when it realistically would take the child 2 1/2 hours to mow the lawn.

Instructional Applications

Although the time allowed for students to complete assigned tasks affects student success, the time factor can be easily neglected or overlooked. Teachers and instructional planners may be more concerned with planning assigned tasks than with the amount of time it takes students to perform the tasks. Moreover, the time it takes to perform some assigned tasks is easier to estimate than other assigned tasks. Estimating how long it will take to do five multiplication problems assigned for homework is easier than estimating how long it will take to complete a report that requires library research. Individual student skill levels also influence the allotment of time for task completion.

Subject Area Examples

Science: Allotting sufficient time for students to complete a lab experiment on their own.

Math: Allotting sufficient time for students to complete a seatwork assignment requiring them to solve a word or story problem using arithmetic.

Social Studies: Allotting sufficient time for students to memorize the names of the 50 states.

Language Arts: Allotting sufficient time for students to read a novel before discussing it in class.

REFERENCES

Anderson, L. W. (1985). Time and timing. In C. W. Fisher & D. C. Berliner (Eds.), *Perspectives on instructional time* (pp. 157–168). White Plains, NY: Longman.

Anderson, S. A. (1994). Synthesis of research on Mastery Learning (Information analysis). ERIC Document Reproduction Service No. ED 382 567.

Gettinger, M. (1984). Achievement as a function of time spent learning and time needed for learning. *American Educational Research Journal*, 21(3), 617–628.

Marliave, R., & Filby, N. N. (1985). Success rate: A measure of task appropriateness. In C. W. Fisher & D. C. Berliner (Eds.), *Perspectives on instructional time* (pp. 217–235). White Plains, NY: Longman.

Utilizing Reminders

ORIENTATION

People commonly use reminders to remember things: for example, a string tied around one's finger might be used to remind someone to do something. In education there is a continuing need for students to recall words and factual information they are taught and are required to recall to pass exams. Teachers need to incorporate reminders in their teaching to help their students remember important information. Reminders may be so elaborate and complex that they are unsuitable for schooling. Other reminders are simple and readily adaptable for classroom practice. Simple reminders, such as highlighting important concepts, should be used by teachers. Students should be taught how to use simple reminders, such as note taking.

Number of Supportive Studies: 89

INSTRUCTIONAL TACTICS

- Identify and teach to students the key ideas that they must remember.
- Use highlighting mechanisms, such as underlining, to emphasize main ideas you want students to remember.
- To help students recall complex ideas and relationships, teach them to use memory joggers such as acronyms, rhyming, catchy phrases or tunes, rules, numerical or alphabetical sequences, and mental imagery.

The following example shows how numerical sequence, rhyming, and mental imagery are used in combination to facilitate recall:

- For this example the student is asked to provide eight possible reasons for the extinction of the dinosaurs.
- The student uses keywords that rhyme with the number associated with each reason (e.g., 1 is bun, 2 is shoe, 3 is tree, and so on).
- The student then forms a mental image that will remind the student of the correct answer (e.g., for reason number 3 the keyword is tree, for which the student might form a mental image of a Christmas tree with an exploding star on the tree, which will remind the student that exploding stars might be an explanation for the extinction of the dinosaurs).
- The student provides the answer.

This type of recall tactic is more applicable to arbitrary facts one is trying to recall than to facts that have a greater relevancy to the person.

ILLUSTRATIONS OF APPLICATIONS

Everyday Applications

The use of reminders is common in everyday practice. Kitchen timers, alarm clocks, "post-it" notes, "in" baskets, and shopping lists are commonly used reminders.

Instructional Applications

Students may be taught how to construct outlines to help them remember major points and to cue recall of details.

Subject Area Examples

Science: Scientific formulas may represent and remind us of procedures to be followed as well as remind us of what the elements of the formula are. An example might be the famous formula derived by Albert Einstein, $\mathbf{E = MC^2}$.

Here the procedural reminder might be that to find $\mathbf{E}$ we must multiply $\mathbf{M}$ by $\mathbf{C}$, which must be squared. Additionally, the letters of the formula may be seen as reminders as to the elements of the formula: Energy ($\mathbf{E}$) equals (=) Mass ($\mathbf{M}$) times the Constant squared ($\mathbf{C^2}$). And we might also see $\mathbf{C}$ as a reminder that for this formula the speed of light is an unchanging constant.

Math: The following reminder is used to teach students how to solve algebra problems: **P**lease **E**xcuse **M**y **D**ear **A**unt **S**ally. It reminds them first to do parentheses (please), second exponents (excuse), third multiply (my), fourth divide (dear), fifth add (aunt), and sixth subtract (Sally).

After students learn this procedure they are taught that sometimes exponents are done before parentheses and how to make the distinction.

Language Arts: Students learn linguistic rules such as "i before e except after c." They may then be told of exceptions.

Social Studies: (1) Students are taught to recite the 50 states alphabetically to improve their recall. (2) The acronym HOMES is used to facilitate recall of the Great Lakes.

Reading: Students are taught to associate the main ideas of reading passages with a numerical order to help them remember the passages and thereby understand the message.

Music: Students are taught the word **FACE** to help them remember the spaces on musical staffs and "**E**very **G**ood **B**oy **D**oes **F**ine" to help them remember the lines.

REFERENCES

Bellezza, F. S. (1996). A mnemonic based on arranging words on visual patterns. *Journal of Educational Psychology*, 78, 217–224.

Carney, R. A., Levin, M. E., & Levin, J. R. (1993). Mnemonic strategies: Instructional techniques worth remembering. *Teaching Exceptional Children*, 25(4), 24–30.

Griffith, D. (1979). *A review of the literature on memory enhancement: The potential and relevance of mnemotechnics for military training* (Technical Report No. 436). Fort Hood, TX: U.S. Army Research Unit for the Behavioral and Social Sciences.

Levin, J. (1988). Elaboration-based learning strategies: Powerful theory = Powerful application. *Contemporary Educational Psychology*, 13, 191–205.

Levin, J. (1993). Mnemonic strategies and classroom learning: A twenty year report card. *The Elementary School Journal*, 94(2), 235–244.

Providing Transfer of Learning Instruction

ORIENTATION

It is incumbent on educators to ensure that students possess the knowledge and skills necessary for them to perform any and every task they are assigned to perform. This is a matter of ensuring student readiness, a prerequisite to further academic achievement.

Academic achievement is additionally enhanced if students are taught how to determine when particular knowledge and skills they possess are relevant and applicable to the performance of an assigned task. The general rule students need to learn is: The more similar a task they have successfully performed in the past is to an assigned task, the more probable it is that the procedure used to perform the prior task will enable them to perform the assigned task. To a great extent teaching students how to transfer learning entails teaching them to select a procedure to perform a new task that has been used successfully to perform similar or analogous tasks in the past.

Number of Supportive Studies: 73

INSTRUCTIONAL TACTICS

The following tactics are derived from the studies that demonstrate the benefits of transfer of learning instruction. Discretion has been used to interpret and reduce overlap in tactics used in different studies and to elaborate tactics.

- Ensure that students possess the readiness characteristics necessary to perform assigned tasks. Students cannot transfer skills they do not possess.
- Teach students to assess the extent to which they are able to perform assigned tasks.
- Teach procedures for performing tasks and the conditions for applying the procedures, relevant to the students' lives.
- Have students determine how procedures they are learning might be applied to perform tasks in the future.
- Teach students to detect correspondence between tasks and procedures.
- Show students how procedures used to perform one task can be used to perform analogous tasks, but not different tasks.
- Teach students to select a procedure to perform an assigned task that has been used successfully to perform analogous tasks.
- Give students practice selecting procedures to perform assigned tasks that have been used successfully to perform analogous tasks. Have students de-

fend their selections based on analogy, then have them test the effectiveness of the procedure they have selected and evaluate the result.

ILLUSTRATIONS OF APPLICATIONS

Everyday Applications

Using a particular fishing lure and presentation of the lure because you have used the lure to successfully catch fish in the past.

Instructional Applications

First, ensure that students have the knowledge and skills to perform any task they are assigned to perform. Second, teach them to select a procedure to perform an assigned task because they have successfully used the procedure in the past to perform similar tasks. Third, if not, they must determine how they can learn to perform the procedure.

When assigned a task to perform, three related transfer of learning skills are almost always essential to successfully perform the task. First, students must be able to identify a procedure by means of analogy that will enable them to perform the task. Second, they must be able to determine whether or not they are presently capable of executing the procedure. Students need to be assured that most often with sufficient time, effort, and instruction they can learn how to perform a procedure they are presently unable to perform. These skills must be emphasized in instruction.

Students especially need practice in using analogies to identify procedures to perform assigned tasks. The paradigm is as follows: Given an assigned task, (1) identify a task(s) successfully performed in the past that is similar to the assigned task, (2) identify a procedure that was used to successfully perform the task(s), and (3) apply the procedure to perform the assigned task. For example, if the task is to treat a cut on a finger, students would (1) recall cut fingers they have treated in the past, (2) recall the procedure they used to successfully treat cuts before, say, application of an antiseptic and a Band-Aid to the cut, and (3) apply an antiseptic and a Band-Aid to their present cut to treat it. Once students apply the paradigm to performing simple tasks of common experience, they can be taught how to find procedures in libraries and data banks to perform tasks they have not performed before.

Although it is not often taught, it is important that students learn to distinguish procedures they are able to perform from procedures they are unable to perform. Young people often fail because they "mistake the wish for the deed" and think they can perform procedures that are beyond their capability. Given practice, they can be taught how to assess their limitations and how they might learn to perform the task. For example, children can be asked to indicate whether or not they can perform tasks that their age group is generally able to perform, such as riding a bicycle or saving money, and tasks they are unable to perform, such as piloting an airplane or performing surgery on people. Discussion and explanations can follow pertaining to their present limitations and what they would need to do to learn how to perform the tasks they cannot presently perform.

Students can also be given problems they cannot solve immediately before they are taught how to solve them. They can be asked to try to solve the problems. The reasons for their failure can be explained to them immediately before they are taught the procedure for solving the problems.

Students can be given the pieces of an object to assemble. The object looks easy to assemble but cannot be readily assembled without following written instructions. Students who think they can assemble the object can volunteer to try. After they struggle, they can be given the instructions so that they can succeed.

Subject Area Examples

Science: Using the scientific method to test an hypothesis because you have used it successfully to test hypotheses in the past.

Math: Using a tape measure to measure the length of a table because you have used it successfully to measure the length of objects in the past.

Social Studies: Writing a letter to your congressman to register a complaint because the congressman has satisfied your complaints in the past.

Language Arts: (1) Buying a new novel written by a particular author because you have enjoyed reading novels by that author in the past. (2) Applying rules of grammar in writing a composition because correct use of the rules of grammar enabled you to earn a high grade on past compositions.

REFERENCES

Farrell, E. (1988). How teaching proportionality affects transfer of learning: Science and math teachers need each other. *School Science and Mathematics*, 88(8), 688–695.

Gott, S. P. et al. (1995, February). *Tutoring and transfer of technical competence.* Report from Armstrong Lab, Brooks AFB, TX. ERIC Document Reproduction Service No. ED 382 817.

Marzolf, D. P., & DeLoach, J. S. (1994). Transfer in young children's understanding of spatial representations. *Child Development*, 65, 1–15.

Misko, J. (1995). *Transfer: Using learning in new contexts*. Learbrook, Australia: National Centre for Vocational Education Research. ERIC Document Reproduction Service No. ED 383 895.

Prawat, R. S. (1989). Promoting access to knowledge, strategy and disposition in students: A research synthesis. *Review of Education Research*, 59(1), 1–41.

Providing Decision-Making Instruction

ORIENTATION

The Socratic method of teaching makes it clear that students can be cued to make accurate decisions by means of appropriate questioning. To enhance decision-making, students are taught how to ask themselves a prescribed sequence of questions to make more accurate decisions. In providing answers to the prescribed questions in the self-questioning sequence, students progressively refine their thinking to derive procedures that are likely to enable them to perform tasks they are attempting to perform. Such is the case whether students are attempting to perform an assigned task or a task they personally want to perform.

Number of Supportive Studies: 79

INSTRUCTIONAL TACTICS

The following tactics are derived from studies that demonstrate the benefits of decision-making instruction. A unique feature of the instructional tactics is that they utilize self-questioning to guide the decision-making. Discretion has been used to interpret and reduce overlap in tactics used in different studies and to elaborate tactics.

- Clarify task assignments. Ask, "What outcome am I to achieve? Are there any constraints, such as time limits?" Ask for clarification of instructions if need be.

- Analyze the assigned task and instructions for clues that suggest the correct procedure to use. Ask, "What am I required to do to accomplish the assigned task?"

- Consider procedures that have been used to accomplish similar tasks. Ask, "Do I know of procedures that have been used to accomplish similar tasks? How can I find out about other procedures?" Students should be assisted in learning about additional procedures.

- Consider the relative merits of alternative procedures you know about or have found out about for accomplishing assigned tasks. Ask, "Which procedure is most likely to accomplish the assigned task? Do I have the ability and resources to execute the procedure?"

- Tentatively select a procedure for accomplishing the assigned task that can be predicted to succeed and is feasible to execute.

- Reevaluate the tentatively selected procedure and attempt to defend that it is feasible to execute and is likely to accomplish the assigned task. Ask, "Am I overlooking any relevant factors or contingencies?"

- Decide on a procedure to test. Ask, "Why do I think the procedure will work?"

Students should be informed that the most considered procedure selected might fail. They can learn from their failure and select a procedure that is likely to succeed on an ensuing attempt.

ILLUSTRATIONS OF APPLICATIONS

Everyday Applications

A boy who wants to buy a bicycle follows the self-questioning sequence to derive a procedure for obtaining the bicycle.

Instructional Applications

Students must be shown how the self-questioning sequence enables them to derive effective procedures for performing any task they may be assigned to perform or may want to perform. The teacher should model the correct decision-making behavior for the students.

Subject Matter Examples

Science: Using the self-questioning sequence to derive a procedure to test a particular hypothesis.

Math: Using the self-questioning sequence to determine the correct statistical formula to use to analyze data.

Social Studies: Using the self-questioning sequence to determine an effective procedure to use to be elected to public office.

Language Arts: Using the self-questioning sequence to derive a procedure for judging the merits of novels.

REFERENCES

Dole, J. A., Duffy, G. G., Roehler, L. R., & Pearson, P. D. (1991). Moving from the old to the new: Research on reading comprehension instruction. *Review of Educational Research*, 61(2), 239–264.

Kucan, L., & Beck, I. L. (1997). Thinking aloud and reading comprehension research: Inquiry, instruction, and social interaction. *Review of Educational Research*, 67(3), 271–299.

Prawat, R. S. (1989). Promotion access to knowledge, strategy, and disposition in students: A research synthesis. *Review of Educational Research*, 59(1), 1–41.

Rosenshine, B., & Meister, C. (1994). Reciprocal teaching: A review of the research. *Review of Educational Research*, 64(4), 479–530.

Rosenshine, B., Meister, C., & Chapman, S. (1996). Teaching students to generate questions: A review of intervention studies. *Review of Educational Research*, 66(2), 181–221.

Saloman, G., & Perkins, D. N. (1989). Rocky roads to transfer: Rethinking mechanisms of a neglected phenomenon. *Educational Psychologist*, 24(2), 113–142.

Facilitating Teamwork

ORIENTATION

Instructing students on teamwork and having students cooperate in achieving group objectives enhances the achievement of group objectives. To be successful in the modern world, students must be able to cooperate with others to achieve work, family, community, club, game, and sports objectives.

Group teaching does not produce the highest individual student academic achievement. One-on-one tutoring produces the highest levels of student achievement—as much as two times more than group teaching. Moreover, the increased individual achievement often reported in group cooperative or teamwork learning research may be due, in part, to the reduced size of the learning group. It has been shown that as class size is reduced below 15, learning increases commensurately. Typically, public school class size ranges from 15 to 30. The recommended size for group cooperative learning and the number used in most research studies on the topic is about five. It should also be acknowledged that group cooperative learning often includes one-on-one tutoring.

Although group instruction has been effective in integrating people from diverse cultures and generating attitudinal changes, our focus is on improving academic achievement. In this regard, the primary benefit of group instruction is that it is the only way to teach teamwork. And since teamwork is essential to success in many, if not most, social functions, the teaching of teamwork needs to be emphasized in school much more than it is now.

Supportive Studies: 165

INSTRUCTIONAL TACTICS

- Students' readiness capabilities should be diagnosed on the basis of their prior performance and/or pretesting, and only those with the potential to succeed as team members should begin the instructional program.

- Students should be assigned to work in four- to five-member teams.

- Before starting a learning program, team-building exercises should be conducted to allow team members a chance to get to know one another and build rapport. This might take the form of the individuals in the teams interviewing one another to get to know their names, interests, common interests, and background. The importance of attaining group goals and rewards should be stressed at this time.

- Initial presentation of the knowledge and skills to be learned should be made to the entire group, and then individual team members should receive the instruction they need to perform their function.

- The group presentation should be followed by team practice, where the entire group works together on assigned tasks. "Brainstorming" within the team and mutual assistance within the team should be encouraged for solving problems.

- Students should be provided assistance any time they need help.

- Evaluation should be conducted of both team and individual performance, with appropriate feedback and opportunity for remediation. Individuals are held accountable for their performance.

- Teams are recognized for their degree of improvement.

ILLUSTRATIONS OF APPLICATIONS

Everyday Applications

For youth to be successful in family relations, community relations, at work, and in playing team games and sports, they must learn how to cooperate with others to achieve group goals.

Instructional Applications

Teamwork can be taught and employed in the classroom to successfully complete assignments such as group projects, learning games, and the enforcement of class rules of conduct. Teamwork can also be taught pertaining to extracurricular activities, such as debating teams and sports teams.

Subject Area Examples

Science: Teamwork can be taught to complete group science projects successfully; for example, constructing a small arboretum or ant colony.

Math: Students can be taught teamwork for solving practical math problems associated with commerce by playing the roles of retail store buyer, salesperson, manager, and bookkeeper cooperating to increase store profits.

Language Arts: Students can be taught teamwork by assigning them roles in a class play to achieve good critical reviews.

Social Studies: Students can be taught teamwork by enacting roles of cabinet members in a U.S. president's cabinet to overcome a national economic recession.

REFERENCES

Johnson, D. W., Maruyama, G., Johnson, R., Nelson, D., & Skon, L. (1981). Effects of cooperative, competitive, and individualistic goal structures on achievement: A meta-analysis. *Psychological Bulletin*, 89(11), 47–62.

Sharan, S. (1980). Cooperative learning in small groups: Recent methods and effects on achievement, attitudes, and ethnic relations. *Review of Educational Research*, 50(2), 241–271.

Slavin, R. E. (1995). *Cooperative learning* (2nd ed.). Boston: Allyn and Bacon.

The references in this chapter are key representative references which provide access to fundamental knowledge pertaining to each effective instructional strategy. For more complete references, see the *Handbook on Effective Instructional Strategies* (Friedman & Fisher, 1998).

5

Promising and Generic
Instructional Strategies

To make our presentation of instructional strategies more complete, promising instructional strategies and generic instructional strategies or programs are described in this chapter. From 50 to over 250 research studies confirm the effectiveness of the instructional strategies presented in the last chapter. In general, there is less research supporting the effectiveness of the instructional strategies described in this chapter. Little or no research could be found to support the effectiveness of some of the generic instructional strategies. There was significant research support for other generic programs.

PROMISING INSTRUCTIONAL STRATEGIES

There is evidence to support the effectiveness of the following two promising instructional strategies presented: (1) enlisting the control motive and (2) providing prediction and problem-solving instruction. However, the evidence is not sufficient as yet to be compelling. These instructional strategies are included primarily because they are distinctive from the others and deal with vital instructional issues. None of the effective instructional strategies described previously prescribe how to enlist student motivation to achieve learning objectives or how to teach students to solve almost any kind of problem relatively simply and efficiently. Teachers need to know how to enlist student motivation to achieve objectives and how to teach students to solve problems. It is advisable at this time to pilot test these strategies to determine whether they are effective in your locality for your purposes. To acquaint you with them the instructional tactics for applying them will be described in greater detail. The summary of the tactics is taken from the *Handbook on Effective Instructional Strategies* (Friedman & Fisher, 1998) and is not readily available elsewhere.

Enlisting the Control Motive

ORIENTATION

Motivation determines what people will pursue and what they will try to avoid. Since in free societies it is generally illegal to coerce people to do another's bidding against their will, there is great interest in inducing people to do willingly what one wants them to do. As a result, huge sums of money are spent on motivational research. Businesses and industries want to know how to entice people to buy their goods and services, and how to encourage their employees to be more productive; welfare agencies want to determine how to get people on welfare to want to work; charities want to know how to entice people to donate more money; crime prevention agencies would like to know how to induce children to cooperate without undue coercion; and educational institutions would like to find ways to enlist students' interest in pursuing the learning objectives they are assigned to achieve.

Students control what they will attend to, focus on, and try to learn. Consequently, an effort must be made to enlist their motivation to learn the knowledge and skills they are assigned to learn. Instruction would be so much easier and more successful if educators were able to induce students to learn eagerly what they are assigned to learn.

The challenge is to identify a motive that can be enlisted to induce students to achieve assigned learning objectives. Such a motive would need to meet certain conditions: (1) it must be a motive that can be enlisted to enhance the pursuit of learning objectives in educational settings without harmful side effects; (2) it must be a stable, prevalent motive inherent in most students most of the time so that it can be reliably enlisted and worked with in group instruction.

Sex is an example of a prevalent motive that cannot be satisfied in a school setting to induce students to achieve learning objectives without deleterious side effects. People are asked to restrain their sexual urges in the workplace and in schools because, as you know, the unbridled expression and satisfaction of the sex motive can be disruptive to achieving both work and learning objectives. Moreover, the open public expression of the sex motive is most often illegal. Hunger is another motive that is not enlisted and satisfied during work and instruction. In free, modern societies people are generally not starving, and it is illegal to starve them. And eating can interfere with work and learning. There are times and places set aside for eating and other times and places set aside for work and formal education.

Other motives are transient, and thus are not sufficiently prevalent to be reliable. For example, anger is frequently fleeting; a parent may be angry with his child one minute and be forgiving the next. Avarice, too, is often fleeting. A child may want a toy and be satisfied when given the toy. If not, the child might be distracted or soon become interested in some other attraction. In addition, bribing children to complete assignments by offering a gift can have adverse side effects. They learn to expect rewards for doing assignments instead of doing assignments because the learning that accrues is inherently beneficial.

INSTRUCTIONAL TACTICS

Unlike most other motives, the control motive can be enlisted reliably to induce students to pursue learning objectives without deleterious side effects on students or schools. The following tactics are prescribed to enlist the control motive.

1. Students need to be taught about control. Since people often have difficulty understanding and coping with their own motivation, it is important to clarify for them the control motive and how it affects behavior.
2. Students need to be taught how to improve their control.
3. The control motive should be enlisted to enhance achievement of learning objectives.
4. Instruction must be designed to engender perceptions of control in students.

CLARIFYING MOTIVATION TO CONTROL

As soon as they are old enough to understand, it can be explained to students that while we tend to be acutely aware of our intense motives, such as hunger and sex urges, other motives are important not because of their intensity but because of their prevalence. Those motives are prompting our behavior a great deal of the time. A most prevalent motive is our motivation to improve our control. Most of the time we are attempting to improve our control of something—be it our weight, our mood, our cholesterol level, other people, or getting food, a car, or money. Unlike many very intense motives, we are not always aware of our motivation to control. When eating delicious food to satisfy our hunger, we are aware of the delightful taste of the food; however, we are much less aware of our desire to control the acquisition of food, getting the food to our mouths, and providing for our future meals.

The important thing to realize is that whatever we may want at the time, be it food, companionship, or a car, we want to control its acquisition. If we are able to control its acquisition, we can make certain that it is available when we want it again in the future. We are interested in controlling all sources of satisfaction. Although the particular things we want change from time to time, we spend most of our waking hours trying to control something. That is why our motivation to control is so prevalent.

We not only want to control in order to get things, we find improving our control satisfying in itself. We feel good about ourselves when we are a "take control" person—in control of our lives. We feel more competent, more capable. Every time we set a goal and control its achievement we are satisfied with ourselves.

To succeed in improving our control it is necessary to understand the nature of control. *By control we mean influencing things or people, including oneself, to bring about desired outcomes.*

For one thing, we are intensely interested in controlling our environment so we can get from it the things we want when we want them. Physical objects we usually control by physically manipulating them—we turn on a stove, ride a bicycle, and close a door through physical manipulation.

People themselves are sometimes controlled by physical manipulation. For example, parents physically manipulate infants to diaper and feed them. Criminals are sometimes controlled by physical manipulation; they are handcuffed and forced into jail. However, when we are dealing with people who can understand what we say, we usually attempt to control them by talking to them. When people are dealing with subordinates, they often give them orders. In the army, drill sergeants give marching orders to their troops; parents give orders to their children when they tell them to finish their food or go to bed; teachers give orders when they give homework assignments or tell their class to be quiet.

On the other hand, when we are dealing with people who are under no obligation to take orders from us, we control them by asking and persuading them to do what we want them to do. If we want to make a date with someone, we ask the person for a date. If a person has something we want, we ask the person for it; for example, we may ask to borrow a pencil from a friend or ask a teacher to answer a question.

Quite often we need to work with others to control an outcome; then cooperation is required. Such is the case when we join a team—members of a sports team must cooperate to win games, and members of work teams must cooperate to manufacture products. If the team we join is to be successful in controlling desired outcomes, team members must place cooperation above conflicting personal preferences.

It is important to realize that self-control is a prerequisite to environmental control. If we want to drive a car, we must control our actions to start the car, shift the gears, and steer the car. If we want to make friends, we must do and say things that are appealing to other people. The bottom line is that if we can't control ourselves, we can't control anything else.

Self-control can have personal as well as environmental benefits. It is required when we want to diet to lose weight, when we want to exercise to build strength, or when we want to rest to recuperate when we are weary.

It is through education that people learn to control outcomes. Learning to speak enables children to ask adults to help them control things they cannot control themselves; for example, learning hygiene and how to obtain medical assistance enables people to control their health; learning how to drive enables people to control a car; and learning an occupation enables people to get and hold a job. People can learn to control some primitive outcomes by themselves, such as crawling, but it is through education that people learn how to control the outcomes primarily responsible for achieving personal aspirations, whatever they may be, and succeeding in society.

TEACHING STUDENTS HOW TO CONTROL OUTCOMES

Students' Motivation to Control Is Elicited. To capture students' interest, they are informed that they are about to be taught a technique that will help them control the achievement of any outcome they may want to achieve. Learning the technique will help them get what they want, whatever that may be.

Students Are Taught to Behave Purposefully. Students are informed that the technique they are about to learn is how to behave purposefully. Purposeful behavior has four defining characteristics: Purposeful behavior (1) is directed toward an outcome rather than aimless, (2) is based on learning rather than instincts, (3) is based on prediction rather than hindsight or ideas of the moment, and (4) is selected rather than predetermined or imposed. Students are informed that the technique involves first selecting an outcome they want to pursue at the time, and then selecting a behavior to achieve the outcome, as follows.

SELECTING AN OUTCOME TO ACHIEVE

The first step in behaving purposefully is to select an outcome to pursue at the time—be it obtaining money, a bicycle, a pet, or a car, or taking a vacation. Although people may want to achieve many outcomes, to be successful they need to establish their preferences and plan to pursue one outcome at a time. Otherwise, they might become confused and ineffectual.

SELECTING A BEHAVIOR PREDICTED TO ACHIEVE
THE OUTCOME

A behavior is selected because it is predicted to achieve the outcome. It must be made clear to students that they frequently and routinely predict the outcomes of their behavior. When turning the page of a novel they predict the story will continue on the next page. They predict that washing will make them and other things clean, that drinking will quench their thirst, that dating a particular person will be satisfying, that dieting and exercise will result in weight loss, that following a particular route will lead them to school. Because particular behaviors have frequently achieved particular outcomes in the past, they have learned to predict with confidence that the behaviors will achieve the outcomes in the future. When their learning does not enable confident predictions, they can consult libraries and data banks to find out whether cumulative learning recorded over the years enables them to make confident predictions. In addition, they can learn statistics to estimate probability in order to make more accurate predictions.

Students must be made aware that when they behave purposefully to control outcomes, they are taking an active part in shaping their own destiny through foresight and preparation, rather than reacting to things that are imposed upon them. When they behave purposefully they are more apt to make things turn out as they choose.

ENLISTING THE CONTROL MOTIVE TO FACILITATE ACHIEVEMENT OF LEARNING OBJECTIVES

Most important, the control motive should be enlisted during instruction to achieve the learning objective being pursued. In order to enlist motivation to control, students would need to be shown how pursuing an assigned learning objective can improve their control of outcomes. In general, this can be accomplished by translating assigned tasks designed to achieve a learning objective into behavior $\rightarrow$ outcome units. The performance of all tasks requires students to execute behaviors to achieve specified outcomes. Breaking down assigned tasks into behavior $\rightarrow$ outcome units during instruction not only conveys to students how their behavior can control outcomes, it simplifies the teaching of task performance. The task of performing long division can be broken down into component behavior $\rightarrow$ outcome units, and so can shopping, developing a household budget, driving a car, writing a composition, and so on. The performance of almost all tasks can be taught in behavior $\rightarrow$ outcome units. Even if students are not especially interested in achieving a particular assigned learning objective, they are interested in improving their control. Hence, if they can see that they are learning behaviors to control outcomes, thereby improving their control, the achievement of the assigned learning objective will be more attractive to them.

Motivation to control can be enlisted when teaching in any subject area, provided students are shown how the to-be-learned subject matter can improve their control of outcomes. It has been said that making instruction relevant to students' lives increases their enthusiasm for learning. By eliciting the control motive in teaching subject matter, the subject matter is not only made relevant to students' lives, it is made useful and important to them because they are being shown how to improve their control of outcomes.

Following are examples of how motivation to control can be enlisted while teaching in a subject area. When teaching social studies, students can be shown how voting (behavior) elects candidates for office (outcome), how writing to a congressman (behavior) can initiate the enactment of a law (outcome), and how breaking the law (behavior) can result in being arrested (outcome). In teaching language arts, students can be shown how learning to write (behavior) enables them to send a message to people they are not in face-to-face contact with (outcome), and how reading books (behavior) can bring them enjoyment (outcome). When teaching science, students can be shown that conducting a lab experiment (behavior) increases their ability to manipulate physical matter (outcome), and how studying the scientific method (behavior) enables them to make discoveries (outcome). In math, students can be shown how learning arithmetic (behavior) enables them to check the change they receive when shopping (outcome), and that learning how to measure (behavior) enables them to follow recipes when cooking (outcome).

ENGENDERING PERCEPTIONS OF CONTROL IN STUDENTS

When students are assigned tasks to perform, it is most important that they perceive that they can control the achievement of the tasks. If they do not, they may well not try at all or they may make a feeble effort to perform the tasks. It is incumbent upon instructional planners and teachers to engender in students the perception that they can control the achievement of assigned tasks so that they will persist in attempting to perform the tasks.

One factor that contributes to students perceiving that they can perform assigned tasks is that they have often performed them successfully in the past. This gives them confidence that they will succeed in the future. Instructional planners and teachers can inspire confidence in students by ensuring student success. This can be accomplished by making certain (1) that students have the readiness ability to perform assigned tasks, (2) that earlier tasks in a task sequence enable the performance of subsequent tasks, and (3) that task sequences are designed in small graded steps or increments.

Second, in providing students feedback on their task performance, they are given a clear understanding of their strengths and weaknesses, they are commended on their efforts and achievements as appropriate, and they are told that they have the ability to perform the next assigned tasks if they make a concerted effort and they will be given the assistance they need to succeed. These assurances must not be in vain or when students fail they will rightfully blame and mistrust the instructional system and refuse to cooperate.

The above explanation of how purposeful behavior is used to improve control explains in part why the instructional tactics prescribed under "Enhancing Decision-Making" facilitates student achievement.

ILLUSTRATIONS OF APPLICATIONS

Everyday Applications

The control motive has been enlisted successfully to improve people's health, attitude toward life, interest in socializing, problem-solving ability, and self-esteem. People need to control outcomes to be able to work successfully and to achieve their own aspirations—whatever they may be. People who are unable to exercise sufficient control become social wards and are often institutionalized.

Instructional Applications

Enlisting the control motive to facilitate achievement of learning objectives is appropriate at all grade levels, in all content areas, for most types of students. There is virtually no conflict with the goals of educational institutions and students are interested in improving their control of outcomes in general. Showing students how the achievement of learning objectives will increase their control of outcomes can only encourage them to strive to achieve the objectives.

Subject Area Examples

Science: Showing students how using a lever will enable them to better control the movement of objects will interest them in learning about levers and leverage.

Math: Showing students how using addition and subtraction will enable them to control the income and outgo of their money will interest them in learning how to add and subtract.

Social Studies: Showing students how they can attain public office will interest them in learning about the election process.

Language Arts: Showing students how effective communication can persuade others to do one's bidding will interest students in learning how to communicate well.

REFERENCES

Banzinger, G., & Roush, S. (1983). Nursing home for the birds: A control relevant intervention test with bird feeders. *Gerontologists*, 23(5), 527–531.

Friedman, M. I. (1993). *Taking control: Vitalizing education*. Westport, CT: Praeger.

Gordon, D. (1977). Children's beliefs in internal-external and self-esteem as related to academic achievement. *Journal of Personality Assessment*, 41(4), 333–336.

Hickson, J., Housely, W. F., & Boyle, C. (1988). The relationship of locus of control to life satisfaction and death anxiety in older persons. *International Journal of Aging and Human Development*, 26(3), 191–199.

Langer, E., & Rodin, J. (1976). The effects of choice and enhanced personal responsibility for the aged: A field experiment in an institutional setting. *Journal of Personality and Social Psychology*, 34, 191–198.

Langer, E., Rodin, J., Beck, P., Weinman, C., & Spitzer, L. (1979). Environmental determinants of memory improvement in late adulthood. *Journal of Personality and Social Psychology*, 37, 2003–2013.

Lefcourt, H. M. (1982). *Locus of control: Current trends in theory and research*. Hillsdale, NJ: Erlbaum.

Lemke, S., & Moos, R. (1981). The suprapersonal environments of sheltered care settings. *Journal of Gerontology*, 36(2), 233–243.

Moos, R. (1981). Environmental choice and control in community care settings for older people. *Journal of Applied Social Psychology*, 11(1), 23–43.

Moos, R., & Ingra, A. (1980). Detriments of the social environments of sheltered care settings. *Journal of Health and Social Behavior*, 21, 88–98.

O'Leary, A. (1985). Self-efficacy and health. *Journal of Behavior Research and Therapy*, 23, 437–451.

Schultz, N. R., & Hoyer, W. J. (1976). Feedback effects on spatial egocentrism in old age. *Journal of Gerontology*, 31(1), 72–75.

Stipek, D. J., & Weisz, J. R. (1981). Perceived personal control and academic achievement. *Review of Educational Research*, 51(1), 101–137.

Toner, J., & Manuck, S. B. (1979). Health locus of control and health related information seeking at hypertension screening. *Journal of Social Science and Medicine (Medical Psychology and Medical Sociology)*, 13A(6), 823–825.

Walker, K., & Bates, R. (1992). Health locus and self-efficacy beliefs in a healthy elderly sample. *American Journal of Health Promotion*, 6(4), 302–309.

Wallston, B., Wallston, K., Kaplan, G., & Maides, S. (1976). Development and validation of the health locus of control scale. *Journal of Consulting and Clinical Psychology*, 44(4), 580–585.

Wolk, S., & DuCette, J. (1974). Intentional performance and incidental learning as a function of personality and task dimensions. *Journal of Personality and Social Psychology*, 29, 90–101.

Providing Prediction and Problem-Solving Instruction

ORIENTATION

Although more studies need to be done, research has shown that predictive ability affects academic achievement, and prediction and problem-solving instruction increases academic achievement. Predictive ability is a great asset not only in achieving learning objectives, but in problem solving of any kind as well.

INSTRUCTIONAL TACTICS

Instructional tactics involve teaching the prediction and problem-solving cycle as an effective means of problem solving in all academic areas as well as daily living.

First, students are given an overview of the prediction and problem-solving cycle so that they can see the parts/whole relationships and how the functions in the cycle are coordinated to solve problems.

Problem solving begins when motivation is aroused and presses for satisfaction.

The Prediction and Problem-Solving Cycle

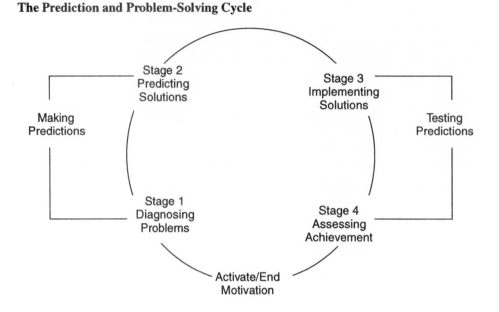

Motivation activates the activities in the prediction and problem-solving cycle, which consists of four stages. Stage 1, Diagnosing Problems, and Stage 2, Predicting Solutions, involve making predictions. Stage 3, Implementing Solutions, and Stage 4, Assessing Achievement, involve testing predictions, as shown in the diagram of the prediction and problem-solving cycle. A brief overview and example of the process follows.

PROVIDING AN OVERVIEW OF THE PREDICTION AND PROBLEM-SOLVING CYCLE

Motivation

People are motivated to satisfy their desires, without knowing initially what to do about them. For example, a student is worried about failing science and is motivated to do something about the situation.

Making Predictions

The student needs to predict a way to alleviate this worry. To proceed the student (1) diagnoses the problem as a basis for (2) predicting a solution.

Stage 1, Diagnosing Problems

Defining the Problem. To satisfy desires it is advantageous to define them as problems. A problem can be defined as a discrepancy between an existing state and a desired state. To continue with our example, existing state: The student is earning a grade of "F" in science. Desired state: The student wants to earn a "B" in science by the end of the school term.

Once the problem is defined, the solution becomes clear: to progress from a grade of "F" to a grade of "B." To complete the diagnosis, factors that need to be controlled to achieve a solution are determined.

Factors to Be Controlled. Factors that need to be controlled are those factors that must be attended to or manipulated to generate progress from the existing state to the desired state.

For example, the student must identify the particular tasks that must be performed competently to raise the science grade to a "B." A conference with the teacher might reveal the following factors to be controlled.

- Earn a "B" on the science project.

- Improve performance on weekly quizzes.

- Earn a "B" on the final exam.

Constraints. In addition to defining the problem and identifying factors to be controlled, constraints are identified so that realistic limitations can be dealt with. Continuing with the example, one constraint would be earning a "B" by the end of the school term.

Stage 2, Predicting Solutions

Once factors to be controlled and constraints are identified to solve the problem, an attempt is made to predict a solution by (1) identifying means of controlling the factors, providing for the constraints, and (2) prescribing procedures to apply the means.

Means of Controlling the Factors.

- Means of controlling the factors are identified through recall and research, if need be.

- Common elements of previous science projects that won awards are identified, and a similar science project is selected.

- Engage a tutor to improve the student's understanding of science and to teach test-taking skills.

- Increase study time.

Prescribing Procedures. A procedure is prescribed to coordinate the means of controlling the factors providing for constraints. For instance, a procedure is derived to implement the science project, engage a tutor and schedule tutoring lessons, and increase study time in time to raise the student's grade to a "B" within the school term.

Testing Predictions

After the problem is diagnosed at Stage 1 and a solution is predicted in Stage 2, it is necessary to test the prediction that the proposed solution will solve the problem. This entails implementing the solution and then assessing the outcome.

Stage 3, Implementing Solutions

To implement solutions, the prescribed procedure is executed according to specifications. For example, the procedure prescribed for completing the science project, being tutored, and increasing study time are implemented exactly as planned.

Stage 4, Assessing Achievement

After implementing the solution, observations are made of the outcome. Then the outcome is compared to the desired state to see the extent to which the desired state has been achieved. If it is achieved, the implemented solution would be considered to be effective. Side effects are also observed, as well as efficiency factors, such as costs of implementing the solution. For instance, at the end of the school term the student notes the grade on his report card to see if he earned the final trade of "B" as desired. He also determines the final cost of the tutoring he received, as well as side effects. Improved study tactics taught by his tutor might have improved his grades in other courses.

This completes the initial execution of the prediction and problem-solving cycle.

Motivation

After the completion of each prediction and problem-solving cycle, motivation is revisited and reappraised. If the desired state is achieved the problem might be considered solved, and there might not be any motivation to continue. In this case, attention would be turned to other problems which people are motivated to solve. This would constitute the end of this problem-solving mission. For example, the student might earn a final grade of "B" and turn his attention elsewhere to solve other disturbing problems that he is motivated to solve. On the other hand, the desired state might be achieved and there might be motivation to recycle to increase efficiency: for example, to reduce the time and money that were required to implement the solution the first time; or recycling might be initiated to remove an undesirable side effect. To recycle, people move to Stage 1 again to diagnose the problem anew and then proceed through the remaining stages to complete the prediction cycle another time.

If the desired state is not achieved, there might be motivation to recycle to try again to solve the problem. Many problems are not solved on the first attempt. Rather, they are solved by successive approximation, when one cycle after another is executed until the problem is solved. Each time the cycle is completed, something new can be learned that makes it more likely that a solution will be achieved on a subsequent attempt. In contrast, there may be no motivation to continue to try to solve the problem. The pursuit might be abandoned because there is no longer any interest in solving the problem or resources are insufficient to continue pursuing a solution.

For whatever reason motivation is sufficient to recycle, the motivation activates the recycling and the four stages of the cycle are repeated in order.

Demonstrating the Relevance of the Prediction and Problem-Solving Cycle

Once an overview of the prediction and problem-solving cycle is represented to students and they understand the parts/whole relationships of the cycle, the relevance of the cycle to solving problems in all subject areas and daily living is demonstrated for the students. This can be achieved by showing students how the cycle can be applied to solve problems in science, math, language arts, and social studies, as well as in their daily lives.

Detailing Each Stage of the Prediction and Problem-Solving Cycle

After students understand how the cycle can be used to solve any kind of problem, it is necessary to teach them how to perform each stage of the cycle in detail. It takes more than a general understanding of the cycle to be able to apply it. Students must become proficient in performing each stage of the cycle. Following are some of the nuances and details students need to learn.

Stage 1, Diagnosing Problems

Defining Problems. Students are taught the advantages of defining a problem as a discrepancy between an existing state and a desired state, rather than just specifying a desired state as a goal or objective. Defining an existing state as a starting point as well as a desired state facilitates predicting solutions at Stage 2 and assessing achievement at Stage 4. It is advantageous to know both the existing state or starting point and the desired state when planning a solution, rather than knowing only the desired state, since the solution must produce progress from the existing to the desired state. It is also advantageous to know both the existing state and the desired state when constructing an observation instrument to detect progress from the existing to the desired state, rather than just knowing the desired state.

Factors to Be Controlled. Many factors that need to be controlled to generate progress from the existing to the desired state are causal agents. Students need to learn about cause–effect relationships so that they can understand that causal agents may need to be identified when the effect being pursued is a specified desired state.

Constraints. Students are taught that desired states cannot be pursued without considering constraints. It is often necessary to avoid harmful side effects when solving problems, and it is often necessary to attempt to solve problems with limited resources.

After students understand in detail how problems are diagnosed, they are assigned to diagnose problems in various subject areas and in their daily lives until they become competent.

Stage 2, Predicting Solutions

To become competent at predicting solutions, students must be able to identify means of controlling the factors that were identified in Stage 1 and prescribe procedures for solving the problem.

Means of Controlling the Factors. Students must be taught how to conduct research to identify means of controlling factors they are interested in controlling. They need to be taught how to access and locate information in libraries and computer data banks. Sophistication can be developed gradually over time.

Prescribing Procedures. Initially students should be taught to find appropriate procedures by searching libraries and data banks. Later they can be taught methods of deriving procedures when standard operating procedures are not available.

Many methods for planning procedures are available: for instance, Project Evaluation and Review Technique (PERT) as well as various methods of deriving computer and other programs. Students are also taught that a predicted solution might be to do nothing but wait. Such is the case when it is predicted that the problem will dissipate with the passage of time.

Students' ability to predict solutions is tested in the various content areas and daily living and remediated as needed until they become proficient.

Stage 3, Implementing Solutions

Students are taught that unless predicted solutions are implemented as prescribed according to specifications, the effectiveness of the solution in solving the problem cannot be tested. Every effort must be made to detect and correct deviations from predicted solution specifications. When predicted solutions are complicated, training is often necessary to ensure that the solution is implemented as prescribed. During training, performance is monitored and corrected until it can be certified as proficient. Monitoring devices such as videotape and audiotape recorders can be used to monitor and analyze performance.

Once students understand how to implement solutions, their ability to implement solutions to problems in science, math, language arts, social studies, and daily living is tested and remediated as needed until they become proficient. Initially, assignments should not require knowledge of monitoring devices or how to estimate the resources needed to implement solutions. Students should eventually learn how to estimate the resources needed to implement solutions.

Stage 4, Assessing Achievement

Students are taught how to make observations of existing states, both quantitative observations by means of measurement and qualitative observations. They should eventually become familiar with the various kinds of instruments that can be used to make observations and how to assess their accuracy (validity, reliability, and objectivity). Students are also taught how to compare existing states with desired states to determine any discrepancies that might be present. Eventually, students should be taught to determine the probability that a derived discrepancy is a chance factor and the importance of a discrepancy (effect size). This requires knowledge of statistics. Students should also eventually learn how to assess side effects and efficiency factors, such as costs.

When students understand how to assess achievement, their ability to assess achievement in science, math, language arts, social studies, and daily living is tested and remediated until they become proficient. Initially, students should not need to know how to use sophisticated instruments to make observations, how to use statistics, or how to assess side effect or efficiency factors.

Developing Student Proficiency in Applying the Prediction and Problem-Solving Cycle

After students have been presented an overview of how the prediction and problem-solving cycle is applied and have become proficient in administering the four stages individually, they are taught how to coordinate the stages in applying the entire cycle. Their ability to apply the cycle to identify and solve problems in science, math, language arts, social studies, and daily living is then tested and remediated as needed until they become proficient.

Student proficiency includes estimating achievement, side effects, and available resources after each cycle is completed as a basis for deciding whether to recycle. Ultimately, it is the authorized decision-maker(s) who use the estimates to decide whether or not to recycle. The decision depends on their motivation, after they are fully informed. Initial applications of the cycle should be kept simple, not requiring students to estimate side effects and available resources or to use sophisticated observation instruments or statistics to estimate achievement.

Illustrations of Applications

Everyday Applications: Good predictors seem to achieve more, whatever they may aspire to achieve. Successful investors are able to predict investments that will increase in value; successful doctors are able to predict medical treatments that will cure patients; successful teachers are able to predict instructional strategies that will increase learning, although this is far too seldom the criteria for judging teaching performance.

Instructional Applications: The self-questioning tactics explicated under "Providing Decision-Making Instruction" (page 114) enable students to derive more cogent decisions. Mastering the application of the prediction and problem-solving cycle enables students to apply the decision-making prowess they developed to systematically make and test predictions to solve problems. Problem solving is applied and/or taught in most content areas. Learning how to apply the prediction and problem-solving cycle enables students to be more effective in problem solving.

Subject Area Examples:

Science: Using the prediction and problem-solving cycle to derive and test hypotheses.

Math: Using the prediction and problem-solving cycle to solve a word or story problem.

Social Studies: Using the prediction and problem-solving cycle to reduce urban blight.

Language Arts: Using the prediction and problem-solving cycle to determine the culprit in a mystery novel, or using the prediction and problem-solving cycle to improve writing instruction.

REFERENCES

Benz, D., & Rosemier, R. (1966). Concurrent validity of the Gates level of comprehension test and the Bond, Clymer, Hoyt reading diagnostic tests. *Educational and Psychological Measurement*, 26, 1057–1062.

Chia, T. (1995). Learning difficulty in applying notion of vector in physics among "A" level students in Singapore. ERIC Document Reproduction Service No. ED 389 528.

Denner, P. R., & McGinley, W. J. (1990). *Effects of prediction combined with storytelling versus listing predictions as prereading activities on subsequent story comprehension.* Paper presented at the annual meeting of the National Reading Conference, Miami.

Dykes, S. (1997). *A test of Proposition One, of prediction theory.* Doctoral dissertation, University of South Carolina.

Freeman, R. H. (1982). *Improving comprehension of stories using predictive strategies.* Paper presented at the Annual Meeting of the International Reading Association, Chicago.

Friedman, M. I. (1974). *Predictive ability tests: Verbal and nonverbal forms.* Columbia, SC: M. I. Friedman.

Friedman, M. I., & Maddock, M. (1980). *Predictive ability instruction.* Research report published for participating school districts in South Carolina.

Greeno, J., & Noreen, D. (1974). Time to read semantically related sentences. *Memory and Cognition*, 2(1A), 117–120.

Henderson, E., & Long, B. (1968). Correlation of reading readiness and children of varying backgrounds. *The Reading Teacher*, 22, 40–44.

Hunt, J., & Joseph, D. (1990). Using prediction to improve reading comprehension of low-achieving readers. *Journal of Clinical Reading, Research and Programs*, 3(2), 14–17.

Hurst, R., & Milkent, M. (1994). *Facilitating successful predictive reasoning in biology through application of skill theory.* Paper presented at the annual meeting of the National Association for Research in Science Teaching, Anaheim, CA, March 19–26. ERIC Document Reproduction Service No. ED 368 582.

Nolan, T. (1991). Self-questioning and prediction: Combining metacognitive strategies. *Journal of Reading*, 35(2), 77–101.

Reutzel, D., & Fawson, P. (1991). Literature webbing predictable books: A prediction strategy that helps below-average, first-grade children. *Reading Research and Instruction*, 30(4), 20–30.

Walker, B. J., & Mohr, T. (1985). *The effects of ongoing self-directed questioning on silent comprehension.* Paper presented at the annual meeting of the Reading Research Conference, Seattle, WA.

Walker, K., & Bates, R. (1985). *The effects of ongoing self-directed questioning on silent comprehension.* Paper presented at the annual meeting of the Reading Research Conference, St. Petersburg, FL.

Zinar, S. (1990). Fifth-graders' recall of proposition content and causal relationships from expository prose. *Journal of Reading Behavior*, 22, 2.

GENERIC INSTRUCTIONAL STRATEGIES

The instructional strategies described previously in this and the preceding chapter are strategies that can be applied individually or in combination in existing instructional programs or instructional programs being planned, usually with very little inconvenience or additional cost. The generic instructional strategies to be described are themselves complete instructional programs that would, when adopted, replace existing instructional programs. Therefore, they can be costly to install and require major changes to present practice. The generic instructional programs to be described are designed to increase student learning. Some of them have proven to be effective and, as you will see, tend to incorporate effective instructional strategies described in the last chapter. This may well be the reason they have proven to be effective; you be the judge. Other to-be-described generic instructional programs designed to increase student learning have not proven to be effective.

Some of the generic instructional programs to be considered are used for teacher training, even though instructional strategies in the program that teachers are being taught have not been shown to enhance student achievement. This raises some serious issues that need to be considered. Ideally, before teachers are trained to use instructional strategies, the strategies would have been tested and proven to be effective. Subsequently, in teacher training teachers or teachers-to-be would first receive lectures and demonstrations on how to use the instructional strategies. Second, they would be supervised and observed as they attempted to apply the strategies in the classroom. The teachers' mistakes would be corrected by their observer/supervisor until the teachers became proficient in applying the strategies. At that point their observer/supervisor would certify their proficiency. Although we cannot expect perfection, there is such a discrepancy between good practice and actuality that we need to be concerned. How can we expect teaching to be effective if in teacher training teachers and teachers-to-be (1) are not taught to apply instructional strategies that have been shown by research to be effective in increasing student achievement, and (2) are not certified to be proficient in applying the strategies in the classroom? Furthermore, how can we have confidence in the results of research studies designed to test the effectiveness of instructional strategies when the proficiency of the teacher in applying the strategies in the study has not been duly certified?

Keeping these questions in mind, the remainder of the chapter describes generic instructional programs to provide a more comprehensive account of the methods available to improve instruction. Each program utilizes a number of instructional strategies or tactics. Generic instructional programs used for teacher training will be labeled "Teacher Training Tactics Employed"; others will be labeled "Instructional Tactics Employed." Descriptions of the generic instructional programs follow.

Learning for Mastery

Introduction: The Learning for Mastery program employs instructional tactics designed to bring all students to a defined level of mastery for intended learning objectives. Students are afforded the time, instruction, and assistance necessary to achieve mastery.

The following description of Mastery Learning and evidence supporting the effectiveness of Mastery Learning tactics is summarized from the work of S. A. Anderson.

Author: Anderson (1994): Synthesis of seven meta-analyses

Students Taught: K–12, college, and other adult students

Intended Learning: Achievement in most academic content areas

Instructional Tactics Employed:

- Students' current level of knowledge in relation to that required for the material to be learned is accurately diagnosed.
- The material to be learned is divided into units, with each unit providing prerequisite skills for subsequent units.
- A mastery level the student must achieve prior to moving on to the next unit is determined.
- Prior to instruction, students are oriented as to procedures to be used, what they are expected to learn, and to what level they are expected to learn.
- Subject matter is divided into small units of learning, following one another as closely as possible in order to enhance the probability of student success.
- Student task performance occurs immediately, or as closely as possible, following instruction on needed knowledge and skills.
- Student learning is tested at the end of each unit as soon as possible after completing the unit.
- Prior to instruction, alternative instructional correctives are developed by

the teacher for each item on a test. The correctives are designed to reteach the material tested in ways different from the original instruction.

- The teacher immediately provides feedback to the students on their errors after each test.
- The teacher assigns the developed alternative correctives as needed after identifying each student's errors.
- In the event a student does not perform a task correctly during the original allocated time, the student is allowed additional time to correctly perform the task.
- Teacher time spent taking attendance, disciplining students, cleaning up, putting away, and moving from activity to activity is minimized.
- The amount of time teachers spend actively teaching in relation to the amount of time available for teaching is maximized.

Findings: Positive achievement gains associated with Mastery Learning were seen in 64–93% of the studies reviewed in the seven meta-analyses.

Interpretation: The efficacy of the Learning for Mastery program in enhancing student academic achievement is well supported by the research.

Direct Instruction

Introduction: The Direct Instruction program places an emphasis on maximizing student engagement in academically related activities, as opposed to unrelated activities. The emphasis is on maximizing teacher-directed instruction, guided practice, and supervised seatwork.

The following description of Direct Instruction and supporting evidence is summarized from the work of Rosenshine and Stevens.

Author: Rosenshine & Stevens (1986)

Students Taught: K–12

Intended Learning: Mathematics, English, science, history, and reading

Instructional Tactics Employed:

- Teachers begin each lesson with a short review of previous, prerequisite learning.
- Skills are taught in a step-by-step manner, with skills learned in one step being applicable to the learning of skills in a subsequent step or steps.
- Teachers begin a lesson with a short statement of goals and objectives.
- Teachers demonstrate what is to be learned, giving explicit, step-by-step directions.

- Student instruction, student practice of assigned tasks, and evaluation of student performance of assigned tasks are incorporated in each instructional segment.
- Student practice immediately follows instruction.
- Teachers prepare a large number of questions relevant to the to-be-learned material.
- During instruction and student practice, teachers ask a large number of questions to check for student understanding.
- Evaluations are frequent, with feedback on evaluations and corrective instruction being administered immediately following evaluation.
- Correct responses to questions are acknowledged as correct.
- The teacher should simply provide the correct response to the student if an incorrect response is determined by the teacher to be a careless error on the part of the student.
- When a student's incorrect response is due to a lack of knowledge or understanding, the teacher has two options to pursue as deemed more appropriate: (1) provide the student with prompts or hints to lead the student to the correct answer, or (2) reteach the material to the students who do not understand.
- Teachers provide praise for correct responses and encouragement after incorrect responses.
- Evaluation of student practice, whether written or verbal, occurs during or immediately following student practice.
- Feedback on evaluations and correctives are administered to students immediately following evaluation.
- Teachers make sure the students are prepared to work alone before assigning them to seatwork.
- Seatwork activity follows directly after the guided practice.
- Seatwork activities are directly relevant to lecture, demonstration, and guided practice activities.

Findings: These Direct Instruction tactics were found to be related to greater academic achievement.

Interpretation: The efficacy of the Direct Instruction program in enhancing student academic achievement is well supported by the research.

Success for All

Introduction: Learning for Mastery and Direct Instruction are generic programs in the sense that they describe instructional techniques that can be used at many different grade levels to teach almost any subject matter. In contrast, Success for All consists of different components designed to teach particular subject matter at particular grade levels. The individual subject area components for language arts, math, science, and social studies and science are marketed to schools individually or in combination.

The presentation of Success for All is an interpretation of convoluted descriptions provided in literature published by the developers of the program(s) (Slavin, 1998; Slavin et al., 1996). The literature describes Success for All and Roots and Wings as being separate entities (Slavin, 1998; Slavin et al., 1994, 1996). However, the individual components are described and marketed under the overall umbrella of Success for All (Slavin, 1998). For that reason, and because it covers a broad range of subject areas and grades, Success for All has been considered a generic instructional program.

Although there are commonalities among the various components, each component of Success for All has its own associated research base, content area(s), grade level appropriateness, and instructional tactics. Therefore, each component will be addressed individually. First, a synopsis of the components of Success for All is provided, and then an interpretation of relevant research is provided.

ROOTS AND WINGS

Language Arts Program

Introduction: The reading program is intended to provide students with the initial necessary basic reading skills and then build on those basic skills through two programs: Reading Roots and Reading Wings.

Reading Roots

Students Taught: Grades K–1

Intended Learning: Reading, writing, and teamwork

Instructional Tactics Employed:

- Letters and letter sounds are introduced to the students orally, and then students move on to written symbols.
- Students are taught to integrate individual letter sounds into words, sentences, and stories.
- Students are provided instruction on story structure.
- Cooperative group reading and story activities are incorporated into instruction.
- Students are provided comprehension skills instruction.

- Students are provided instruction on self-assessment and self-correction.
- Reading and writing are progressively integrated.
- Students receive one-on-one tutoring as necessary.

Reading Wings

Students Taught: Grades 1–6

Intended Learning: Reading writing, and teamwork

Instructional Tactics Employed:

- Cooperative learning activities are assigned so that students can work together to learn.
- Students receive instruction and practice in story structure, prediction, summarization, vocabulary building, and story-related writing.
- Teachers provide direct instruction in reading comprehension skills, followed by student team practice of these skills.
- Students are grouped by reading level for reading practice and tutoring.

Mathematics Program

Introduction: The mathematics program is intended to enhance student mathematics achievement by balancing instruction in problem-solving skills with concept development.

Math Wings

Students Taught: Grades 1–6

Intended Learning: Mathematics and teamwork

Instructional Tactics Employed:

- Students work in cooperative learning groups to discover and apply the ideas of mathematics.
- Games, discovery, creative problem solving, manipulatives, calculators, and computers are used by teachers to teach mathematics.
- Shared student hands-on activities are employed.
- Student performance is frequently assessed by teachers.

Social Studies and Science Program

Introduction: The social studies and science program, named World Lab, is intended to enhance student academic achievement by integrating the social studies and science content with reading, writing, mathematics, and fine arts skills.

World Lab

Students Taught: Grades 1–6

Intended Learning: Academic achievement in general and teamwork

Instructional Tactics Employed:

- Students engage in simulations playing the roles of people associated with the social studies and science topics.
- Students work in small cooperative groups to investigate topics.
- In their groups, students read books and articles and write broadsides, letters, and proposals.
- Students use fine arts, music, computers, video, and other technology to prepare newspapers and multimedia reports.

SUPPORTIVE EVIDENCE

Research was available pertaining to specific instructional techniques used to teach particular subject matter to particular grades. Relevant research studies are reported accordingly without attempting to establish correspondence between the research and particular components of Success for All as marketed.

Language Arts Program

Authors: Paris, Lipson, & Wixson (1983): A logical synthesis with 68 study citations

Students Taught: Grades Pre-K–5

Intended Learning: Reading comprehension

Instructional Tactics Employed: The following instructional tactics were inferred from the research results of the studies analyzed by Paris, Lipson, and Wixson (1983).

- Young children's oral skills were developed prior to their learning to read print.
- Beginning readers were taught to apply letter sounds to letter combinations to identify words.
- Students were taught to ask questions, to take notes, and to use a dictionary.
- Students were taught to evaluate their reading and to correct their own errors.

- Students were taught story structure.
- Students were taught how to summarize reading material.
- Students were taught how to use mnemonics as an aid to remembering what they have read.
- Students were taught the value of rereading, analyzing word parts, and context.
- Students were taught that they can succeed if they keep trying.
- Students' reading was evaluated frequently and feedback provided on their performance.

Findings: The above-listed tactics have been found to be related to greater student reading comprehension and recall.

Authors: Short & Ryan (1984)

Students Taught: Grade 4

Intended Learning: Reading comprehension and recall

Instructional Tactics Employed:

- Students were taught to use self-questioning to identify story main ideas.
- Students were taught to underline and take notes on story main ideas.
- Students were given feedback on their performance.
- Students were provided review of and practice in using the reading strategies.

Findings: Use of the above tactics by students resulted in significantly greater main idea recall.

Authors: Fitzgerald & Spiegel (1983)

Students Taught: Grade 4

Intended Learning: Reading comprehension and recall

Instructional Tactics Employed:

- Students were taught to identify story parts.
- Students were provided a review of story parts learned in the previous lesson prior to giving an overview of the upcoming lesson.
- Students were taught to use self-questioning to identify story parts.

Findings: Use of the preceding tactics resulted in significantly greater levels of reading comprehension.

Author: Slavin (1983)

Students Taught: Grades 3–12

Intended Learning: Teamwork and academic achievement

Instructional Tactics Employed:

- Students are formed into small, heterogeneous learning groups.
- Students are taught to help one another in learning.

Findings: The above cooperative learning tactics have been shown to be related to achievement.

Authors: Slavin et al. (1996)

Students Taught: Grades 1–5

Intended Learning: Language arts achievement

Instructional Tactics Employed:

- Letters and letter sounds are introduced to the students orally, and then students move on to written symbols.
- Students are taught to integrate individual letter sounds into words, sentences, and stories.
- Students are provided instruction on story structure.
- Group reading and story activities are incorporated into instruction.
- Students are provided comprehension skills instruction.
- Students are provided instruction on self-assessment and self-correction.
- Reading and writing are progressively integrated.
- Students receive one-on-one tutoring as necessary.
- Cooperative learning activities are administered.
- Students receive instruction and practice in story structure, prediction, summarization, vocabulary building, and story-related writing.
- Teachers provide direct instruction in teaching reading comprehension skills, followed by student team practice of these skills.
- Students are grouped by reading level for reading practice and tutoring.

Findings: Over a six-year period, language arts achievement was higher for students in grades 1–5 as compared to students in matched control schools.

Mathematics Program

Authors: Carpenter et al. (1989)

Students Taught: Students of first grade teachers

Intended Learning: Mathematics

Teacher Training Tactics Employed:

- Teachers were familiarized with research on children's solutions of addition and subtraction problems.
- Teachers learned to classify problems and to identify the process that children use to solve different problems.
- Teachers were taught that instruction should develop understanding by stressing relationships between skills and problem solving, with problem solving serving as the organizing focus of instruction.
- Teachers were taught that instruction should be organized to facilitate students' active construction of their own knowledge and understanding.
- Teachers were taught that each student should be able to relate problems, concepts, or skills being learned to the knowledge the student already possesses.
- Teachers were taught that it is necessary to continually assess student performance.

Findings: Students of first grade teachers who received instruction performed significantly better on complex addition and subtraction word problems than did students of first grade teachers who did not receive instruction.

Authors: Slavin, Madden, & Leavey (1984)

Students Taught: Grades 3–5

Intended Learning: Mathematics and teamwork

Instructional Tactics Employed:

- Students are formed into four- to five-member heterogeneous teams.
- Students in groups assist and evaluate each other's performance.
- Based on initial testing, individual students are placed in an individualized sequence and allowed to work at their own pace.
- Teachers instruct students in homogeneous groups drawn from heterogeneous teams.

Findings: Students in the cooperative learning condition achieved at significantly higher levels on mathematics achievement measures than did control students.

Social Studies and Science Program

No references to supportive literature were provided by the developers of the program. No supportive literature was located.

Interpretation: Research support for Success for All in its original form, as well as for the components of the reading and language arts program, is substantial. Research support for the added mathematics program is adequate. No research support for the social studies and science components was located.

For a more recent report on cooperative learning, see Slavin (1995).

Accelerated Schools Program

Introduction: The Accelerated Schools Program is intended to improve the academic achievement of at-risk students. Acceleration, moving through the curriculum at a faster pace, is the main instructional focus of the Accelerated Schools Program. The program includes parental involvement, local governance, and instructional strategies intended to accelerate learning.

Students Taught: K–12 at-risk students

Intended Learning: Achievement in all academic areas

Instructional Tactics Employed:

- The pace of instruction is accelerated to keep the students focused on and engaged in learning.
- Remedial instruction is curtailed.
- Peer tutoring is utilized following cooperative learning specifications.
- Interesting applications are developed that relate to the daily lives and experiences of students and that demonstrate the usefulness of the methods and concepts presented to them.
- Students are asked to discover for themselves applications of the concepts taught.
- Students are provided the conceptual and analytical tools that will enhance their capacity to learn more advanced material.
- Substantial attention is given to the arts and physical activity.
- Outside assignments or homework is mandatory.
- Teaching time and student engaged time are maximized.

Findings: H. M. Levin (1988), the initiator and advocate of the Accelerated Schools Program, acknowledges that very little research has been done on accelerating instruction for students other than on the gifted and talented student. Effectiveness is claimed for the Accelerated Schools Program because he contends that it incorporates "Learning for Mastery," "Direct Instruction," and "cooperative learning" techniques. However, this claim is questionable.

Interpretation: The Accelerated Schools Program as designed has very serious flaws. According to the research, an effective instructional program must provide for student remediation of incorrect performance. Mastery Learning, Direct Instruction, and cooperative learning all provide for remediation of incorrect student performance. Research by Denhem and Liebeman was cited as support for accelerating the pace of instruction. Their research is taken into account in the Brophy and Good (1986) research report, which concludes that student incorrect performance should be remediated, students should be allowed ample time to perform assigned tasks, and that additional time should be allowed if the student does not have enough time to perform the task. In short, no research support was found for curtailing remediation of student incorrect performance, or for accelerating the pace of instruction for other than gifted and talented students. Moreover, the Accelerated Schools Program gives inadequate attention to the use of other effective instructional tactics (described in Chapter 4) that have been shown by research to increase academic achievement.

The CABAS Program

Introduction: The Comprehensive Application of Behavior Analysis to Schooling program (CABAS) is described as a research-based, student-centered education initiative that has been effective in small schools for children with behavioral anomalies as well as normal children (Greer, 1996).

As reported, the program includes teacher training, teacher accountability, and teacher supervision, and encourages parental involvement. Seven major characteristics of CABAS were identified:

1. Comprehensive individualized instruction.
2. New conceptions of curriculum and pedagogy based on the epistemology of behavior selection.
3. A system-wide perspective that is learner-driven.
4. Schools that engender a sense of community.
5. Total redesign of schools based on the individual and what science tells us works.
6. A system that works because there is a continuous measurement of the

important behaviors of each member of the system, and measurement drives the system.

7. Teachers function as strategic scientists of the system.

SUPPORTIVE EVIDENCE

Authors: Selenski & Greer (1991)

Students Taught: Visually and mentally impaired students aged 3 to 21

Intended Learning: Number of correct student responses

Teacher Training Tactics Employed:

- Initial evaluation of students to identify deficits.
- Development of objectives and curricula tailored to the needs of the child in the form of learn units.
- Students are taught using continuous assessment.
- Advancement to the next objective is based on the student attaining criterion performance.
- Number of student correct and incorrect responses is graphed and posted daily in a prominent location.
- Trials (evaluations) include a teacher antecedent, a student response, and a consequence or reward (praise, edible reward, or time to play with a favorite toy).

Findings: As the number of trials increased, the number of student correct responses increased, with the proportion of correct responses remaining essentially unchanged.

It should be noted that a major focus of this study was the effect of teacher training and bonuses given for exceptional teacher performance in terms of the number of modules completed, the number of evaluations given, and the number of objectives met.

Authors: Ingham & Greer (1992) (Two identical studies with the same students but different teachers)

Students Taught: Severely mentally deficient students aged 6 to 21 with I. Q. scores ranging from 8 to 49

Teacher Training Tactics Employed:

- Student correct response is reinforced by the teacher.
- Student incorrect response is corrected by the teacher.

Findings (both studies): As the number of correct actions by the teacher increases (number of times the teacher correctly reinforces or corrects student responses), the number of correct responses by the student increases.

It should be noted that the major focus of this study was the effect of supervisor observations and guidance of a teacher on the teacher's performance rate and accuracy in correctly reinforcing or correcting student responses.

Interpretation: Research conducted on mentally deficient students cannot be generalized to public school students who are, for the most part, not mentally deficient. The emphasis in all three studies reviewed was on developing teacher efficiency in reinforcing and correcting students.

Cited research does not support the effectiveness of CABAS in enhancing student academic achievement in general. There is no evidence that CABAS is effective in teaching what they refer to as "normal students," and the evidence supporting the effectiveness of CABAS in teaching mentally deficient students is highly limited and questionable.

The following programs were developed primarily to improve teacher preparation in the teaching of math and science.

New Mexico Collaborative for Excellence in Teacher Preparation (CETP)

Introduction: The reported goal of the New Mexico Collaborative for Excellence in Teacher Preparation (CETP) is to improve the science, mathematics, and technology preparation of future K–12 teachers. CETP supports the concept of pre-service teachers learning from experienced teachers, exploring new technologies, and applying innovative teaching strategies (CETP, 1998).

Students Taught: Pre-service, mathematics, science, and engineering teachers

Intended Learning: Instructional strategies

Teacher Training Tactics Employed:

- The program works toward reforming pre-service teachers' curriculum content and teaching.
- The program is tailored to suit regional needs. It incorporates mentoring, advising, professional development opportunities, and a materials/resource loan program.

The program is under development. No specific curriculum or instruction information was provided or found, and no references to supportive research literature were provided.

Discovery

Introduction: Discovery is a teacher professional development program for Ohio middle school mathematics and science teachers. The mission of the program is to improve middle school mathematics and science instruction (Discovery, 1998).

Students Taught: Middle school mathematics and science teachers

Teacher Training Tactics Employed:

- Collaborative programs between colleges of education and colleges of arts and science were initiated for the education of prospective teachers of science and mathematics.
- Collaborations among public and independent universities and large school districts were initiated for the induction and professional development of science and mathematics teachers.
- High-quality research and development activities were initiated to guide Ohio's reform of science and mathematics education.
- Articulation across elementary, middle, and high schools, Tech Prep, and two- and four-year colleges and universities was initiated to provide quality education in science and mathematics for students from elementary grades through the undergraduate years.

No specific curriculum or instruction information was provided or found, and no references to supportive research literature were provided.

Mathematics and Science Teacher Education Program (MASTEP)

Introduction: The MASTEP Collaborative is a five-year systemic project to improve mathematics and science teacher education in the greater San Francisco Bay Area and is housed at San Jose State University (MASTEP, 1998).

Students Taught: In-service and pre-service mathematics and science teachers

Teacher Training Tactics Employed:

- A support network and professional development program is provided for newly graduated math and science teachers.
- An innovative curriculum and instructional program was developed for teaching math and science.
- A network of local K–12 schools was formed that will participate in the education of future teachers.

The program is under development. No specific curriculum or instruction information was provided or found, and no references to supportive research literature were provided.

Textbooks

An attempt was made to find research on the effectiveness of textbooks in enhancing academic achievement. None could be found. Evidently textbooks are not adopted because of their proven contribution to academic achievement.

REFERENCES

Anderson, S. A. (1994). *Synthesis of research on Mastery Learning* (Information analysis). ERIC Document Reproduction Service No. ED 382 567.

Brophy, J., & Good, T. (1986). Teacher behavior and student achievement. In M. C. Wittrock (Ed.), *Handbook of research on teaching* (3rd ed., pp. 328–375). New York: Macmillan.

Carpenter, T. P., Fennema, E., Peterson, P. L., Chiang, C., & Loef, M. (1989). Using children's mathematics thinking in classroom teaching: An experimental study. *American Educational Research Journal*, 26(4), 499–531.

Discovery. (1998). (on-line) Available at: http://www.discovery.k12.oh.us/.

Fitzgerald, J., & Spiegel, D. L. (1983). Enhancing children's reading comprehension through instruction in narrative structure. *Journal of Reading Behavior*, 15(2), 1–16.

Greer, R. D. (1996). The education crisis. In M. Mattainy & B. Thyer (Eds.), *Finding solutions to social problems: Behavioral strategies for change* (pp. 113–146). Washington, DC: American Psychological Association.

Ingham, P., & Greer, R. D. (1992). Changes in student and teacher responses in observed and generalized settings as a function of supervisor observations. *Journal of Applied Behavior Analysis*, 25(1), 153–164.

Levin, H. M. (1988). *Accelerated schools for at-risk students.* New Brunswick, NJ: Center for Policy Research in Education. ERIC Document Reproduction Service No. ED 382 567.

Mathematics and Science Teacher Education Program (MASTEP). (1998). (on-line) Available at http://www.mastep.sjsu.edu/.

New Mexico Collaborative for Excellence in Teacher Preparation (CETP). (1998). (on-line) Available at http://www.enmu.edu/cetp/.

Paris, S. G., Lipson, M. Y., & Wixson, K. K. (1983). Becoming a strategic reader. *Contemporary Educational Psychology*, 8, 293–316.

Rosenshine, B., & Stevens, R. (1986). Teaching functions. In M. C. Wittrock (Ed.), *Handbook of research on teaching* (3rd ed., pp. 376–391). New York: Macmillan.

Selenski, J. E., Greer, R. D., & Lodhi, S. (1991). A functional analysis of the comprehensive application of behavior analysis to schooling. *Journal of Applied Behavior Analysis*, 24(1), 107–117.

Short, E. J., & Ryan, E. R. (1984). Metacognitive differences between skilled and less skilled readers: Remediating deficits through story grammar and attribution training. *Journal of Educational Psychology*, 76(2), 225–235.

Slavin, R. E. (1983). When does cooperative learning increase student achievement? *Psychological Bulletin, 94,* 429–455.

Slavin, R. E. (1995). *Cooperative Learning* (2nd ed.). Boston: Allyn and Bacon.

Slavin, R. E. (1998). *Success for All.* (on-line) Available at http://www.successforall.net.

Slavin, R. E., Madden, M. A., Dolan, L. J., & Wasik, B. A. (1994). Roots and Wings: Universal excellence in elementary education. *Educational Leadership, 52*(3), 10–13.

Slavin, R. E., Madden, M. A., Dolan, L. J., & Wasik, B. A. (1996). *Every child, every school: Success for all.* Thousand Oaks, CA: Sage.

Slavin, R. E., Madden, M. A., & Leavey, M. B. (1984). Effects of team assisted individualization on the mathematics achievement of academically handicapped students and non handicapped students. *Journal of Educational Psychology, 76,* 813–819.

6

Empowering Students to Learn on Their Own

Of all the learning people acquire in their lifetime, none is more valuable than learning how to learn on their own. People who know how to learn on their own can do much better in school because they are better able to augment the classroom instruction they receive, gain more from classroom assignments, and earn higher grades. In addition, people who know how to learn on their own are able to acquire the knowledge and skill of personal interest to them outside of school. People are lifelong learners; they may be bored or frustrated with school and still spend large amounts of time investigating and learning about things that intrigue them. For humans learning is necessary for survival and success.

Despite the vast amount of time people spend attending to television and other forms of entertainment, they appreciate it when the entertainment is also educational. And many people enjoy spending time learning about things that enrich and benefit their lives. Everyone is aware of the importance of reading as a means of learning and enjoyment. However, the importance of reading as a self-teaching technique is most often overlooked or underemphasized. Yet through reading people can teach themselves almost anything recorded in libraries and data banks. Similarly, the computer is acknowledged as a great advancement, yet it is rarely lauded as the self-teaching device it can be.

Of all the gifts that schooling can bestow upon students, nothing is more important than teaching them how to learn on their own. Instead of self-teaching skills developing incidentally as a by-product of planned curriculum and instruction, an instructional program needs to be constructed for the sole purpose of teaching students how to learn on their own and should be included in the required course of study. Empowering students to learn on their own extends significantly beyond teaching the usual study skills.

Maturing in life entails progressing from total dependence toward independence. Schools play a large role in freeing children from total dependency on their parents or guardians and making them increasingly more able to take care of themselves, to contribute to society, and to succeed in family life and in the workplace. Schools are much less successful in weaning students from teachers and enabling them to learn on their own. This neglect needs to be remedied.

One of the major benefits of the effective instructional strategies described in the last two chapters is that many of them can be adapted to enhance students' ability to learn on their own. Moreover, they can be fashioned into an instructional program to teach students how to teach themselves anything they may need or want to learn. Of course, other important self-teaching skills, such as reading, are already incorporated in the school curriculum. Although necessary, they are insufficient to the development of proficient self-teaching.

The purpose of this chapter is to identify effective instructional strategies reported in the last two chapters that are pertinent to self-teaching, then to show how they can be adapted to formulate guidelines for instructional programs on self-teaching. Rather than repeat the tactics of strategies as reported previously, concise rules or tactics are derived for self-teachers to apply to control and advance their own learning. Not only can the application of the strategies advance their learning, it will additionally save time and effort and produce better results. To be effective, instructors who are administering the self-teaching program will need to provide sufficient guided practice for students to master the application of the strategies. This will ensure that the students are able to learn on their own.

Rules or tactics for the following strategies will be summarized in this chapter.

- Utilizing Repetition
- Utilizing Contiguity
- Clarifying Communication
- Utilizing Subject Matter Unifiers
- Staying on Task
- Providing Ample Teaching Time
- Providing Ample Learning Time
- Utilizing Reminders
- Facilitating Transfer of Learning
- Facilitating Decision-Making
- Facilitating Problem Solving
- Accessing Information

These titles have been changed slightly from the titles in the last chapters to be more appropriate references for self-teaching.

UTILIZING REPETITION

Students are aware of some of the benefits of repetition. Many have been told by their parents and other teachers to practice a musical instrument, reading, or the multiplication tables. Many have voluntarily practiced a game or sport they are interested in and have seen the benefits of practice. However, there is a great deal more about repetition they need to know to improve their school grades and to learn what they wish on their own.

To begin teaching students how to profit from repetition, it is advantageous to discuss what they already sense or know about the merits of repetition—that is, practice improves performance in the learning of any skill. Then they need to be informed that there are other forms of repetition they can use to control and further their own learning—whatever they may choose to learn.

The general rules students need to learn are:

- Frequent repetition enhances learning, provided the repetitions do not become boring and/or exhausting.

- To avoid boredom, novelty or variety must be introduced from one repetition to the next. For example, context can be changed with each repetition.

- Boredom can be averted and learning can be enriched at the same time. The novelty that is introduced with each repetition can provide important new information about the concepts or skill being learned to increase their knowledge. For example, when learning about a pear, students can feel, taste, see, and smell the pear.

- To increase their skills, say for example in playing a piano, a variety of musical compositions can be practiced and learned.

- To avoid exhaustion, study sessions should not be too long. Students need respite from repetition. Frequent spaced repetition is preferred.

- Once achievement of a learning objective has been mastered, students need to address new challenges.

- Two modes of repetition improve learning:

  1. *Repeated exposure*. Repeated exposure to to-be-learned information enhances the learning of the information. For example, to avoid boredom and add enrichment with repetition in learning the meaning of a word, the word can be looked up in different dictionaries.

  2. *Practice*. Repeated performance of to-be-learned tasks increases skill in performing the tasks. For example, to avoid boredom and add enrichment when practicing the solving of word problems in math, students can practice solving a variety of math word problems with different content in different contexts.

- Repeated exposure to information and practice can be used in combination
  to enhance learning. For example, students can repeatedly read instructions
  on how to use a telescope before practicing to perfect using it.

After students know the rules for using repetition appropriately, they should
select information and skills they want to learn and practice applying them until
they master applying them.

UTILIZING CONTIGUITY

If there is any "law of learning" that students should know about and apply to
enhance their own learning, it is the law or rule of contiguity. There is so much
research evidence confirming the validity of the rule of contiguity that it might
rightfully be called the "law of contiguity."

Students should be informed of the law of contiguity and that it specifies: For
events to be associated they must be experienced close together in time and space.
Moreover, they should be informed that much of learning is the learning of relationships, and they can take an active part in facilitating their learning any relationship they may want to learn by arranging to perceive the to-be-related events close
together in time and space. This would include, for example, the learning of cause–
effect relationships. To be associated appropriately the causal agent and its effect
must be perceived in proximity to one another.

The following are applications of contiguity students can be taught to use:

- *Studying for exams*. Studying or cramming immediately before an exam
  can improve their performance on the exam. This does not mean that there
  is no need to study earlier. As shown, there is a need to repeatedly study to-
  be-learned material. It does mean that the final study session should be as
  close to exam time as possible.

- *Correcting mistakes*. Students should be taught to correct their mistakes as
  soon as possible after they make them so that they are more likely to perform correctly in the future. This applies to any mistakes they may make,
  whether they be mistakes someone else (such as a teacher) may point out or
  a mistake they may detect. Suppose, for example, students were practicing
  a speech and recording their own presentation. They should check their
  recording immediately, and when they detect a mistake while replaying their
  presentation they should correct it immediately. They should also immediately check and correct any mistake they may find when reading their first
  draft of a written presentation.

- *Practicing*. When practicing a procedure students want to learn to perform,
  they should perform the steps of the procedure close together in time so that
  they will be able to associate the steps with one another. It may be necessary

to learn to perform individual steps before attempting to integrate them, but once students are ready to integrate the steps to perform the entire procedure they should not allow large time gaps between their performance of steps.

- *Communicating their ideas.* Students should be taught that when communicating their ideas in speech or in writing, the ideas they want their audience to associate should be presented in close proximity. Students should not leave gaps in the message they want to convey. They can expect better grades on compositions, essay exams, and term papers if the topics within them are close enough to be associated. For example, facts presented to corroborate a conclusion should be presented sufficiently close to the conclusion so that they can be associated with the conclusion.

- *Arranging for contiguity.* Students need to be taught to arrange for contiguity among the things they need to associate to complete their projects. The tools and materials they will need to complete a project should be arranged close together in their perceptual field so that they will be able to associate and use them readily as needed (for instance, when conducting a lab experiment).

- *Utilizing replicas.* Students should be taught that replicas such as maps, pictures, models, and diagrams are created so that relationships among distant and imperceptible events can be associated. Diagrams of the solar system are drawn to condense relationships among distant planets, stars, and other solar entities so they can be associated. X-ray pictures are taken to show imperceptible relations among inner body organs. The statement, "A picture is worth a thousand words" is true partly because pictures often reveal contiguous relations better than words can.

    When students are having difficulty understanding relationships they want to learn, they should try to find replicas created to make the relationships clearer. They may find the replicas they need in atlases, encyclopedias, and textbooks, or on web sites.

    Students should be taught to create their own replicas to help them learn relationships. Drawing their own diagrams, time lines, and pictures can serve as clarifying replicas of relations they are trying to learn. Students can create their own replicas to display the configurations they have in their minds. Architects draw tentative diagrams to develop and conceptualize ideas for shopping malls. When they finalize their conceptualizations as blueprints, they build miniature model replicas of the shopping malls for their clients.

CLARIFYING COMMUNICATION

The advantage of teachers clarifying communication to their students is that their students will learn more. There is also an advantage of students clarifying communication. Students who can communicate clearly are better able to obtain from others information they need to further their learning and to solve problems they want to solve. In addition, the more able students are to communicate clearly to teachers, the more likely they are to earn higher grades. Students can know the right answers and still get low grades because they are unable to communicate their knowledge to their teachers.

Ability to communicate clearly is very helpful to students in both oral and written communications. Students who can clearly convey their knowledge on oral exams and in answering teachers' questions in class discussion are more likely to receive higher grades. Similarly, students capable of communicating clearly in writing on essay exams, reports, and compositions will score higher.

Success comes more easily and more often to people who have natural talent for communicating. However, aptitudes for communicating in different modes vary. Some people are gifted speakers; others are gifted writers. It is less often the case that gifted speakers are also gifted writers.

In any event, all students can be *taught* to communicate their ideas more clearly. They can be taught general communication rules which will serve them well when communicating in any mode or media. It is well to keep in mind as we explore rules for communicating clearly that communication rules are not the same arbitrary rules of grammar taught in language arts programs. People can use rules of grammar perfectly and not be able to communicate clearly.

In teaching communication skills it is important to keep in mind that the primary goal of communication is to transfer one's ideas to others. To discuss communication one does not focus entirely on punctuation, parts of speech, and other grammatical issues. One refers to senders and receivers of messages and of encoding and decoding messages. Moreover, communication can be said to be effective when senders accurately transfer their ideas to receivers. Thus, good communication is functionally defined. On the other hand, being grammatically correct is a matter of applying arbitrary formal rules accurately, whether or not complying with the rules results in accurate communication.

It is not that students should not learn grammar; it is that grammar continues to be taught from first grade into college and communication is taught too infrequently, if at all. Moreover, teaching communication is quite different than teaching grammar. Perhaps an abbreviated example of how a teacher might teach effective communication would clarify the issue.

Consider an example of teaching oral communication to a class of students. A student, say Henry, is given a picture of a building to describe orally to the class. Each member of the class has pictures of four similar buildings including the one Henry is to describe to them. The teacher listens to Henry's description of the building with the class. After Henry has finished, the class and the teacher attempt to select the picture Henry has described from the four pictures before them. The percentage of students choosing the picture Henry is supposed to describe is calculated. The higher the percentage, the higher the score Henry is given on his communication. Finally, the class (with the teacher's guidance) discusses what Henry might have said or done to communicate more clearly and increase his score.

This example focuses on and illustrates pragmatically how students can be taught to communicate orally more accurately. The main difference in teaching written communication would be that the students and teacher would choose a picture based on Henry's written description. Afterward, the class would discuss what Henry might add or delete from his written description to improve his communication and his score.

In any discussion, recommendation for improving performance would be based on rules of good practice. Changes in grammar, such as punctuation, might be recommended, but only if the changes were deemed to improve communication. Obviously, some violations of rules of grammar would affect written communication more than others. Whether or not it was necessary to discuss applications of rules of grammar, it *would always* be necessary to discuss applications of rules of good communication to recommend improvements in any communication.

The following are rules for clarifying communication that need to be taught to students. The rules are excerpted from Chapter 4, "Making Instruction More Effective," and modified to apply more specifically to students.

Communication Rules for Students

- Provide examples and illustrations of concepts the receiver needs to know to understand your message.

- When speaking, avoid halts in the flow of your speech, such as "uh," "er," "your know," and so on.

- Avoid irrelevant interjections and relevant interjections at inappropriate times.

- Avoid vagueness by being precise and adding relevant detail in your message.

- Use transitional terms such as "next," "therefore," "in conclusion," and "to begin" to denote progressions in your message.

- To clarify cause–effect relations you are discussing, provide explanations of why the causal agent brings about the effect.

- Show the relevancy of the points you are making to the receivers' or audience's lives.

- Use multiple and diverse approaches to convey your message. For example, use a variety of illustrations and media that involve different senses, such as taste and touch.

- Use simple, commonly understood language.

UTILIZING SUBJECT MATTER UNIFIERS

Students can facilitate their own learning appreciably if they are taught how to obtain, create, and use unifying schemes that highlight the parts/whole relationships they are interested in understanding.

Important unifying schemes are (1) textual summaries, (2) hierarchical tree diagrams, (3) subject matter outlines, (4) pictorial or graphic representations, and (5) matrices.

First, students should be acquainted with the five types of unifying schemes mentioned above. Illustrations of an outline and matrix are in Chapter 4. Other illustrations are in Chapter 9 of the *Handbook on Effective Instructional Strategies* (Friedman & Fisher, 1998).

Next, students should be taught how to find unifying schemes of the subject matter they are interested in learning. They should be shown how to find them in textbooks, encyclopedias, "Skinnys," videotapes, and computer data banks.

Finally, students should be given subject matter that contains topics and subtopics and be taught how to create unifying schemes that highlight parts/whole relationships in the subject matter. They should be taught how to create subject matter outlines, hierarchical tree diagrams, textual summaries, and pictorial representations.

It is probably true that unifying schemes other than the five described above that relate linguistic terms also increase learning. Unifying schemes such as maps show parts/whole space relationships and clock faces that show parts/whole time relations probably enhance the learning of relationships, although research has not yet corroborated the effectiveness of these unifying schemes. It should be pointed out to students that in effective unifying schemes, the parts/whole relationships are presented contiguously.

STAYING ON TASK

There is a preponderance of evidence showing that the more time students spend concentrating on to-be-learned tasks, the more probable it is that they will learn to perform the tasks. In Chapter 4, the importance of teachers keeping students on task is stressed, and ploys teachers can use to keep students on task are described. In addition, it is pointed out that students control what they will attend to and learn and will not focus on tasks if they choose not to. What was not stressed in that chapter is what students can do for themselves to focus on to-be-learned tasks without distraction.

The importance of students keeping themselves focused on tasks they want to learn must be emphasized, and they need to be shown what they can do to keep themselves focused on the tasks. The following are rules students can be taught to employ to keep themselves on task.

- Students should plan and organize their study. In general, disorganization is disruptive to learning.

- Students should arrange for a place to study that is comfortable and quiet, with ample light.

- Students should arrange for a time to study that will be free of interruptions and intrusions.

- Students should allot a sufficient amount of study time to make significant progress without becoming exhausted. One-half to two-hour study periods are advisable, depending upon the students' age.

- Students should have nearby the books, tools, and equipment that are needed to complete the learning tasks at hand. Continually getting up to get what you need interferes with needed continuity of study.

- Students should make certain that they have the prerequisite know-how or readiness to complete the learning task at hand.

PROVIDING AMPLE TEACHING TIME

Providing ample teaching time is almost entirely the responsibility of instructional planners and teachers. There is abundant evidence showing that more teaching time enhances learning. However, students can further their own learning if they aggressively seek and avail themselves of the teaching they need when they do not know how to complete an assigned task. Even if students are reluctant to make their own ignorance public, they become acutely aware of their lack of know-how when they are assigned tasks and do not know how to proceed. At such times, they can relieve their anxiety, conserve time and energy, and maximize their chances for success if they compose germane questions and ask their teacher or other experts on the subject (such as a parent) for the answers.

Students need to be reassured that they are not expected to have mastered material they are being taught at the time they are being given task assignments. To help them learn, they should be told that they are expected to ask questions to improve their performance.

Of course, making tutoring available to students any time they may need it lets them know that they are expected to take advantage of it whenever they need help. This removes the psychological barriers that can make students reluctant to impose upon their already overburdened teacher who is not usually assigned time specifically for out-of-class tutoring.

PROVIDING AMPLE LEARNING TIME

In Chapter 4, the importance of instructional planners and teachers allotting ample time for students to complete assigned tasks was emphasized, including seatwork assignments, homework, library projects, and laboratory assignments. Allowing students ample time to complete assigned tasks was shown by research to improve task performance.

It is implicit that students can improve their own performance of tasks they are assigned to perform out of class if they allot themselves ample time to complete the tasks. It may be quite natural for students to want to rush through homework assignments to engage in recreational activities they prefer. Still, many students, especially as they become more mature, see the need to do well in their schoolwork and should be taught to estimate how long it takes them to perform various assigned tasks. They need to learn how long it takes to write compositions and term papers that require library research, as compared to compositions and term papers that do not require library research. Also, students need to be taught to estimate the amount of time it takes to complete science and other projects. In addition, students need to be able to gauge how many pages they can write and how many textbook pages they can read and assimilate in an hour.

Most important, students need to be taught to allot enough time in performing assigned tasks to be thorough. Cursory performance of assigned tasks impairs learning and grades. Students need to invest the time required to do their best work. They need to allow time for review and repetition to enhance their performance, and when developing a product they need to allow time to perfect the product. When writing a composition they should not be satisfied with the first draft; they should take time to analyze, critique, and improve their first draft. Similarly, when completing science and other projects, they should take time to refine and perfect their project.

Estimating and allocating sufficient time to do their work well is an important time management skill that all students need to learn. Older students can be taught to project time lines to help them estimate the time it takes to complete the segments of protracted tasks.

UTILIZING REMINDERS

Students, as well as teachers, can utilize reminders to increase learning. Students need to be informed that reminders are an effective tool they can use to facilitate their recall of important information. Students should be reminded that using reminders is common practice. People use alarm clocks, kitchen timers, and "post-its" as reminders, as well as date and appointment books.

Students should also be acquainted with the use of reminders in school. Scientific formulas are reminders of procedures to be followed. Many math symbols (such as +, −, ×, and ÷) also serve as reminders of particular operations that are to be performed. In language arts linguistic rules are used: for example, "i before e except after c." In music, FACE is used to remind students of the spaces on musical staffs.

Most important, students need to be taught how to *create* their own reminders to help them remember things they need to know. After learning how reminders are created they should receive guided practice in creating the following reminders.

- Outlines to remind them of subject matter.
- "Get and do" lists to remind them of materials they will need and tasks they need to perform (for example, when they are planning to conduct lab experiments).
- Acronyms to remind them of names they need to remember (as stated earlier, the acronym HOMES was created to help people remember the names of the Great Lakes).
- Rhymes and songs to remind them of arbitrary symbols that have no inherent meaning (for example, songs that facilitate the recitation of the alphabet).

The final four instructional strategies to be covered in this chapter are (1) facilitating transfer of learning, (2) facilitating decision-making, (3) facilitating problem solving, and (4) accessing information. They are presented and should be taught in that order because transfer of learning is incorporated in decision-making, and decision-making is incorporated in problem solving. Moreover, decision-making is more complex than transfer of learning, and problem solving is more complex than decision-making, at least as they are conceptualized in the following presentation. As "thinking skills" decision-making would be considered a higher-order skill than transfer of learning, and problem solving would be considered a higher-order skill than decision-making.

FACILITATING TRANSFER OF LEARNING

In Chapter 4, an attempt was made to show instructional planners and teachers (1) how to prepare instruction to enable students to transfer prior learning to achieve instructional objectives and (2) how to teach students to be successful in transferring learning to perform assigned tasks. Here the focus is on teaching students how to apply transfer of learning skills to learn on their own—whatever tasks they are interested in learning to perform.

After thoroughly learning how to transfer learning, students can use the following guidelines to help them effectively transfer learning to enable them to perform tasks they are interested in performing.

Transferring Learning from Memory

1. Recall procedures you have used in the past to successfully perform tasks that are similar to the task you presently are interested in performing.

2. To perform the present task of interest, apply the procedure used to perform the task most similar to the present task.

When applicable procedures cannot be recalled from memory or they do not work, try the following.

Transferring Learning from Libraries and Data Banks

1. Identify in libraries and data banks tasks that are similar to the task you are interested in performing.
2. If successful, identify procedures used to successfully perform the tasks you have identified.
3. If successful, determine the procedures you are able to perform.
4. To perform the present task, from among the procedures you are able to perform apply the procedures used to perform the task most similar to the present task.

When transferring knowledge from libraries and data banks, it will necessary to abort the quest at steps 1 and 2 if the information sought is unavailable.

When transferring knowledge from memory, it is implicit that if you can recall procedures you performed in the past, ability to perform the procedures is not at issue. On the other hand, when identifying procedures from libraries and data banks, ability to perform the procedures is at issue and must be assessed.

FACILITATING DECISION-MAKING

In Chapter 4, the focus was on teaching students to identify procedures to perform assigned tasks. Here the emphasis is on teaching students to identify procedures on their own to perform any tasks they may be interested in performing. To accomplish this they must learn to apply the following self-questioning sequence in order to derive a procedure to perform the task that interests them. Students should be taught how to facilitate their own decision-making after they learn how to facilitate transfer of learning because, as you will see, facilitating transfer of learning is incorporated in the self-questioning sequence used to make decisions.

After thoroughly learning the decision-making process, students can use the following self-questioning guidelines when attempting to derive procedures to perform tasks they are interested in performing.

Define the task. Answer the questions:
• What is it I am to achieve?
• Are there any constraints I need to conform to?

Identify procedures that have been used to accomplish similar tasks in the past. Answer the questions:

- Can I recall a procedure I have used in the past to successfully perform similar tasks?
- Can I identify procedures in libraries and data banks that have been used to perform similar tasks?

Tentatively select a procedure. Answer the questions:

- Which of the identified procedures, when executed, is most likely to accomplish the task?
- Which of the identified procedures do I have the ability and resources to execute?

A procedure is tentatively selected that is deemed feasible to perform and likely to accomplish the task.

Decide on a procedure to test. Answer the questions:

- Why do I think the tentatively selected procedure will work?
- Are there any relevant factors or contingencies I have overlooked?

FACILITATING PROBLEM SOLVING

Decision-making as described is a linear process that terminates when a decision is made. Problem solving is a cyclical process that continues on and on until the problem has been solved or the decision is made to abort efforts to solve the problem. The problem-solving cycle entails making a number of decisions in a prescribed order each time the cycle is executed. The diagram on the following page depicts a problem-solving cycle that has had some success in enhancing problem solving and learning. Instructions for teaching students how to use the cycle were described in detail in Chapter 5.

It is important that students learn that formal problem solving requires a long-term commitment, and that it is not possible to know beforehand if or when the problem will be solved. Few problems are solved on the first attempt. Most problems are solved by successive approximation as one cycle after another is completed leading to a solution.

ACCESSING INFORMATION

It is difficult, if not impossible, for students to learn on their own if they are not proficient in accessing the information they need. Almost all learning includes the acquisition and retention of new information, whether the purpose of the acquisition is to learn new facts or to obtain information for decision-making. In school

The Prediction and Problem-Solving Cycle

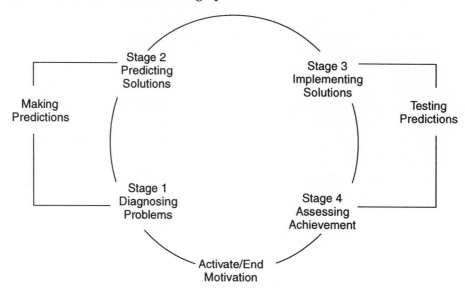

teachers often provide the information they want students to assimilate, but this does not improve the students' ability to obtain information on their own. In fact, it precludes the need for students to obtain information themselves. If students are to become proficient, independent learners, a most important skill for them to acquire is skill in accessing information.

Of course, by the time students reach adulthood they will have learned some techniques for accessing information, whether or not they were taught the techniques by their teachers as a part of the planned school curriculum. For example, in the process of reading books people eventually will learn about a table of contents and index without being taught. However, they may not learn as many benefits that can be derived from the use of indexes and tables of contents as they might be taught through planned instruction.

Because accessing information is so important in the development of independent learners it should not be left to chance, nor should it be taught sporadically. Many teachers outline a particular technique for accessing information when the technique is pertinent to the primary subject they are teaching at the time. Information access should be taught as a vital curricular skill, as reading and writing are taught. Reading and writing are not and should not be taught only as an adjunct to another scheduled topic; neither should accessing information be taught as an adjunct topic. Accessing information is a key skill that enables learning and should be stressed as a separate curricular topic.

Major topics that should be covered in an "Accessing Information" curriculum include techniques for accessing information in books, on microfiche, on audiotapes and videotapes, in libraries, and in computer data banks. Naturally, these major topics would break down into sub-topics. Another related topic is techniques for accessing information from people by means of questioning, interviewing, and correspondence. This list is meant to be more suggestive than exhaustive.

The decision on what to teach in an "Accessing Information" curriculum should be left to experts on the subject. And if there are no experts that know how to teach all facets of "Accessing Information," experts should be developed. There are expert librarians who know how to access information from libraries, and there are computer experts who know how to access information from computer data banks. We need to develop experts who know how to access all kinds of information by all means and methods.

It was mentioned at the beginning of this chapter that other skills students can apply to learn on their own are important. Some of those skills, such as reading, listening, and computer applications, are taught as a part of the required curriculum. In a self-teaching program these skills need to be addressed and students need to be taught how they are applied in self-teaching. For instance, students may know how to read but not know how to choose and organize reading material to develop a self-teaching program. The use of other self-teaching devices should also be dealt with in programs involving audio and video equipment.

In conclusion, this chapter contains guidelines for empowering students to learn on their own so that they can teach themselves. The guidelines do little more than suggest how the effective instructional strategies described in Chapter 4 can be modified and adapted for self-teaching. It may be that experts in teaching study skills might add significantly to these guidelines. In any event, the guidelines have been formulated for your consideration, should you be interested in developing an instructional program to teach self-teaching skills.

7

Preventing Impediments to Learning

In the preceding chapters, instructional strategies were prescribed that research shows to increase academic achievement. In this chapter, factors other than instructional strategies are considered that, if not dealt with, can impair academic achievement. Although instruction has the most direct and potent effect on academic achievement, other insidious factors can undermine learning, even if the most effective instructional techniques are used. These impediments pertain to organizational, environmental, and student control factors that define the conditions under which instruction takes place. They include student/teacher ratio, controlling classroom disruptions, and preventing school violence. Other commonly used practices will also be discussed, not because they preclude learning, but because research shows that they do not work and are for the most part a waste of time. They impede learning because they divert attention, funds, and effort away from the employment of practices that research shows are effective in enhancing academic achievement. They encroach on an already overcrowded school day, during which all available resources must be devoted to practices that are known to work. From what is known at present, the following factors have been shown to have an inconsequential effect on academic achievement: reinforcement, ability grouping, whole language instruction, some teacher characteristics as opposed to teaching characteristics, and matching students and teachers on certain factors. The remainder of the chapter is divided into two major parts: (1) impediments to learning and (2) questionable practices.

Impediments to Learning

STUDENT/TEACHER RATIO

Reducing student/teacher ratio is being advocated across the nation, and many school systems are reducing student/teacher ratios haphazardly, without understanding the implications of the research findings on the subject. There is no doubt that reducing student/teacher ratio will make teachers' jobs easier. Teaching, testing, controlling, and ministering to the needs of fewer students is simply less burdensome. And the fact that teachers are both overworked and underpaid is sufficient justification for reducing student/teacher ratio. It's no wonder that most teachers and teachers' organizations advocate it. The problem is that many advocates who support a reduction claim that it will increase academic achievement, and this assertion is both a serious overgeneralization and oversimplification. It is time to set matters straight so that informed, effective decisions can be made.

To begin with, it's important to recognize that there is some truth to the adage that "there are lies, damn lies, and statistics." When the research on a chosen topic is extensive, it is usually the case that a research study can be found to support almost any position an advocate may wish to take. There are over 100 studies on student/teacher ratio, and advocates pushing for a reduction have cited one or two studies to buttress their stance, ignoring the findings from the other studies. One such statement often heard is, "Reducing student/teacher ratio to 15:1 has been proven to increase academic achievement." Rather than debunk the many incorrect and partially correct statements on the subject, let us consider warranted inferences that can be drawn taking into account the more than 100 available studies (see Friedman & Fisher, 1998).

The following generalizations are tenable. However, any educator who establishes a student/teacher ratio for classes without considering the subsequent discussion of specific factors that should be taken into account is likely to make a mistake.

- Reducing student/teacher ratio from a larger ratio down to 15:1 does not appreciably increase academic achievement.
- The more the student/teacher ratio is reduced below 15:1, the more academic achievement tends to increase.
- Academic achievement is approximately two standard deviations higher when students are tutored one-on-one than when students are taught in groups.

After fully digesting these three generalizations, consider the relevance of the following factors to your particular situation before making a decision.

Cost. Reducing student/teacher ratio is very expensive. It requires hiring additional teachers and providing additional classrooms, equipment, and supplies for them. In contrast, implementing all of the effective instructional strategies described earlier simply requires that teachers presently employed learn and use more effective techniques when planning and executing instruction. Teachers can be taught to implement all of the effective instructional strategies in routinely scheduled staff development sessions in a short period of time. It is also important to keep in mind that the greatest gains in academic achievement begin as student/teacher ratio is reduced below 15:1. In most public school classes the student/teacher ratio is considerably above 15:1. The large amount of public school funds it would take to reduce student/teacher ratio to 15:1 probably would not increase academic achievement significantly, if at all.

Corrective Instruction. When students' performance is inadequate and, consequently, corrective instruction is needed, one-on-one tutoring is preferred. Feedback on evaluation results must be given to students individually and privately. Individual failures should not be broadcast to the class, and classes do not fail, individual students fail. To maximize a student's opportunity to recover from failure, teachers must point out to them personally what their failures were and what they must do individually to remediate their failure. Then teachers must prescribe corrective instruction for them individually and give them the guidance they need to succeed. Initial instruction can be given to the class as a whole. Corrective instruction is best individualized.

Grade Level. The development level of students needs to be taken into account when determining student/teacher ratio. Very young children have shorter attention spans. It takes more time and management to keep them focused on tasks. Furthermore, they are less able to take care of their personal needs and to exercise self-control. For these reasons, teachers' aides are assigned to assist teachers in preschool. Adolescents can be more difficult for teachers to manage. The internal eruptions generated by increased intense urges often cause disruptive outbursts and delinquent behavior. At the college level, students are becoming better able to control and satisfy their desires. Consequently, they are less difficult to manage.

Handicapped Students. The handicapping conditions of students need to be considered when determining student/teacher ratio. Handicapped students require more time and management than students who do not suffer from handicapping conditions. Accommodating the Individual Education Plans that are devised for each handicapped student presents an enormous challenge to teachers.

Instructional Mode. The mode of instruction is a primary consideration when determining student/teacher ratio. When the purpose of instruction is simply to impart information to students, the *lecture* mode is adequate. Students receiving information by means of a lecture need only to listen, observe demonstrations, take notes, and try to remember essential aspects of the lecture. Under lecture conditions there is very little reason to limit student/teacher ratio.

When the purpose of instruction is the exchange of information and viewpoints, the *discussion* mode is more suitable. The discussion mode requires that participants interact with each other in conversation. Group size is usually held below 20 so that all of the participants have an opportunity to be heard and to rebut others' assertions.

When the purpose of instruction is to provide on-the-job experience, student/teacher ratio is kept small so that the teacher can monitor and correct students' job performance. This mode of instruction is sometimes called *clinical instruction, practicum instruction*, or *apprenticeship instruction*.

When the purpose of instruction is for students to confirm facts for themselves, the mode of instruction is *laboratory work* or *field work*. Students may be working with expensive equipment and/or under dangerous conditions and need close supervision. In addition, their behavior needs to be closely monitored. As a result, student/teacher ratio should be kept small.

REFERENCES

Glass, G. V., Cahen, L. S., Smith, M. L., & Filby, N. W. (1982). *School class size: Research and policy*. Beverly Hills, CA: Sage Publications.

McGivern, J., Gilman, D., & Tillitski, C. (1989). A meta-analysis of the relation between class size and achievement. *The Elementary School Journal*, 90(1), 47–56.

Molnar, A., Smith, P., & Zahorik, J. (1999, December). *1998–99 Evaluation Results of the Student Achievement Guarantee in Education* (SAGE Program). www.uwm.edu/SOE/centers&projects/sage/.

Mosteller, F. (1995). The Tennessee study of class size in early school grades. *The Future of Children*, 5(2), 113–127.

Word, E. R. et al. (1990). *The State of Tennessee's Student/Teacher Achievement Ratio (STAR) Project: Technical Report*. Review of literature (pp. 199–205). Nashville: Tennessee State University, Center of Excellence for Research in Basic Skills.

CONTROLLING CLASSROOM DISRUPTIONS

Teaching is difficult. Teaching in the midst of classroom disruption is impossible. Even if teachers persist in their efforts to teach when disruptions are occurring, students will be distracted and unable to attend to the teacher's presentation. Some background noise from traffic or heating and air conditioning apparatus can be adjusted to and filtered out without disrupting the teaching–learning process, but blatant classroom disruptions will inevitably preclude learning and must be prevented. Some blatant disruptions can be easily prevented. For example, a simple administrative regulation can prevent messages from blaring into the classroom over loudspeakers during class. On the other hand, preventing student behavior from disrupting the class is more difficult to manage and depends on teacher know-how. It takes skill to manage student outbursts, infringements on classmates, acting out, and unruly and attention-seeking behavior. However, student disruptions can be managed by establishing and enforcing student rules of conduct. Moreover, research shows how to establish and enforce rules of conduct. Student disruptions vary in intrusiveness and the harm they can do, ranging from passive disruptions, such as tardiness and failure to be seated promptly, to aggressive disruptions, such as verbal harangues and violence toward the teacher or another student—all of which must be dealt with. Teachers who are successful in controlling disruptive behavior differ from unsuccessful teachers in the way they introduce classroom rules and provide consequences for violations, and in their consistency in invoking consequences when rules violations occur.

Tactics

The following are tactics for establishing and enforcing student rules of conduct that research shows to be effective. The tactics have been inferred from 50 studies. Students in the studies range from grades 1 to 12. Grade level and ability level of students must be taken into account when determining how to teach rules to students.

- Rules of conduct and consequences for violating them need to be established, clarified, and justified during the first meeting with students, before academic instruction begins.
- Rules need to be few in number (about five) and of sufficient brevity and clarity to be memorized by the students involved.
- Students' knowledge of rules and the consequences for violating them must be ensured as soon as possible.
- Consequences for violations of rules need to be given promptly and briefly, with as little disruption to instruction as possible.
- Prompts need to be used to maintain order and prevent rules violations. Prompts may be (1) nonverbal, such as direct eye contact, gestures, or proximity to disruptive students, or (2) verbal, ranging from simple prompts such as "shh," "stop," or "no" to more assertive desist commands such as "return to your seat" or "keep your hands to yourself."

Cautions and Comments

Student rules of conduct established for a classroom do not exist in isolation. They must be compatible with the rules and laws of the social milieu in which the classroom exists. School and school district regulations as well as city, county, state, and federal laws must be taken into account when establishing rules for a class. And if students are old enough, they should be informed of the importance of rules and laws for civilized intercourse among people. In addition, the relationship between class rules and the regulations and laws of governing social institutions might be discussed briefly. When establishing classroom rules, it is important to keep in mind that there is no evidence that student participation in the process is of any advantage in reducing classroom disruptions. The crucial factor is that class rules of conduct be established and enforced as specified. However, no system of rules can consistently control student inappropriate and disruptive behavior if instruction is not proficient or is inadequately matched to students' needs and abilities. It is also important to make the rationale for the rules clear to students (for example, to enhance learning and to promote safety).

REFERENCES

Ball, S. J. (1980). Initial encounters in the classroom and the process of establishment. In P. Woods (Ed.), *Pupil strategies: Exploration in the sociology of the school* (pp. 143–161). London: Croom Helm.

Blumenfeld, P. C., Hamilton, V. L., Wessels, K., & Falkner, D. (1979). Teaching responsibility to first graders. *Theory into Practice*, 18(3), 174–180.

Bremme, F., & Erickson, F. (1977). Relationships among verbal and non-verbal classroom behaviors. *Theory into Practice*, 5, 153–161.

Brooks, D. M., & Wagenhauser, B. (1980). Completion time as a non-verbal component of teacher attitude. *Elementary School Journal*, 81(1), 24–27.

Carter, K., & Doyle, W. (1982, March). *Variations in academic tasks in high- and average-ability classes.* Paper presented at the annual meeting of the American Educational Research Association, New York.

Cartledge, G., & Milburn, J. (1978). The case for teaching social skills in the classroom: A review. *Review of Educational Research*, 48, 133–156.

Cazden, D. B. (1981). Social contexts of learning to read. In J. T. Guthrie (Ed.), *Comprehension and teaching: Research reviews* (pp. 118–139). Newark, DE: International Reading Association.

Cone, R. (1978, March). *Teacher decisions in managing student behavior.* Paper presented at the annual meeting of the American Educational Research Association, Toronto.

Doyle, W. (1979). Making managerial decisions in classrooms. In D. L. Duke (Ed.), *Classroom management* (78th yearbook of the National Society for the Study of Education, Part 2) (pp. 42–74). Chicago: University of Chicago Press.

Doyle, W. (1984). How order is achieved in classrooms: An interim report. *Journal of Curriculum Studies*, 16(3), 259–277.

Eder, D. (1982). The impact of management and turn-allocation activities on student performance. *Discourse Processes*, 5, 147–159.

Emmer, E., Evertson, C., & Anderson, L. (1980). Effective classroom management at the beginning of the school year. *Elementary School Journal*, 80(5), 219–230.

Emmer, E. T., Sanford, J. P., Clements, B. S., & Martin, J. (1982). *Improving classroom management and organization in junior high schools: An experimental investigation* (R & D Center Rep. No. 6153). Austin: University of Texas, R & D Center for Teacher Education.

Emmer, E. T., Sanford, J. P., Evertson, C. M., Clements, B. S., & Martin, J. (1981). *The classroom management improvement study: An experiment in elementary school classrooms* (R & D Center Rep. No. 6050). Austin: University of Texas, R & D Center for Teacher Education.

Erickson, F., & Mohatt, G. (1982). Cultural organization of participation structures in two classrooms of Indian students. In G. Spindler (Ed.), *Doing the ethnography of schooling* (pp. 132–174). New York: Holt, Rinehart, & Winston.

Evertson, C. M. (1982). Differences in instructional activities in higher and lower achieving junior high English and math classes. *Elementary School Journal*, 82, 329–350.

Evertson, C. M. (1985). Training teachers in classroom management: An experimental study in secondary school classrooms. *Journal of Educational Research*, 79, 51–58.

Evertson, C. M. (1987). Managing classrooms: A framework for teachers. In D. C. Berliner & B. V. Rosenshine (Eds.), *Talks to teachers* (pp. 54–74). New York: Random House.

Evertson, C. M. (1989). Improving elementary classroom management: A school-based training program for beginning the year. *Journal of Educational Research*, 83(2), 82–90.

Evertson, C. M. (1995). *Classroom organization and management program*. Revalidation Submission to the Program Effectiveness Panel, U.S. Department of Education.

Evertson, C. M., & Emmer, E. T. (1982). Effective management at the beginning of the school year in junior high classes. *Journal of Educational Psychology*, 74, 485–498.

Florio, S., & Shultz, J. (1979). Social competence at home and at school. *Theory into Practice*, 18, 234–243.

Gettinger, M. (1988). Methods of proactive classroom management. *School Psychology Review*, 17, 227–242.

Gordon, T. (1974). *Teacher effectiveness training*. New York: Peter H. Wyden.

Griffin, P., & Mehan, H. (1979). Sense and ritual in classroom discourse. In F. Coulman (Ed.), *Conversational routine: Explorations in standardized communication situations and prepatterned speech*. The Hague: Mouton.

Gump, P. V. (1967). *The classroom behavior setting: Its nature and relations to student behavior*. Washington, DC: U.S. Office of Education, Bureau of Research.

Hargreaves, D. H., Hester, S. K., & Mellor, F. J. (1975). *Deviance in classrooms*. London: Routledge & Kegan Paul.

Humphrey, F. M. (1979). *"Shh!": A sociolinguistic study of teachers' turn-taking sanctions in primary school lessons*. Unpublished doctoral dissertation, Georgetown University, Washington, DC.

Johnson, M., & Brooks, H. (1979). Conceptualizing classroom management. In D. L. Duke (Ed.), *Classroom management* (78th yearbook of the National Society for the Study of Education, Part 2) (pp. 1–41). Chicago: University of Chicago Press.

Johnson, T., Stoner, G., & Green, S. (1996). Demonstrating the experimenting society model with classwide behavior management interventions. *Research into Practice*, 25, 199–214.

Jones, V. F., & Jones, L. S. (1981). *Responsible classroom discipline*. Boston: Allyn & Bacon.

Kounin, J., & Gump, P. (1958). The ripple effect in discipline. *Elementary School Journal*, 59, 158–162.

Kounin, J. S. (1970). *Discipline and group management in classrooms*. New York: Holt, Rinehart, & Winston.

LeCompte, M. D. (1980). The civilizing of children: How young children learn to become students. In A. A. VanFleet (Ed.), *Anthology of education: Methods and applications* (pp. 105–127). Norman: University of Oklahoma Press.

McDermott, R. P. (1976). *Kids make sense: An ethnographic account of the interactional management of success and failure in one first grade classroom*. Unpublished doctoral dissertation, Stanford University, Stanford, CA.

McGinnis, C., Frederick, B., & Edwards, R. (1995). Enhancing classroom management through proactive rules and procedures. *Psychology in the Schools*, 32, 220–224.

McKee, W. T., & Witt, J. C. (1990). Effective teaching: A review of instructional and environmental variables. In T. B. Guitkin & C. R. Reynolds (Eds.), *The handbook of school psychology* (2nd ed., pp. 821–846). New York: Wiley.

Metz, M. (1978). *Classrooms and corridors*. Berkeley: University of California Press.

Moskowitz, G., & Hayman, J. (1975). Success strategies of inner-city teachers: A year-long study. *Journal of Educational Research*, 69, 283–289.

O'Leary, K. D., Becker, W. C., Evans, M. B., & Saudargas, T. (1969). A token reinforcement program in a public school: A replication and systematic analysis. *Journal of Applied Behavior Analysis, 2*, 3–13.

Paine, S. C., Radicchi, J., Rosellini, L. C., & Darch, C. B. (1983). *Structuring your classroom for academic success*. Champaign, IL: Research Press.

Phillips, S. U. (1972). Participation structures and communicative competence: Warm Springs children in community and classrooms. In C. B. Cazden, V. F. Johns, & D. Hymes (Eds.), *Function of language in the classroom* (pp. 370–394). New York: Teacher's College Press, Columbia University.

Pittman, S. I. (1985). A cognitive ethnography and quantification of a first grade teacher's selection routines for classroom management. *Elementary School Journal, 85*, 541–557.

Rhode, G., Jenson, R. J., & Reavis, H. K. (1993). *The tough kid book: Practical classroom management strategies*. Longmont, CO: Sopris West.

Rosenburg, M. S. (1986). Maximizing the effectiveness of structured classroom management programs: Implementing rule-revue procedures with disruptive and distractible students. *Behavioral Disorders, 11*, 239–248.

Sanford, J. P., Emmer, E. T., & Clements, B. S. (1983). Improving classroom management. *Educational Leadership, 40*, 56–60.

Sieber, R. T. (1976). *Schooling in the bureaucratic classroom: Socialization and social reproduction in Chestnut Heights*. Unpublished doctoral dissertation, New York University.

Smith, L. M., & Geoffrey, W. (1968). *The complexities of an urban classroom*. New York: Holt, Rinehart, & Winston.

Shultz, J., & Florio, S. (1979). Stop and freeze: The negotiation of social and physical space in a kindergarten/first grade classroom. *Anthropology and Education Quarterly, 10*, 166–181.

Thomas, A., & Grimes, J. (Eds.). (1990). *Best practices in school psychology—II*. Washington, DC: National Association of School Psychologists.

Wallat, C., & Green, J. L. (1979). Social rules and communicative contexts in kindergarten. *Theory into Practice, 18*(4), 275–284.

Yinger, R. J. (1977). *A study of teacher planning: Description and theory development using ethnographic and information processing methods*. Unpublished doctoral dissertation, Michigan State University, East Lansing.

REDUCING SCHOOL VIOLENCE AND CRIME

School violence is not so much a critical problem because of its frequency, but rather because of its dire consequences and high profile. In 1996, about 26 out of every 1,000 students were victims of violent crimes away from school, as compared to 10 of every 1,000 students in school; school-related homicides account for approximately 1% of all homicides for schoolchildren aged 5–19 (U.S. Department of Justice, Bureau of Justice Statistics, 1999). So youth are much less likely to be victims of violent crimes in school than away from school. Furthermore, there has been a reduction in violent crimes in schools over the past 10 years (*National Report on School Safety*, 1999). However, students' perception and fears of school violence exacerbate the problem. Student reports indicate a higher incidence of violent crimes (Everett & Price, 1995) and a greater fear of being victimized by violent crimes than is substantiated by the evidence (U.S. Department of Justice, Bureau of Justice Statistics, 1999).

Violent crimes against teachers were higher than against students. Thirty-one teachers out of 1,000 were victims of school-related violent crimes (U.S. Department of Justice, Bureau of Justice Statistics, 1992–1996).

As seldom as they may occur, violent crimes in school almost always make media headlines and stay in the news for a while, for two reasons. First, they have dire, long-lasting consequences resulting in the destruction of life, limb, and property. Second, they tend to be sensational news. The public is much more accustomed to youth being the victims rather than the perpetrators of atrocities. When youth commit atrocities associated with sociopathic adult criminals it is surprising and shocking. The crimes draw and fixate attention for some time. Shootings at Jonesboro, Arkansas, and Littleton, Colorado, are cases in point.

In the final analysis, no matter how rare violent crimes may be in school, because of their catastrophic nature schools beset by violence or fear of violence are compelled to attack the problem. Fundamentally, three approaches have been used to reduce violent crime in schools: (1) establishing and enforcing student rules of conduct, (2) securing the physical environment, and (3) modifying student attitudes and behavior.

Establishing and Enforcing Student Rules of Conduct

The value of establishing student rules of conduct is not nearly as well established for reducing violent crimes in school as it is for reducing classroom disruptions. As shown previously, 50 research studies demonstrated that when teachers establish and enforce student rules of conduct, disruption in their classrooms is significantly reduced. Moreover, specific classroom tactics were prescribed that teachers can employ to aid in the reduction of classroom disruptions.

Reducing classroom disruption is a problem teachers must manage; reducing violent crimes in school is the responsibility of school administrators. Since classrooms are contained in schools, what administrators do to manage violent crimes indirectly affects teachers' ability to manage the behavior of students in their classes. Students who feel free to be violent in the school environment would naturally be more difficult for classroom teachers to control. So it is very important to establish and enforce student rules of conduct that work in the school environment. The problem is that available research is insufficient to support particular rule enforcement tactics for reducing school violence.

Of existing rule enforcement tactics used to reduce school violence, zero-tolerance policies and research come closest to suggesting particular tactics. Zero-tolerance policy was defined as school or district policy that mandates predetermined consequences for specific offenses (U.S. Department of Education, 1997). Offenses listed include violence and possession or use of alcohol, drugs, weapons other than firearms, and firearms. It was easier to identify offenses than it was to identify rule enforcement tactics for reducing them. Only one study could be found that prescribes such tactics for reducing the incidence of these offenses. The *Safe Schools Study* (U.S. Department of Health, Education, and Welfare, 1978) examined 600 schools to determine conditions necessary for safe schools and found the best predictors of safe schools to be:

- fair, firm, and consistent rule enforcement
- quality of academic instruction
- student involvement in decisions
- student/teacher ratio

Although this study is suggestive, it is hardly a sufficient basis for prescribing a particular set of rule enforcement tactics to reduce school violence.

There are traditional rule enforcement tactics commonly adopted and practiced for many years: (1) in-school suspension, (2) out-of-school suspension, and (3) expulsion. They are often applied conditionally in that order. Typically, in-school suspension is usually used first, out-of-school suspension is used when in-school suspension fails to work, and expulsion is used as a last resort.

When in-school suspension is used, students are removed from class and assigned elsewhere in school. Students may be tutored, counseled, or simply warehoused with little attention to their learning deficits or behavior needs. Frequently some form of punishment is added: for instance, students may be deprived of participation in extracurricular activities. Allegedly the benefits of in-school suspension depend on the degree to which the student is helped in school rather than warehoused (Florida Department of Education, 1995). Although logic suggests that it is advantageous to try and help students rather than to warehouse them, there is no hard evidence that tutoring, counseling, or other tactics will cause violent students to become nonviolent. However, evidence was presented showing that tutoring can be expected to remediate the learning deficits these or other students may have.

Out-of school suspension (OSS) has the advantage of being easy to administer, requires little planning or resources, and can be applied for a number of infractions. It has the additional advantage of removing the violent student from the school (U.S. Department of Justice, 1986).

Research has shown that OSS has no demonstrated positive effect on disruptive behavior (Comerford & Jacobson, 1987). Wheelock (1986) charges that suspension is perhaps the most powerful message of rejection that contributes to student disengagement from school. Other disadvantages of OSS cited in the research literature include:

- Suspended students are often the most in need of instruction and often fail required courses as a result of being suspended.
- High school dropouts are twice as likely to have been suspended as non-dropouts.
- Suspended students may regard suspension as a reward.
- Removing students from school may contribute to delinquency, as many suspended students are left unsupervised.

Expulsion, the permanent removal of a student from school, is reserved only for the most serious discipline problems when all else fails. Minority group members are suspended or expelled in disproportionately high numbers (Hodgkinson, 1993; Silva, 1992; Task Force on School Discipline, 1990; U.S. Department of Justice, 1986; Wehladge & Rutter, 1986), giving rise to the accusation that ethnic and race origin determine whether students are suspended or expelled as much as undesirable behavior.

The increased emergence of alternative schools has provided an alternative to suspension and expulsion as a means of reducing school violence. When a school transfers a violent student to another school, a problem is solved for that school, but the transfer does not necessarily result in the rehabilitation of the violent student. It takes more than placing violent students with their own kind to rehabilitate them. Moreover, the techniques presently used to rehabilitate violent students and other juvenile delinquents still leave a great deal to be desired.

There is reason to hypothesize that establishing and enforcing school rules for student conduct will reduce violence and crime in school. Rules need to be formulated and tested to see which ones work, keeping in mind that students must learn the rules and school personnel must enforce the rules consistently for them to have a chance of working. When consequences for violating rules are known by students, they are more likely to be accepted as consequences of their own actions, rather than arbitrary punishment administered at the whim of authority figures. This helps to teach students that they are responsible for their own actions and the consequences their actions may bring.

When formulating school rules of conduct, it is wise to keep in mind that school rules must be compatible with governmental laws, and that when a criminal law is violated schools are obligated to report the violation to the police and collaborate with the police to honor the law. A study of Chicago public school discipline procedures found that police were called in for only 6.5% of 106 criminal acts including aggravated assault, weapons possession, and sexual assault. In every case students received less than the minimum required days of suspension for the crimes committed (Menacker, Weldon, & Hurwitz, 1990). Such practice is a dubious deterrent to school crime. Rapp, Carrington, and Nicholson (1992) found that when school discipline practices are lax, students are more apt to feel threatened and bring weapons to school to protect themselves. Goldstein (1999) recommends that schools adopt the "catch it low to prevent it high" policy used by many police departments to control street crime. The policy advocates that punishment for violations be promptly enforced for minor offenses so that students do not receive benefits for their commission, encouraging them to escalate their offenses.

However schools decide to establish and enforce student rules of conduct, it is good to remember that classroom rules must be consistent with school rules and school rules must be consistent with governmental laws. Furthermore, teachers, school administrators, and police must cooperate in enforcing regulations.

The search of students and seizure of their property by school officials has always been a controversial means of enforcing school rules and laws. It creates apprehension and is in need of clarification. Student search practices were initially clarified by *New Jersey v. T.L.O.* (1985). In that case, an assistant vice-principal opened and searched the purse of T.L.O. (as the student involved was identified to protect her identity) after she had been accused of violating the school's policy of smoking a cigarette on school property. His search disclosed not only a pack of cigarettes, but also marijuana, drug paraphernalia, a large sum of money, and documents which were related to drug trafficking. The court rejected the former doctrine of in *loco parentis*, stating that educators were more like government agents than parents, and therefore subject to Fourth Amendment restrictions on illegal search and seizure. However, the court allowed the search under a doctrine of "reasonable suspicion," declaring searches must pass a test of being (1) reasonable in inception and (2) reasonable in scope to avoid the need for a search warrant. The T.L.O. rule has since been interpreted to include the following acts as permissible behavior of school officials:

- Search of students' school lockers to look for contraband or illegal materials (*S. C. v. State*, 1991; *Student Searches and the Law*, 1995).

- Search of a student's car in the school parking lot (*State v. Slattery*, 1990; *Student Searches and the Law*, 1995).

- Searches by drug-sniffing dogs (*Doe v. Renfrow*, 1980; *Horton v. Goose Creek Independent School District*, 1982; *Jones v. Laxtero Independent School District*, 1980).

- Use of metal detectors (*People v. Dukes*, 1992; *National Treasury Employees Union v. Van Raab*, 1989).

- Performance of a visual or manual body cavity search (*Student Searches and the Law*, 1995).

The U.S. Supreme Court (*Veronia School District 47J v. Acton*, 1995) supported the random drug testing of students wishing to participate in extracurricular activities, such as athletics, and stated a preference for random-based, as opposed to suspicion-based, testing. The court found that suspicion-based tests would stigmatize innocent students and also permit teachers to arbitrarily test "troublesome but not drug likely students."

With respect to students' rights in school, the current direction of Fourth Amendment law increasingly supports the security concerns of educators at the expense of student civil rights issues (Beyer, 1997). Finally, a zero-tolerance policy can create significant, often unforeseen problems. It can substantially increase the number of students who are disciplined and as a result overburden school personnel. It can also reduce school attendance and interfere with student learning.

Securing the Physical Environment

The average public school in America is 42 years old, according to the National Center for Education Statistics (NCES) released in 1999. A recent report (GAO Report Number HEH-95-61) estimates that one-third of all public schools need extensive repair or replacement. According to this report, it would cost $112 billion to bring the nation's schools into good overall condition. These costs do not include security items. Thus, analysts conclude that any modification of physical surroundings for security purposes will be done in addition to, or at the expense of, these needed repairs. On the other hand, consider that schools in foreign countries, where violent crimes are less frequent and academic achievement is higher, typically are older. Some foreign countries take pride in the age of their schools and are not compelled to throw older things away for the new and improved. And although schools are contained in physical plants, physical plants do not have a direct or potent effect on student learning. Moreover, securing the school environment does not necessarily require costly construction.

In *Reducing School Violence* (1999), the authors published a checklist for creating a safe school building:

- Light all hallways adequately during the day.
- Close off unused stairways, or do not leave areas of the school unused.
- Install all lockers in areas where they are generally visible, or remove lockers altogether.
- Minimize blind spots; use convex mirrors to allow hall monitors to see around corners.
- Prohibit posters on classroom windows.
- Install an alarm system and/or a closed-circuit television monitoring system.
- Keep buildings clean and maintained.
- Locate playground equipment where it is easily observed.
- Limit roof access by keeping dumpsters away from buildings.
- Cover drainpipes so they cannot be climbed.

- Avoid decorative hedges; plant trees at least 10 feet from buildings.

- Trim trees or hedges to limit outside hiding places for people or weapons.

- Keep school grounds free of gravel or loose rock surfaces.

- Ensure vehicle access around the building(s) for night surveillance and emergency vehicles.

- Design parking lots to discourage through traffic; install speed bumps.

- Mix faculty and student parking.

- Create a separate parking lot for students and staff who arrive early or stay late, and monitor these lots carefully.

- Use fencing and gates with discretion, and choose attractive wrought-iron styles instead of chain-link fences. Secure access with heavy-duty padlocks.

- Establish a policy to have the school campus fully lighted or totally dark at night.

- Keep a complete list of staff member(s) who have keys to the building(s).

- Do not allow graffiti to linger on walls. Follow the three "Rs" after discovery—read, record (i.e., photograph or videotape), and remove. Inflammatory bathroom graffiti needs to be removed daily.

- Offer school- or community-based activities for students after school and on the weekends. Institute after-school academic and recreation programs for latchkey students.

- Conduct a thorough background check on anyone applying to work in the school to assure that no one is hired who has been convicted of sexual assault, child molestation, or pornography, or has a history of violent criminal behavior. Do not make hiring decisions before the check is completed (California State Department of Education, 1989; Centers for Disease Control, 1992; Gaustad, 1991; May, 1992; National School Safety Center, 1989, 1990; Prophet, 1990; Rapp et al., 1992; Speck, 1992).

It may be noted that the above list does not include the use of metal detectors or physical search of entering students. Ross et al. (1995) report that 96% of schools implement at least one type of security measure, including closed campuses (78%), bag, desk, and locker searches (61%), and locked outside doors (53%). Everett and Price (1995) report a 7% use of metal detectors.

In spring 1999, President Clinton announced the Safe Schools/Healthy Students Initiative, a grant program jointly administered by the U.S. Departments of Education, Health and Human Services, and Justice (*National Report on School Safety*, 1999). Fifty-four grants were given, with amounts ranging from $1 million to $3 million. An analysis of these grants revealed that only two included the installation of metal detectors. By comparison, nearly one-half included increased use of school resource police officers or heightened community policing, and nearly all grants mentioned student and community programs including counseling, parental skills instruction, and after-school programs.

Modifying Student Attitudes and Behavior

The third approach to the reduction of school violence is intervention programs that attempt to modify students' attitudes and behavior. At least 300 of these programs are commercially available. However, most developers and advocates of the programs have done little to validate their effectiveness in reducing school violence. Howard, Flora, and Griffin (1999) identified only 44 that even attempted scientific validation. Butler et al. (1998) found that only 20% of the ones they inspected provided for an outcome evaluation of any kind. Thus most programs are not worth considering.

The following are summaries of a few of the more scientifically evaluated programs marketed to reduce school violence. The "Good-Behavior Game," a program to reduce shy and aggressive behaviors, was studied by Dolan et al. (1993). This program was integrated into regular classroom curriculum. Teams of students were encouraged to minimize disruptive or inappropriate behavior and to work together to solve problems. Their "good behavior" resulted in rewards, such as stickers or recess. Nineteen schools in Baltimore, Maryland were randomly chosen to participate in the experiment. Within the 19 schools participating, comparable schools were grouped in units of three, with one school participating in the "Good-Behavior Game," another participating in the Mastery Learning Program, a reading skills and academic achievement program, and a third school receiving no treatment. There were also control classes within the two treatment schools which received neither treatment.

From the fall semester to the spring semester, teachers regularly reported that students in the "Good Behavior Game" displayed significantly less shy and aggressive behaviors. However, teachers may well have been biased because they were assigned to administer the game by superiors and were invested in achieving the desired outcome. Student peers failed to record a similar improvement in behavior. The children in the reading program had improvements in reading, but no change in behavior. A follow-up study (Kellam et al., 1994) found the only residual effect to be a lessening of aggressive behavior for sixth grade boys who had participated in the "Good Behavior Game" as first graders.

A pilot test of The Fighting Fair Model, conducted by a Miami, Florida elementary school, was evaluated by Powell, Muir-McClain, and Halasyamani (1995). The Fighting Fair Model is designed to promote conflict resolution and peer mediation. Fourth through sixth grade students utilized role-playing, classroom discussion, and peer mediation to gain positive behaviors to deal with conflict. Three teachers agreed to have their classes participate. Randomly chosen classes comparable to the three volunteer treatment classes were used as a control. The treatment was integrated into existing language arts and social studies curricula during almost daily 30-minute sessions for a seven-week period. Outcome measures included student self-reports describing their responses to hypothetical situations involving conflict, and school staff reports of student negative behavior including rudeness, hitting another student, and defiance of adult authority.

Immediately following the intervention there were significant positive changes in responses to hypothetical situations for students in the intervention group, and no significant changes for the control group. Both groups reported (school staff response) a decrease in negative behavior, with a larger effect for the treatment group. Desirable behaviors reported for the entire school during the two years of implementation included increased faculty attendance from 92% to 95% and increased student attendance from 92% to 95%. Disciplinary suspensions fell from four the year before the project to one during each of the two years of the project. Referrals to the principal's office declined from 103 before the project to 93 and 80, respectively, in the two years of the project. No statistical records were kept for fighting or hitting, and suspension and referral counts were not categorized. The authors conclude that no assurance exists that reductions occurred in violent or aggressive acts.

Orpinas et al. (1995) assessed the effectiveness of a curriculum called Second Step: A Violence Prevention Curriculum, which is distinctive because of its use of peer leaders. The goal was to increase social skills and reduce impulsive and aggressive behaviors. In four middle schools in a Texas city, three sixth grade classes from two schools were assigned (nonrandom) to either the curriculum administered by the teacher, the curriculum assisted by two peer leaders, or the control group. The curriculum consisted of 15 50-minute lessons that covered knowledge about violence; training on empathy, anger management, and interpersonal problem solving to reduce impulsive and aggressive behavior; and practice applying skills to hypothetical situations through behavior modeling and role-playing. Knowledge about violence, violence-prevention skills, and self-reported aggressive behaviors were assessed.

Both interventions (with and without peer instruction) significantly increased knowledge about violence and skills to reduce violence. Self-reported aggressive behavior (reported in instances per week) decreased during the program implementation, but increased to baseline levels on a three-month follow-up assessment. Student results on a follow-up test about violence prevention did show improvement, but were not reflected in statistics about actual aggressive behavior. This prompted the authors to suggest that future studies should limit the outcome variable to actual aggressive or violent behavior. There was a statistically significant improvement in attitudes about violence only in the peer-instructed classes, leading to the conclusion that the careful selection and training of peer leaders was necessary to increase the effectiveness of program implementation. There was no objective evidence of any reduction in actual violent behavior.

Another version of Second Step: A Violence Prevention Curriculum was evaluated by Grossman et al. (1997) in an elementary setting. This curriculum was designed to teach second and third grade students about social skills via discussion, role-playing, and conceptual activities related to anger management, impulse control, and empathy. Six matched pairs of elementary schools in King County, Washington were chosen for the intervention. Trained teachers in the intervention schools taught 30 35-minute classroom lessons over one semester. Student behavior was evaluated in three periods: (1) before the start of the curriculum in fall 1993, (2) two weeks after conclusion of the curriculum during spring 1994, and (3) six months after the conclusion of the curriculum in fall 1994. Three sources of data were used to evaluate the effect of the curriculum on child behavior: teacher ratings, parent ratings, and direct observation of students by trained observers in three settings: the classroom, the playground, and the cafeteria.

There was no reported difference in the two conditions from parents or teachers. There was a reported difference in student behavior by the trained observers, who reported a significant decline in physical aggression for the intervention-based children. Negative behaviors were recorded on an incident per hour basis. The interobserver agreement was .92 for pro-social, or neutral behavior, .50 for physical negative behavior, and .45 for verbal negative behavior. The conclusion that this program is beneficial is dependent on the acceptance of these direct behavior observations and the denial of competing data from parents and teachers. However, the statistics show that observers did not agree very consistently on their observations of negative behavior.

In conclusion, of the 300 commercially available programs designed to reduce school violence, most are not worth considering because there is no attempt to scientifically validate their effectiveness. Of those programs that were scientifically evaluated, none that were reviewed provided compelling proof that the program was effective in reducing school violence. In some cases there were flaws in the methodology of the study; in other cases there was some evidence of increased knowledge of tactics that might prevent violence. But in no case was evidence presented showing that students in a particular program actually committed fewer acts of violence than students who were not in the program, or that students who had committed acts of violence became less violent after being subjected to a particular program.

REFERENCES

Beyer, D. (1997). School safety and the legal rights of students. In *Preventing youth violence in urban schools: An essay collection.* New York: Columbia University.

Butler, E. W., Adams, M. A., Tsunokai, G. T., & Neiman, M. (1998). *Evaluating evaluations of anti-violence programs.* Riverside, CA: Office of Community Research Projects, Department of Sociology, University of California.

California State Department of Education. (1989). *Safe schools: A planning guide for action.* Sacramento, CA: Author.

Centers for Disease Control. (1992). *The prevention of youth violence: A framework for community action.* Atlanta: Division of Injury Control.

Comerford, D. L., & Jacobson, M. G. (1987, April). Suspension–capital punishment for misdemeanors: The use of suspension at four suburban junior high schools and viable alternatives that could work. Paper presented at the annual meeting of the American Educational Research Association, Washington, DC.

Doe v. Renfrow, 632 F. 2d 91, 7th Cir. (1980).

Dolan, L. J., Kellam, S. G., Brown, D. H., Werthamer-Larsson, L., Rebok, G. W., Mayer, L. S., Laudolff, J., Turkkan, J. S., Ford, C., & Wheeler, L. (1993). The short-term impact of two classroom based interventions on aggressive and shy behaviors and poor achievement. *Journal of Applied Development Psychology,* 14, 317–345.

Everett, S. A., & Price, J. H. (1995). Students' perception of violence in the public schools: The Metlife Survey. *Journal of Adolescent Health*, 17, 345–352.

Fish, S. (1993, January 31). Students on the outs may stay in. *The Orlando Sentinel*, A1, A8.

Florida Department of Education (1995). *School safety report 1995–96: School environmental safety incident reporting system handbook*. Tallahassee, FL: Safe & Drug-Free Schools Program.

Gaustad, J. (1991). Schools respond to gangs and violence. Special issue, *Oregon School Study Council (OSSC) Bulletin*, 34(9).

Goldstein, A. P. (1999). Aggression reduction strategies: Effective and ineffective. *School Psychology Quarterly*, 14(1), 40–58.

Grossman, D. C., Neckerman, H. J., Koepsell, T. D., Liu, P. Y., Asher, K. N., Beland, K., Frey, K., & Rivara, F. P. (1997). Effectiveness of violence-prevention curriculum among children in elementary school: A randomly controlled trial. *Journal of the American Medical Association*, 277, 1605–1611.

Hodgkinson, H. (1993). *Southern crossroads: A demographic look at the Southeast*. Tallahassee, FL: SERVE.

Horton v. Goose Creek Independent School District, 690 F. 2d 475, 5th Cir. (1982).

Howard, K. A., Flora, J., & Griffin, M. (1999). Violence-prevention programs in schools: State of the science and implications for future research. *Applied & Preventive Psychology*, 8, 197–215.

Indicators of School Crime and Safety (1999). National Center for Education Statistics and the Bureau of Justice Statistics. *Journal of School Health*, 65, 426–431.

Jones v. Laxtero Independent School District, 499 F. Supp. 223 E.D. Texas (1980).

Kellam, S. G., Rebok, G. W., Ialingo, N., & Mayer, L. S. (1994). The course and malleability of aggressive behavior from early first grade into middle school: Results of a developmental epidemiologically-based preventive trial. *Journal of Child Psychology and Psychiatry and Allied Disciplines*, 35, 259–281.

May, J. (1992). In tragedy's wake, students build esteem. *Detroit Free Press*, 10A.

Menacker, J., Weldon, W., & Hurwitz, E. (1990). Community influences on school crime and violence. *Urban Education*, 1, 68–80.

National report on school safety. (1999). A joint report prepared by the U.S. Department of Education and the U.S. Department of Justice. Washington, DC: Author.

National School Safety Center. (1989). *Student and staff victimization*. Malibu, CA: Author.

National School Safety Center. (1990). *School crisis prevention and response*. Malibu, CA: Author.

National Treasury Employees Union v. Van Raab, 489 U.S. 668 (1989).

New Jersey v. T.L.O., 1055 Ct. 731 (1985).

Orpinas, P., Parcel, G. S., McAlister, A., & Frankowski, L. (1995). Violence prevention in middle schools: A pilot evaluation. *Journal of Adolescent Health*, 17, 360–371.

People v. Dukes, 580 NY 2d 850, New York Crim. Ct. (1992).

Powell, K. E., Muir-McClain, L., & Halasyamani, L. (1995). A review of selected school-based conflict resolution and peer mediation projects. *Journal of School Health*, 65, 426–431.

Prophet, M. (1990). Safe schools in Portland. *The American School Board Journal*, 177(10), 28–30.

Rapp, J. A., Carrington, F., & Nicholson, G. (1992). *School crime and violence: Victim's rights*. Malibu, CA: National School Safety Center.

Reducing school violence: Building a framework for school safety. (1999). Greensboro, NC: SERVE.

Ross, J. G., Einhaus, K. E., Hohenemser, L. K., Greene, B. Z., Kann, L., & Gold, R. S. (1995). School health policies prohibiting tobacco use, alcohol and other drug use, and violence. *Journal of School Health*, 65, 333–338.

S. C. v. State, 583 S.2d 188, Miss. (1991).

Silva, T. (1992, August 16). Does suspending students help or hurt? *Gainesville Sun*, 1A, 4A.

Speck, M. (1992, May). *Tokay high school proactive school safety plan*. Paper presented at the National School Safety Conference, Seattle, WA.

State v. Slattery, 56 Wash. App. 820, Wash. Ct. App. (1990).

Student searches and the law. (1995). Malibu, CA: Pepperdine University, National School Safety Center.

Task Force on School Discipline. (1990). *Report of the Task Force on School Discipline*. Tallahassee, FL: Florida Department of Education.

U.S. Department of Education, National Center for Education Statistics. (1997). Fast Response Survey System, Principal/School Disciplinarian Survey on School Violence, FRSS 63. Washington, DC: Author.

U.S. Department of Education, National Center for Education Statistics. (1999). Washington, DC: Author.

U.S. Department of Health, Education, and Welfare. (1978). *Violent schools, safe schools: The safe schools report to Congress*. Washington, DC: Author.

U.S. Department of Justice. (1986). *Reducing school crime and student misbehavior: A problem solving strategy*. Washington, DC: National Institute of Justice.

U.S. Department of Justice, Bureau of Justice Statistics. (1992–1996). National Crime Victimization Survey. Washington, DC: Author.

U.S. Department of Justice, Bureau of Justice Statistics. (1999). Washington, DC: Author.

Veronia School District 47J v. Acton, No. 115 S.Ct. (1995).

Webster, D. W. (1993). The unconvincing case for school-based conflict resolution programs for adolescents. *Health Affairs*, 12, 126–141.

Wehlage, G., & Rutter, R. (1986). Dropping out: How much do schools contribute to the problem? *Teacher's College Record*, 87, 3.

Wheelock, A. (1986, November). *The way out: Student exclusion practices in Boston middle schools*. Boston: Massachusetts Advocacy Center.

Questionable Practices

The common questionable practices that are to be described have not so much been proven to impede academic achievement as they have been proven not to enhance academic achievement. In other words, the practices have not been proven to work, even though they may not do any harm. At the very least, they may in a sense be considered a waste of time and resources. On the other hand, they may eventually be proven to have undesirable side effects.

REINFORCEMENT

A great many teachers have been taught in pre-service and in-service education to adopt and use reinforcement in their teaching, with the expectation that reinforcement will enhance academic achievement. Although reinforcement is commonly practiced in schools, there is no scientific basis for the generalization that reinforcement increases academic achievement. However, the term reinforcement has so many different meanings, and issues pertaining to the term are so complicated and misunderstood, that clarification and explanation are needed.

The term reinforcement emanates from conditioning psychology. In this context, reinforcement entails repeatedly rewarding behavior that a conditioner/trainer considers desirable to condition a subject to perform the behavior automatically. To be a reward, the thing given to the subjects must satisfy an internal motive. For instance, food is a reward because and when it satisfies the motive hunger. Reinforcement may be the most widely researched psychological phenomenon of all. Fundamental laws of reinforcement were derived by conditioning psychologists, ranging over time from Pavlov to Skinner, who did research using food to shape the behavior of captive, starved lower animals. Such laws are as applicable to shaping the behavior of infrahumans today as they ever were, and are widely applied to successfully condition lower animals.

In one type of experiment that was conducted to prove that reinforcement shapes behavior, rats are starved by depriving them of food for a certain amount of time or until they lose a certain amount of weight. This ensures that they are hungry and that food will serve as a reinforcer. They are then placed in a small Skinner box with only a bar or lever protruding. A slot is built in to dispense food pellets. Because the rats are hungry and actively searching for food, they soon press the lever and are rewarded with a food pellet. This causes them to continue to press the bar to receive additional food pellets. Conditioners then reward the rats for pressing the bar in the manner they desire until the rats habituate to pressing the bar as the conditioner desires, thereby shaping the rats' behavior. It was by means of tightly controlled experiments such as this that laws of reinforcement were derived, and that reinforcement was proven to shape behavior of lower animals.

After the laws of reinforcement were established, it became common practice to use reinforcement accordingly to shape the behavior of lower animals. Consider two familiar examples. Captive confined porpoises and whales are conditioned in seaquariums to perform tricks for paying audiences. The animals are rewarded with food when they perform the behavior desired by their trainer until they are able to perform the behavior automatically on command. When not being trained their activity is controlled as well as their intake of food to prepare them for conditioning. Similarly, obedience trainers repeatedly give dogs food the dogs like for sitting when the trainer gives the command to sit, until the dogs sit habitually on command. While being trained the dog is kept in a restricted environment, where its activity and intake of food are controlled. The same conditioning principles are followed in the conditioning of all lower animals, although accommodation must be made depending on the characteristics of the animal and its environmental requirements.

Although there is little doubt that reinforcement is effective in shaping the behavior of captive, hungry lower animals, the generalizability of laws of reinforcement is quite limited. Laws of reinforcement derived from research conducted under such contrived, restrictive environmental conditions have not been proven to be generalizable to rats in their natural environment or to human beings in any environment. However, it might be speculated that if humans were held captive, confined, and starved, reinforcement might be effective in shaping their behavior.

With this background in mind, let us now consider some limits to the generalizability of the reinforcement principles discussed. It is generally known to be risky to generalize research results from lower animals to humans, and such attempts have often proven to be mistaken. However, the focus of this discourse is restricted to the effect of reinforcement on academic achievement, so our inquiry will not consider effects of reinforcement on anything else but the academic achievement of human beings.

Most important, the generalization that reinforcement increases academic achievement is not supported by the sizable amount of classroom research that has been done on the subject. Reinforcement appears only to enhance the academic achievement of less mentally competent students, that is, young children and mentally retarded youth. This is a conclusion of the well-respected educational researchers Brophy and Good (1986) after considering the available research. The present author came to the same conclusion based on his independent review of more inclusive, up-to-date research. Since the majority of students are not mentally retarded or very young, the conclusion that reinforcement increases academic achievement is a gross overgeneralization. The remainder of this section will be devoted to explaining why the laws of reinforcement are not generalizable to enhancing the academic achievement of mentally competent people and how reinforcement has been confused with other educational terms.

One reason the laws of reinforcement are more generalizable to less competent humans and lower animals than competent humans is that mentally competent people are less likely to respond as automatons to prompts. They are more astute and more likely to use their knowledge to deliberate alternatives before deciding on a course of action. More mentally competent people are not as habit-bound and are not as prone to be conditioned to react as robots in a particular way to a particular stimulus.

Another reason laws of reinforcement have limited generalizability is because the captive lower animals used in traditional research are placed in highly confining environments, which severely restrict their movement and free choice. Most humans are not subjected to such confinement, except perhaps some prisoners and slaves. In addition, laws of reinforcement derived from rewarding starved lower animals with food are not generalizable to human educational environments because human students are rarely, if ever, purposefully starved to prepare them to be conditioned. The above reinforcement ploys are certainly not tolerated where human rights are honored.

Furthermore, laws of reinforcement are not generalizable to classroom learning because they are derived from conditioning individual animals one at a time, not from conditioning groups of animals. Therefore, the laws are not generalizable to the group instruction of lower animals or human students. It is not only unwarranted, but impractical as well, for teachers to administer reinforcement to a class of students. The teacher would be required to reward every student in the class for the performance of every desirable behavior. Punishment is not allowed, so the teacher must await every desirable behavior from all students, say a class of 20, and promptly reward them without being able to punish misbehavior. This is a recipe for chaos, as many classroom teachers who have been trained and required to administer reinforcement in their classroom report. Besides, the practice is inconsistent with what is known to be effective in reducing classroom disruptions, that is, establishing and enforcing student rules of conduct.

Still another reason the laws of reinforcement are not generalizable to classroom instruction is because most of the learning produced by reinforcement is the learning of automatic behaviors or habits. Although reinforcement evidently can be used to condition habits in young and mentally retarded students, only a small percentage of the learning objectives pursued in school pertain to the conditioning of habits. Such learning objectives would include the automatic recognition of words, numbers, letters of the alphabet, and significant others by name. In addition, while students may be expected to be able to recite the multiplication tables automatically, as well as the Pledge of Allegiance to the American flag and to sing "The Star-Spangled Banner," such learning pertains primarily to the basic indoctrination of young children into society. More advanced learning, such as problem solving, requires students to deliberate options as the basis for choosing a solution. Young children's automatic responses are often impulsive and impair deriving tenable solutions. To advance their learning and competence they are prompted not to act impulsively, but rather to think before they act.

The teaching of automatic behavior is much more in keeping with totalitarian governments, where people are to obey commands without questioning them, and in communist states, where individual penchants are to be sacrificed for the common good. In the United States, where students have the freedom to pursue happiness as they choose and are encouraged to think for themselves, conditioning students to perform as robots is frowned upon and is illegal when it deprives them of their legal rights to free choice. Moreover, education pertains to more than performing desired behaviors habitually. It pertains to the acquisition of knowledge—knowledge people can apply as they deem appropriate and desirable. Conditioners are concerned primarily with the shaping of behavior, not with the acquisition of knowledge.

In addition to the many limitations to the generalizability of the laws of reinforcement that have been discussed, there are some practical problems as well. Reinforcement can only be successful for any purpose if the proposed rewards actually satisfy internal motives of the subjects being conditioned. So far the only reward found to be unambiguously generalizable across people is food, but only to hungry subjects. Subjects satiated with food are indifferent to it; subjects glutted with food find food repugnant at the time. Not being able to starve students, the challenge is to identify other offerings that satisfy the motives of most students most of the time.

The would-be rewards that have been tried on students have not been nearly as successful as the food used to condition hungry lower animals. Oral forms of reinforcement, such as words of praise and encouragement, as well as indulgent attention for desired behavior, have achieved mixed, inconsistent results on humans. On reflection, it can be understood that attention and praise in general are not rewarding. Praise from a white teacher to a black student or from a female teacher to a male teenager in the company of his gang may not be rewarding. Furthermore, repeated praise is often regarded as insincere.

To ensure that students will be motivated to receive offerings, tokens are offered as rewards for desired behavior. The tokens can be cashed in for one of a number of options of the students' choice. Tokens seem to work best when students can choose from among a wide variety of attractive options so that students are more certain to find an option they consider rewarding. The rationale is akin to the "Green Stamp" promotion that allowed customers to choose merchandise from a vast array of options in a catalog. This is hardly feasible in a school setting.

It might be more effective to offer money to students as a reward for desired behavior. Money is certain to be more rewarding to students than tokens; students can trade the money for a much greater variety of treats and merchandise. However, many consider giving money to students for achieving learning objectives to be bribery, more so than giving tokens. Other professionals feel that learning is intrinsically rewarding because it empowers students, and that offering extrinsic rewards like candy, praise, or attention for achieving learning objectives is diverting and subverting to the learning process and to schooling.

In addition to the problems of finding a broadly generalizable reinforcing agent, if indeed it is desirable to find one at all, there are serious problems in confusing reinforcement with other terms. It is exceedingly important not to confuse feedback and reinforcement. Some professionals contend that feedback provides, or at least should provide, reinforcement if done appropriately. They believe that it is reinforcing for students to find out that their response is correct, and that encouraging students to proceed with their next assigned task, whether they succeeded or failed in performing their last task, is also reinforcing. This blunts and perverts the important distinction between the functions of feedback and reinforcement. The purpose of reinforcing a behavior is to increase the probability that the behavior will recur. Typically, the desired behavior is rewarded repeatedly until it becomes a habit. To be reinforcing the offering given or said to a student must satisfy an internal motive, as food satisfies the hunger motive. However, as indicated, the verbal endorsement of a behavior cannot be relied upon to satisfy students' motives, so it is doubtful that telling students anything will reliably act as reinforcement.

The purpose of feedback is quite different from reinforcement. The purpose of feedback is to impart to students one of two things: (1) their behavior is correct and they are ready to attempt to perform the next more advanced task, or (2) their behavior is incorrect and they need to perform remedial tasks until they master the behavior. In both cases the underlying purpose is to advance the knowledge and skills of students. In short, the function of reinforcement is to induce habits; the function of feedback is to enable students to continually advance their capabilities.

One reason reinforcement and feedback become intermingled, if not confused, is because the difference in the ability of humans and lower animals is not fully appreciated and taken into account. Since humans are more intelligent than infrahumans and are capable of understanding more sophisticated linguistic communication, when they perform correctly they can be informed through language that they have performed correctly and are ready for the next challenge; and when they perform incorrectly they can be informed of their incorrect behavior. In addition, and most significant, they can be informed of and told how to perform the desired behavior.

In contrast, reinforcement of a correct behavior of a porpoise encourages the porpoise to repeat the behavior to be reinforced again. This may be said, in a sense, to inform a porpoise that it has performed correctly. In addition, punishment of a porpoise for incorrect or undesirable behavior will tend to dissuade the porpoise from repeating the behavior. However, in contrast to humans, and most important, conditioners cannot tell a porpoise what the correct behavior is and how to perform the correct behavior. This explains in part why conditioners use reward in conditioning animals, but not punishment. Reward communicates to them that their behavior is desirable. Punishment communicates that their behavior is undesirable but does not indicate the desired behavior. Moreover, continuous punishment can be harmful and can cause the animal to flee or attack.

It is also important not to confuse reinforcement (such as food) used to condition captive lower creatures to do what the conditioners desire with the sophisticated tactics used by free humans to influence other people to do what they desire. For instance, doing favors for others influences them to return favors, and complimenting others tends to be ingratiating and influences them to do one's bidding, while insulting others tends to alienate them. However, compliments are not equivalent to reinforcements such as food, nor are insults equivalent to punishments such as intense electric shock. In the final analysis, efforts to persuade free people to do one's bidding and to discourage them from doing what one dislikes will succeed only if they want to comply or they feel obligated to comply.

In instruction it is more productive to refer to task performance as either correct or incorrect, rather than behavior that the teacher desires or does not desire. This places the emphasis where it belongs, on performing tasks correctly in order to achieve a learning objective, rather than on pleasing the teacher, even though the two may often be congruent. In addition, the emphasis should be on encouraging students to try to perform the next assigned task correctly in order to achieve the learning objective. When completing a task, students who perform it correctly may be complimented on their success and encouraged to meet the next challenge. Students who perform the task incorrectly cannot be complimented on their achievement. This would be encouraging them to fail. When they strive to succeed but fail, they can be complimented on their effort and encouraged to undertake remedial tasks with assurances that they will succeed. This presupposes that the teacher has had success in the past when using the remedial tasks. It would also be helpful if the teacher showed students how achieving the learning objective benefits and empowers them.

In conclusion, research results confirm conclusively that reinforcing captive, starved, individual lower animals repeatedly with food for performing behavior the conditioner deems desirable will condition the animals to perform the desired behavior. However, these reinforcement conditions do not have sufficient generalizability to be applicable to the education of most children and adults when the goal is academic achievement. Moreover, the conditions have virtually no generalizability to the educational environments of humans living in free modern nations such as England, Switzerland, and the United States, to name a few. Other so-called reinforcements such as toys, praise, attention, candy, and tokens have not been consistently effective on human students when used as reinforcing agents to achieve academic objectives. Moreover, bribing students to achieve academic objectives might dissuade them from learning for personal advantage and empowerment. Whatever other effects reinforcement may have, research indicates that it does not, in general, increase academic achievement.

ABILITY GROUPING STUDENTS

The grouping of students according to ability level for the purpose of facilitating instruction and learning has been practiced and researched for approximately 70 years. The research covers the following ability grouping formats:

- Students are grouped according to ability, and instruction is provided in separate classrooms for each ability group. Instruction may be for one, multiple, or all subjects. In high school this most often takes the form of academic, general, and vocational tracks. In middle school this frequently occurs in the form of advanced, basic, and remedial tracks (Kulik & Kulik, 1992; Slavin, 1990).

- Students from several grade levels are grouped together, regardless of their grade level, according to their level of academic achievement in a particular subject matter area. This tactic is used most often in elementary reading and is often referred to as the Joplin Plan (Kulik & Kulik, 1992; Slavin, 1987).

- Students within a classroom are formed into groups based on ability, and the teacher provides instruction appropriate to each group's level of ability. This tactic has been used primarily for elementary school mathematics (Kulik & Kulik, 1992).

- High-ability students are placed in groups separate from other students and instructed using a different curriculum.

In general, the many research studies that have been conducted on ability grouping indicate that it is not effective in increasing the academic achievement of students. There is no scientific basis for adopting and using ability grouping for the purpose of enhancing academic achievement. However, as is the case with most generalizations, some qualifications need to be taken into account for a more complete understanding of ability grouping.

An insufficient number of studies have been conducted on ability grouping prior to grade 4 and after grade 9 to conclude about its effects on either lower elementary school students or high school students. Furthermore, there is evidence that in middle school, gifted and talented pull-out programs that accelerate and enrich instruction do enhance academic achievement. Thus it appears that ability grouping can have a more positive effect on the academic achievement of high-ability students than of low-ability students when the curriculum of high-ability students is enriched. There is also very weak evidence suggesting that ability grouping may have a positive effect on academic achievement in particular subject areas, specifically in the areas of reading (cross-grade ability grouping) and mathematics (within-grade ability grouping). But the effectiveness of ability grouping in enhancing learning is not generalizable across content areas.

The body of research on teacher expectancy offers one explanation for the failure of ability grouping. Reviews of this body of research have shown that teachers' teaching and grading is influenced according to their perception of their students' ability level (Cooper, 1979; Dusek, 1975; Hamachek, 1995; Jamieson et al., 1987). Studies have been conducted which demonstrate that when teachers are led to believe that high-ability students are of low ability, the resulting student achievement is consistent with that of low-ability students and vice versa, when low-ability students were identified as high-ability (Dusek, 1975). Still, ability grouping of students for the purposes of enhancing student learning continues to be a common practice at many levels of education.

Some efforts have been made to reduce ability grouping on the high-school level with dubious success. Tech Prep and School-to-Work programs are examples. Although their intention is to prepare all students for some form of postsecondary education, most often they result in the formation of high school academic and vocational tracks. Academic tracks tend to prepare students for college, and vocational tracks prepare students for the world of work. This is unfortunate since, with the extension of longevity, learning has become a lifelong enterprise for many, and workers tend to change jobs, even careers, a number of times during their work life. It is more important than ever that all students be prepared for postsecondary education.

REFERENCES

Brophy, J., & Good, T. L. (1986). Teacher behavior and student achievement. In M. C. Wittrock (Ed.), *Handbook of research on teaching* (3rd ed., pp. 328–375). New York: Macmillan.

Cooper, H. M. (1979). Pygmalion grows up: A model for teacher expectation communication and performance influence. *Review of Educational Research*, 49(3), 389–410.

Dusek, J. B. (1975). Do teachers bias children's learning? *Review of Educational Research*, 45(4), 661–684.

Hamachek, D. (1995). Expectations revisited: Implications for teachers and counselors and questions for self-assessment. *Journal of Humanistic Education and Development*, 34(2), 65–74.

Jamieson, D. W., Lydon, J. E., Stewart, G., & Zanna, M. P. (1987). Pygmalion revisited: New evidence for student expectancy in the classroom. *Journal of Educational Psychology*, 79(4), 461–466.

Kulik, J. A., & Kulik, C. C. (1992). Meta-analytic findings on grouping programs. *Gifted Child Quarterly*, 36(2), 73–77.

Sipe, T. A., & Curlette, W. L. (1997). A meta-analysis of factors relating to educational achievement. *International Journal of Educational Research*, 25(7), 591–698.

Slavin, R. E. (1987). Ability grouping and student achievement in elementary schools: A best-evidence synthesis. *Review of Educational Research*, 57(3), 293–336.

Slavin, R. E. (1990). Achievement effects of ability grouping in secondary schools: A best-evidence synthesis. *Review of Educational Research*, 60(3), 471–499.

WHOLE LANGUAGE INSTRUCTION

Whole language instruction has been advocated and practiced for approximately 30 years. Practitioners who use whole language instruction to teach language consider whole language instruction to be a philosophy rather than a specific instructional method, making it difficult to define the term precisely or to prescribe unambiguously how to teach it. Advocates characterize whole language instruction as indirect and unsystematic and avoid the use of skill sequences in the organization of instruction. Individual word recognition and sound–symbol relationships are taught only in the context of the whole text. Many pre-service and in-service teacher education programs continue to teach the whole language approach, and many classroom teachers use it to teach language beginning in kindergarten.

Proponents' insistence that whole language instruction is a philosophy rather than a method of instruction makes it difficult to arrive at a list of employed instructional tactics. However, the following derived tactics appear to be utilized by many, if not most, whole language approaches to language instruction.

- Skill sequences are not used to organize instruction.
- Children move from oral to written language using words they know the meaning of.
- Individual words and sound–symbol relationships are taught only if they are needed to understand the whole lesson and not in isolation.
- Children are encouraged to use invented spelling.

The interrelationships among and the interdependence of reading, writing, speaking, and listening are stressed.

In general, research shows that whole language instruction is an ineffective means of teaching language. The evidence does not support its continued use for teaching language. Having made this generalization, there is a need to discuss specific applications to provide a fuller understanding of whole language instruction.

The most that can be said in favor of whole language instruction is that there is weak evidence supporting its use in the earliest stages of language instruction, primarily in kindergarten. However, it is difficult to conceive of whole language instruction being applicable in kindergarten. To a great extent students are learning to recognize and pronounce letters and words in kindergarten. Is it possible to recognize and pronounce words in the context of the whole text, as prescribed in whole language instruction? Is whole language instruction really possible at the kindergarten level?

Moving beyond the beginning stages of language instruction, there is no evidence supporting the use of whole language instruction through the sixth grade. Research has fairly consistently found no difference between whole language and traditional forms of language instruction for student achievement in grades K–6. No evidence is provided, one way or the other, for students beyond the sixth grade.

Whole language instruction is allegedly intended to enhance learning in areas of reading, writing, speaking, and listening. The research pertains primarily to basic reading and writing skills taught through the sixth grade.

It may be worthwhile to consider one explanation of why whole language instruction is an ineffective way to teach language. Several of the effective instructional strategies discussed previously highlight or at least imply the importance of clarifying parts/whole relationships to students, including defining instructional expectations, providing contiguity, clarifying communication, utilizing reminders, utilizing subject matter unifiers, facilitating decision-making, facilitating prediction and problem solving, and keeping students on task. Although whole language instruction stresses the importance of the parts/whole relationships of reading, writing, speaking, and listening to the overall whole of communication, it neglects the important parts/whole relationships within each of these areas. Does not a competent writer understand fundamental relationships among the component acts of writing? Does not problem solving in any area require that students be able to see the relationships between specific tactics necessary to the solution of a problem? Could not whole language deprive students of a thorough understanding of individual communication skills and impair their performance?

REFERENCES

Sipe, T. A., & Curlette, W. L. (1997). A meta-analysis of factors relating to educational achievement. *International Journal of Educational Research*, 25(7), 591–698.

Stahl, S. A., & Miller, P. D. (1980). Whole language and language experience approaches for beginning reading: A quantitative research synthesis. *Review of Educational Research*, 59(1), 87–116.

TEACHER CHARACTERISTICS

A substantial portion of this book has been devoted to the description of instructional strategies that research shows improve academic achievement. Students whose teachers employ these instructional strategies can be expected to learn more than students whose teachers do not use these strategies. Furthermore, pre-service and in-service teacher education programs will develop more successful teachers if they teach these effective instructional strategies. These are conclusions warranted by the research on instructional strategies. And based on this research, it can be recommended that all teacher education programs teach these strategies. This puts the emphasis where it belongs, on the instructional skills of the teacher rather than the personal characteristics of the teacher. Still, it is obvious that teacher characteristics cannot be completely discounted.

There are evidently certain teacher characteristics that need to be taken into account when recruiting teachers for pre-service teacher education programs and for employment, but these characteristics have little to do with people's appearance, their smile, color, shape, height, or the clothes they wear. The most important selection criteria for teachers pertain to personal characteristics that affect people's ability to apply the effective instructional strategies described in this book. A person who has personal characteristics that prevent them from "clarifying communication," one of the effective instructional strategies described, is unlikely to be a successful teacher. For instance, a person with a serious speech impediment cannot be expected to communicate well orally, even though the person may learn how to execute the tactics required for clarifying communication. Also, people who cannot explain relationships are unable to effectively "facilitate transfer of learning," "utilize reminders," "facilitate decision-making," or "utilize subject matter unifiers." Similarly, people who are flighty, vacillate, change their mind excessively, or are unreliable are unlikely to be consistent in "establishing and enforcing student rules of conduct." These are a few examples of personal characteristics that should be considered when selecting teachers, but only because they prevent people from effectively applying instructional strategies that were proven to be effective. Preoccupation with personal traits for other reasons is not justified.

Some people believe that a teacher's personality affects his or her teaching effectiveness, but this does not appear to be the case. In an expansive study conducted by able researchers Jacob Getzels and Phillip Jackson (1963), personality characteristics were shown not to enhance student achievement. There seem to be many misconceptions of the significance of teachers' personalities. It may be argued that entertaining persons with a good sense of humor excel as teachers because they captivate students' attention, but entertaining teachers may spend too much time amusing students, diverting their attention from the learning they should be focused on. Similarly, teachers with pleasing personalities may be thought to be superior teachers. However, a teacher's job is to teach students, not to please students. Such teachers may be more successful in parents' conferences and job interviews than they are in the classroom.

The scope of teachers' knowledge is thought by some to affect their teaching, but this was not proven to be the case (Shulman, 1986). Teachers do not need encyclopedic minds; they need only to have mastered the content of the subjects they teach. In addition, they must know how to teach to instill the content they have mastered. Subject matter mastery is necessary but not sufficient for successful teaching. Subject matter specialists also need to have learned and mastered effective instructional strategies.

Teacher characteristics have been thought to be important in increasing academic achievement in another way. It has been contended that student achievement would be enhanced if students and teachers were matched on particular characteristics. Teachers with particular characteristics would be more successful teaching students with the same characteristics than teaching students who did not have the same characteristics, and it would be worthwhile in school to test and diagnose students and teachers to determine whether or not they possess these characteristics. If they did, classrooms should be reorganized so that teachers with particular characteristics would teach only students with those characteristics. Despite the impracticality and cost of implementing such a program, it has been advocated and tested with respect to a particular characteristic thought to be important. The results of the research showed that matching on student–teacher field-dependent/field-independent cognitive styles does not work.

Witkin et al. (1977) identify field-dependence-independence as representing one dimension of cognitive style. They define this dimension as being

> the extent to which the person perceives part of a field as discrete from the surrounding field as a whole, rather than embedded in the field; or the extent to which the organization of the prevailing field determines the perception of its components; or, to put it in everyday terminology, the extent to which the person perceives analytically. Because at one extreme of the performance range perception is strongly dominated by the prevailing field, that mode of perception was designated "field dependent." At the other extreme, where the person experiences items as more or less separate from surrounding fields, the designation "field independent" was used. (p. 7)

Matching student–teacher cognitive styles in this way employs the following instructional tactics regardless of grade level or content area:

- Identify students and teachers as either field-independent or field-dependent in cognitive style.
- Match field-independent students with field-independent teachers.
- Match field-dependent students with field-dependent teachers.

There is no evidence to support the use of matching student–teacher cognitive styles in this way at any age or grade level. The limited amount of research that has been conducted has found no difference in student achievement between matching and mismatching student–teacher cognitive styles for the grades K–college. Matching student–teacher cognitive styles cannot be regarded as a generalization that is applicable to students at any level of instruction. In addition, no evidence was found to indicate that matching student–teacher cognitive styles enhances student achievement in any content area.

From the evidence to date, it can be concluded that the emphasis on teacher education and recruitment should be on teaching competence rather than teacher characteristics. We need to ensure that teachers' education emphasizes the development of competency in implementing effective instructional strategies, not personal traits. Unfortunately, the one-room "little red school house" with one teacher responsible for the learning of a few students is no more. We now have enormous educational bureaucracies in the form of school districts which operate many schools and are responsible for the education of a great number of students. Nowadays, in addition to student learning, attention is paid to teacher management, counseling, staff meetings, busing, buildings, equipment, student delinquency, custodial staff, and educational administration. Although the only purpose of education is to produce desired learning, the amount of time school personnel focus on and discuss student learning has diminished drastically. Educators need to be reminded that although many other factors may be essential to schooling, instruction has the greatest and most direct impact on learning. If we want to increase desired learning we need to focus on implementing effective instructional strategies.

REFERENCES

Garlinger, D. K., & Frank, B. M. (1986). Teacher–student cognitive styles and academic achievement: A review and mini-meta-analysis. *Journal of Classroom Interaction*, 21(2), 2–8.

Getzels, J. W., & Jackson, P. W. (1963). The teacher's personality and characteristics. In N. L. Gage (Ed.), *Handbook of research on teaching* (pp. 506–582). Chicago: Rand McNally.

Loughlin, E. C. (1992). Classroom physical environments. In M. C. Alkin (Ed.), *Encyclopedia of educational research*, vol. I (6th ed., pp. 161–164). New York: Macmillan.

Shulman, L. S. (1986). Paradigms and research programs in the study of teaching: A contemporary perspective. In M. C. Wittrock (Ed.), *Handbook of research on teaching* (3rd ed., pp. 1–36). New York: Macmillan.

Sipe, T. A., & Curlette, W. L. (1997). A meta-analysis of factors relating to educational achievement. *International Journal of Educational Research*, 25(7), 591–698.

Witkin, H. A., Moore, C. A., Goodenough, D. R., & Cox, P. W. (1977). Field-dependent and field-independent cognitive styles and their educational implications. *Review of Educational Research*, 47(1), 1–64.

8

Effective Preschool Instruction

A book entitled *Ensuring Student Success* would not be complete without dealing with preschool instruction—more specifically, the primary challenge addressed throughout the book is to increase the number of youth who achieve high school learning objectives. And research shows conclusively that preschool attendance significantly increases the likelihood of high school graduation (Barnett, 1995). Preschool instruction is the means of instilling learning when children are in their most malleable and formative years, and it has been recognized throughout the world that early learning is most important. However, the reasons why early learning is so very important are not so clear. Clarification is in order before proceeding.

First, the amount of learning that takes place in the first five years is much greater than in any other five-year period in the span of life. Benjamin Bloom (1964) in his book *Stability and Change in Human Characteristics* demonstrated this rather conclusively. He scientifically analyzed data on human learning over much of the life span and established that learning during the first five years is greater in amount by far than during any comparable time period.

Second, early learning is potent. It takes place at a time when people are most impressionable and vulnerable. One of Freud's greatest contributions was explaining the enormous impact early learning has on people's lives and the trauma it can create. Freud's initial stages of emotional learning and development (the oral, anal, and phallic stages) occur during the first five years of life. Although his disciples add stages of emotional development through adulthood, he built his theory on the preeminence of experience and learning during the first five years. It seems that during the first five years parents are responsible for ministering to their offspring and ensuring their survival. Parents are the primary teachers, and the young child, being aware of its own dependence, regards obeying its parents' edicts to be a matter of life and death. Thus, the potency of early learning emanates from the abject dependence of the young child on its parents for its very existence.

Third, early learning tends to be permanent. Later learning builds upon early learning rather than replacing it. Freud also offers an explanation for this contention. Although many early experiences are not available for immediate conscious recall, they reside in unconscious memory and continue to have an impact on people throughout their lives. Memories of very traumatic experiences remain repressed in the unconscious but disrupt the functioning of adults and can cause mental disorders. The clergy, too, seem to be aware of the permanence of early learning. Allegedly they have claimed something like the following, "Give a child to the church until he is six and he will belong to the church ever after." Yes, for the most part, early learning is indelible.

Although learning is lifelong, early learning is special. It provides the foundation for future development. A solid learning foundation provides a head start, opens the door to opportunity, and facilitates success in all of life's pursuits. Deficits in early learning form weak links in the chain of development that cause problems throughout life. Nothing is more important than understanding early learning and its consequences so that education can be planned to maximize its benefits and minimize its potential detriments.

Respected theories which explain the trauma that young children can experience and the effect it can have in later life do have important implications for understanding learning. They explain why people have learning blocks and inhibitions that prevent and distort subsequent learning. Thus, they explain primarily why people do not learn; they do not explain how and why people learn. Moreover, they focus on the emotional rather than the cognitive attributes of learning.

It is important to remember that cognitive development is mainly responsible for human superiority. Humans do not seem to be superior to lower creatures in their emotional attributes. They do not appear to be any more motivated to find pleasure or to avoid pain. In fact, other animals may be better able to endure emotional assaults. They fight for their very survival most of the time and may well be more resilient to and less incapacitated by emotional trauma. Humans certainly are not superior to other creatures because of their physical attributes. Other animals are far stronger, faster, and more agile than humans. Humans are superior because of their cognitive attributes. That is, they are more intelligent than other animals; they simply have greater knowledge and know-how. But those attributes are not present at birth. Although newborn humans have the potential for great achievement, at birth they are among the most helpless of creatures. It is through instruction and learning over time that they acquire the knowledge that not only enables them to dominate their environment, but to excel in competition with other people.

The knowledge that is instilled through planned instruction in modern societies represents the lore, technology, and wisdom that have accumulated over the years. Knowledge that was passed on from generation to generation and recorded in libraries and data banks has become greater in volume as civilization has progressed. In modern societies, school curriculum is designed primarily to impart this knowledge to students so that they and society can benefit from it. Toward this end, basic curriculum emphasizes what has been commonly called academic subject matter: math, science, language, and social studies. Although nonacademic learning is important, academic learning is largely responsible for people's success in modern society, as well as the perpetuation and advancement of society itself. For this reason, this entire book is devoted to methods and means of improving academic achievement, and this entire chapter is dedicated to improving the academic learning of preschoolers. We have not as yet begun to provide the academic instruction preschoolers are able to absorb and benefit from.

The research on early childhood programs was not very helpful in prescribing specific instructional techniques that have proven to be effective in increasing academic achievement. Typically, preschool programs are much broader in scope. They may include parenting education, establishing community support and services for preschoolers, health care, baby sitting, and social and emotional development programs. Many preschool programs do not have a component that prescribes teaching techniques to increase academic achievement. However, there is substantial evidence demonstrating the long-term beneficial effects of more broadly conceived preschool programs. W. Steven Barnett (1995), in his scholarly review of 36 early childhood development programs, shows that they can produce large effects on I. Q. during the early childhood years and stable, persistent effects on achievement, grade retention, special education, high school graduation, and socialization. Fewer students in these programs are retained in grade, assigned to special education programs, or have behavior problems. More graduate high school. The evidence on persistent achievement, however, is very weak. This is no great surprise, since there is little evidence showing a short-term gain in academic subjects such as science, math, social studies, and language arts. It is also worth considering that any academic gain that might be generated by preschool programs cannot endure under present conditions, because children who are ahead academically initially are subjected to elementary school curricula that tends to reduce rather than maintain their lead. In classroom instruction, students who have a head start tend not to advance further academically until the rest of the class catches up to them. They can only maintain their lead if they continue to be taught more advanced content than they already know.

It is very difficult to identify specific causes of the beneficial effects of preschool programs, especially causes of beneficial academic effects. Studies do not tend to isolate effective instructional techniques. The programmatic comparisons they make are home visits versus center-based programs, model interventions versus large-scale programs such as Head Start or traditional child care, and programs that start at birth versus those that begin at age three or four years (Barnett, 1995). In her sophisticated study *Child Care Experiences and Development Outcomes*, Margaret Burchinal (1999) concludes, "Further work is clearly needed to identify and clarify the mechanisms by which these global measures of quality (in early childhood programs) are related to children's cognitive and social development."

Still, we appear to know more about effective preschool instructional techniques than is revealed in the research on broad-based early childhood programs.

It is time to give preschoolers the academic head start they deserve. As you will see in the remainder of this chapter, preschoolers are capable of learning fundamentals of math, science, language, and social studies—even basic problem solving. Moreover, the instructional techniques for instilling academic learning have been established through research and are described in the coming pages.

First, under the heading "Student Beneficiaries," the students this investigation pertains to are delimited and defined. Second, the type of learning of concern is delineated. Third, the types of instructional tactics found to be effective are introduced. Fourth, an in-depth analysis of effective preschool instructional strategies is provided. Fifth, summaries of exemplary preschool research studies that describe effective instructional techniques are provided. (Statistical data supporting the conclusions of these studies can be found in the appendix at the end of this book.) Sixth, references are provided so that you can read more about the studies and familiarize yourself with the scope of academic preschool research.

STUDENT BENEFICIARIES

The students of interest in this investigation of instructional strategies that enhance the academic achievement of preschoolers are students of kindergarten age or younger. Some of the studies encountered in this search did include students of kindergarten age, but not many. Many conclusions about preschool instruction were drawn from studies that included mostly older children. It was thought that an intensive search of studies that focused entirely on students of kindergarten age and under would be productive, and this suspicion turned out to be correct. Many studies on instructional strategies that increase academic achievement of students this age have been located and reported on. The subjects in those studies are referred to as students because the focus is on academic achievement, which frequently requires more studious attention of the children than typical child care and play activities.

LEARNING ACHIEVED

The learning assessed in this chapter is solely academic learning, such as the learning of math, language, and science. This book focuses entirely on academic achievement and does not delve into other kinds of learning that occurs in art, music, and physical education classes and in school-related extracurricular activities. We are aware that preschool programs teach very important nonacademic subjects, including self-control, personal hygiene, play, self-care, cooperation, coordination, and interpersonal relations. However, nonacademic learning is beyond the scope of this book.

INSTRUCTIONAL TACTICS

In this search for instructional tactics that research shows are effective in increasing the academic achievement of preschoolers, the tactics in the *Handbook on Effective Instructional Strategies* were reviewed. It was found that the following tactics described in the *Handbook* were supported by research at the kindergarten level as well as higher grade levels: "Taking Student Readiness into Account," "Defining Instructional Expectations," "Providing Effective Evaluation," "Providing Contiguity," and "Providing Ample Learning Time." This intense review of individual preschool studies confirmed the applicability of those instructional strategies at the preschool level and revealed the applicability of additional effective instructional strategies described in the *Handbook*. In addition, an instructional strategy was found that is effective at the preschool level, although its effectiveness has not been confirmed to be generalizable across higher grade levels.

The following review of instructional strategies that research shows to be effective at the preschool level is based on all of the research studies found on the preschool level that met the selection criteria. In general, the selected studies present a clear description of the instructional strategies employed so that they can be reproduced by the reader, and they provide evidence that the strategies are effective in increasing academic achievement. Details on selection criteria are provided later in the chapter. The ways in which the instructional tactics pertain specifically to preschool instruction are also discussed. A summary of the eight most informative research studies found at the preschool level is presented at the end of the chapter for your perusal. They are both exemplary research studies and provide instructional prescriptions that work.

Effective Preschool Instructional Strategies

The following is a review of the effective instructional strategies discussed in previous chapters and their application to preschool instruction. The review is written with the presumption that the reader understands the effective instructional strategies described earlier in the book.

REDUCING STUDENT/TEACHER RATIO

There should be as few preschool students per teacher as feasible for the following reasons. The research shows, in general, that (1) students who are tutored one-on-one achieve two standard deviations higher than students taught in groups, and (2) the lower the student/teacher ratio is below 15, the higher the academic achievement tends to be (see pages 171–174 for more detail). In addition to those warranted general inferences, preschool children require more personal attention and care than older children.

The most important inference that can be made from the preschool research is that students be given as much one-on-one tutoring as they may need to achieve a learning objective. Although preschool class sizes varied, and teachers presented information to the class as a whole, students were given as much one-on-one tutoring as they needed to master each task assignment. And, of course, the amount of one-on-one tutoring required to master performance of a task varies from student to student. The following studies (summarized at the end of this chapter) illustrate how student/teacher ratio can be reduced in effective instruction: Carnine (1977); Lawton and Fowell (1978); Rickel and Fields (1983). Most often in their studies, reducing student/teacher ratio in preschool pertains to providing one-on-one tutoring to enhance learning.

DEFINING INSTRUCTIONAL EXPECTATIONS

Defining instructional expectations for students turns out to be at least as important in preschool instruction as it is in more advanced grades, with some modifications needed in preschool. In general, the research shows that academic achievement increases when prior to instruction students are told (1) what the learning objective is, (2) what procedures are necessary to perform the tasks required to achieve the learning objective, and (3) what the criteria are for successful achievement of the learning objective. Although these specifications are appropriate for older students, they are too stringent, complex, and overwhelming for preschool instruction. Instead of defining the educational objectives in detail for preschoolers, they can be told in simple language what they are about to be taught. Instead of specifying in detail the procedure they are to employ to achieve the objective, they can be told in simple language beforehand what they are going to do to learn it. As feasible the teacher should model or demonstrate the behavior the preschoolers will be performing. Finally, preschoolers are too young to comprehend fully criteria of successful performance and to take the responsibility for conforming themselves to the criteria. Instead, the teacher should know the criteria for successful performance of assigned tasks and guide and facilitate preschoolers to conform to the criteria, most often by successive approximation and practice.

Instructional expectations are defined for each task students are assigned to perform, and all task assignments are based on student readiness. The following studies (summarized at the end of this chapter) illustrate how defining instructional expectations can be used in effective preschool instruction: Carnine (1977); Lawton and Fowell (1978); Perlmutter and Meyers (1975); Stipek et al. (1995); Toyama, Lee, and Muto (1997); Wolff (1972).

TAKING STUDENT READINESS INTO ACCOUNT

Student readiness is taken into account at three different times:

1. *Instructional Planning.* Task sequences must be constructed for students with particular readiness or entry-level characteristics. Since preschoolers cannot be expected to have prior academic experience, the entry-level task of a sequence must be based on maturational readiness more than academic readiness. To be ready for instruction of any kind, preschoolers must be sufficiently mature to take simple directions from a teacher and to perform according to the directions. This assumes, of course, that the preschoolers have been weaned sufficiently from their parents or guardians to relate to the teacher and have sufficient attention spans and coordination to perform the simple tasks in a sequence designed for them.

2. *Placement.* Students are placed in task sequences being considered for them when their readiness characteristics match the entry-level tasks of the sequences. If academic task sequences designed for preschoolers are to require only maturational readiness, academic readiness is not an issue. Adjustments might need to be made when an initial placement reveals that students already have learned to perform the assigned tasks from home schooling. Typically, at the preschool level placements are made initially at the lowest level of an academic sequence and adjusted afterwards, if need be. In contrast, at more advanced grade levels student placements are based on test results and other academic data in the student's file, making placement more complex.

3. *Task Assignment* (after placement). After preschoolers are assigned to tasks and their performance is evaluated, there is a basis for determining their readiness for the next task assignment. In general, if their task performance is adequate, students are ready to be assigned to the next more advanced task in the sequence. If students' task performance is inadequate, they are assigned corrective tasks until their inadequacies have been remediated and they are ready to advance. Lawton and Fowell's study (1978) (summarized at the end of this chapter) illustrates how readiness can be taken into account in effective preschool instruction.

PROVIDING EFFECTIVE INSTRUCTIONAL EVALUATION

Instructional evaluation was defined as the comparison of a student's performance of instructional tasks with standards of adequate performance and the diagnosis of inadequacies in task performance. In higher grades evaluation is often conducted after teaching, using an evaluation instrument constructed for the purpose of determining the extent to which the lessons previously taught have been learned. Standards of adequate performance on the instruments are often determined as cutoff scores. And in formal test development the validity, reliability, and objectivity of the testing instruments need to be established. In preschool, evaluation is quite different. Most often evaluation of preschoolers' task performance is conducted during teaching as the teacher guides and facilitates the students' per-formance of the assigned task and evaluates the students' performance attempts. Evaluation is most often conducted by the teacher's direct observation of the stu-dents' attempts. As teachers watch and listen to students' performance, they evalu-ate student progress and diagnose students' inadequacies as a basis for adjusting their teaching to maximize the students' opportunity to succeed. The following studies (summarized at the end of this chapter) illustrate how effective evaluation can be provided in successful preschool instruction: Carnine (1997); Lawton and Fowell (1978); Stipek et al. (1995).

PROVIDING CORRECTIVE INSTRUCTION

At higher grade levels, corrective instruction is prescribed based on students' performance on testing instruments. In grading testing instruments, teachers make note of students' inadequacies and prescribe for corrective instruction accordingly. However, corrective instruction is not administered until after the teachers provide feedback to the students to acquaint them with their inadequacies and to explain the plans for corrective instruction.

In contrast, at the preschool level evaluation, feedback, and corrective instruc-tion tend to occur one after the other during the teaching process. The teacher sees an inadequacy in the students' performance, tells the students their performance is incorrect, informs them of or models the correct performance, and guides the stu-dents to the correct performance. On occasion corrective instruction may be sepa-rated from evaluation on the preschool level. Teachers may detect an incorrect performance and not know how to provide corrective instruction at the moment. They may need time to seek advice on how to conceive of a prescription to correct the inadequacy. The following studies (summarized at the end of this chapter) illus-trate how effective corrective instruction can be provided in successful preschool instruction: Carnine (1977); Lawton and Fowell (1978); Stipek et al. (1995). At the preschool level, corrective instruction is almost always one-on-one.

Defining instructional expectations, taking student readiness into account, pro-viding effective evaluation, and providing corrective instruction represent compo-nents of the teaching process that teachers need to coordinate. The following instructional strategies represent other techniques teachers can apply to improve academic achievement.

PROVIDING AMPLE TEACHING TIME

It is generally the case that academic achievement is enhanced when teachers spend more time preparing students to perform assigned tasks, guide and facilitate their performance, and monitor their attempts in order to detect and correct inad-equacies in their performance, rather than assigning students to independent activi-ties.

Preschoolers require more teacher guidance than older students. Older students are more self-reliant and have acquired study skills that enable them to learn on their own. Preschoolers need teacher guidance almost all of the time. Furthermore, they require more one-on-one teacher guidance. Older students can be taught as a class more effectively than preschoolers. About the only things that can be done to teach preschoolers as a class is defining simple instructional expectations and modeling or demonstrating behavior required to perform the assigned tasks. Most other teaching needs to be conducted one-on-one.

The following studies (summarized at the end of this chapter) illustrate how ample teaching time can be provided in effective preschool instruction: Hong (1996); Toyama, Lee, and Muto (1997).

KEEPING STUDENTS ON TASK

It has been proven rather conclusively that academic achievement is increased when students stay focused on assigned tasks that enable the achievement of the learning objectives being pursued. This generalization is as valid for preschoolers as it is for older students. The problem in teaching preschoolers is that it is much more difficult to keep preschoolers focused on assigned tasks; they are more easily distracted by activities around them and by their personal needs and urges at the moment. It is also probably the case that it is easier to keep preschoolers focused on the task at hand when teaching them to play fun games than when teaching them fundamentals of academic subjects, such as math and language. The study by Stipek et al. (1995) (summarized at the end of this chapter) illustrates how students can be kept on task in effective preschool instruction.

UTILIZING REPETITION EFFECTIVELY

In general, the repetition of to-be-learned information and behavior enhances the learning of the information and behavior. Most educators seem to know that repetition facilitates learning and attempt to use it. However, many educators are not proficient at incorporating repetition in their teaching. Teachers need to be able to (1) incorporate repetition in the presentation of to-be-learned information, (2) plan for students to repeat or practice to-be-learned behavior, and (3) combine repeated presentation and student practice in their lessons. Quite often repeated presentation and student practice are planned for and used separately. For example, a teacher may plan a lecture with the main points summarized at the end without being concerned with student practice at the time. Student practice might be considered later when students are required, in homework assignments, to write compositions incorporating the to-be-learned information.

Consider another example, in which practice is planned without considering the repeated presentation of information at the time. A teacher models or demonstrates the correct behavior for using a microscope and then has the students practice the behavior to perfect it. In considering this example, it is important to realize that the repeated presentation of information could have been incorporated in the teacher's plan. For instance, before modeling the correct behavior for using a microscope, the teacher might have distributed a handout which describes the correct procedure before showing a sequence of pictures depicting the correct use of a microscope.

The purpose of the above example is to show that although repeated presentation and student practice can be and are used separately, they can often be used advantageously in combination. Teachers need to know how to plan for and use repeated presentation and student practice in combination and to be well enough informed about the uses of repetition to use enlightened discretion when planning instruction.

Now in preschool education, repetition of teacher demonstrations and student practice are often used in combination. In teaching phonics, for example, teachers first demonstrate the correct pronunciation of letters and words a few times before requiring students to mimic their pronunciation over and over until the students' pronunciation is accurate. Repeated demonstration and student practice are frequently used together when it is desirable for students to learn habits. Such is the case when students are required when seeing a letter or word to pronounce it correctly, automatically. Reciting the multiplication tables automatically is another example of the learning of a habit.

Much of preschool academic education requires the use of both repeated presentation and student practice. However, the excessive teaching of habits through drill or practice can be detrimental to effective development. Students need to acquire and use knowledge as well as habits. Human capacity extends far beyond the limits of habitual behavior. Students begin to acquire knowledge in preschool and continue as they progress through school, and they are taught to use their knowledge to consider alternative behaviors before acting. As they become more proficient at deliberating alternatives, they are taught to think before they act rather than responding habitually to the impulse of the moment. So much of early learning is the learning of habits because fundamentals of language and math must be learned as habits. In addition, early learning begins to plant seeds of knowledge to be used to deliberate alternatives as a basis for making decisions. This brings us to a very important application of repeated presentation and student practice in combination.

Repetition needs to be used to teach know-how as well as behavior. To explain, first, repetition in presentation is used to teach students to conceptualize procedures for executing desired behavior. This may be done by describing the to-be-conceptualized procedure in words. Then a graphic presentation of the procedure can be provided for the students in one form or another. Once students have conceptualized the procedure accurately, they can begin practicing its execution and continue until they execute the procedure smoothly with little or no error.

Conceptualizing a procedure accurately before attempting to execute it enables students to guide their own behavior and monitor, detect, and correct their own mistakes. When students are trained like lower animals to execute a behavior without being taught to conceptualize the correct execution of the behavior first, they cannot guide their own behavior or detect and correct their own mistakes. Trainees in the armed services were once taught to assemble and disassemble guns by seeing and copying demonstrations. It has since been found to be more effective prior to demonstration to show soldiers diagrams of the guns' assembly and to explain the relationship between the gun's parts, its form, and its function. Golfers and batters in baseball are frequently taught to visualize the correct swing as they attempt to execute it.

Although preschool children are too young to be able to conceptualize complex procedures, they can be taught to conceptualize simple behaviors before attempting to execute them. They can be told how to play a simple game before seeing a demonstration or attempting to play it. In one study stories were used to help preschoolers conceptualize solutions to problems they were asked to solve. Preschoolers were able to transfer the solution described in a story to solve the problem confronting them (Rickel & Fields, 1983). Preschoolers can and do learn to conceptualize simple procedures to guide their behavior, even when the procedures are conveyed in words rather than pictures, providing they understand the meaning of the words.

Utilizing repetition in teaching is most important at the preschool level. As explained, many math and language fundamentals need to be learned as habits, and repetition is vital in the teaching of habits. Furthermore, preschool teachers need to become proficient at applying repetition (1) in the presentation of information, (2) in assigning and guiding student practice, and (3) in utilizing repetition in presentations and student practice in combination. The following studies (summarized at the end of this chapter) illustrate how repetition can be utilized effectively in successful preschool instruction: Carnine (1977); Hong (1996); Lawton and Fowell (1978); Stipek et al. (1995); Rickel and Fields (1983); Toyama, Lee, and Muto (1997); Wolff (1972).

PROVIDING CONTIGUITY

It has generally been established that for associations to be learned, the events to be associated must be perceived sufficiently close together in space and time. This applies to the association of occurrences in the students' environment, the association of teacher or teaching behaviors, and to the association of the students' behavior with resulting consequences. For preschoolers, to-be-associated events must be arranged closer in space and time than for older students. Preschoolers cannot abstract and extrapolate as well as older children; they learn best through concrete experiences in the here and now. They cannot make associations when to-be-associated events occur too far apart in either space of time; it is best to present to-be-associated events together in their immediate perceptual field. The following studies (summarized at the end of this chapter) illustrate how contiguity can be provided in effective preschool instruction: Carnine (1977); Hong (1996); Lawton and Fowell (1978); Perlmutter and Meyers (1975); Rickel and Fields (1982); Stipek et al. (1995). Successful preschool instruction must provide contiguity of to-be-associated events. Although at times contiguity may be provided inadvertently, effective teachers need to provide it purposefully.

PROVIDING SUBJECT MATTER UNIFIERS

Academic achievement is increased when parts/whole relationships in the subject matter being taught are conveyed and displayed to students. This generalization is as true in preschool instruction as it is at other grade levels. In the previous discussion of providing contiguity it was pointed out that to-be-associated events must be presented close together in time and space. However, the examples of providing contiguity given required learning simple relationships between two events. Contiguity must be ensured when providing subject matter unifiers. But most often in providing subject matter unifiers the relationships being taught are more complex. Students are being taught a pattern of relationships. For example, graphic subject matter unifiers, perhaps in the form of pictures, are used to teach the complex parts/whole relations of human body parts.

Although subject matter unifiers convey more complex relationships, they are as useful in teaching preschoolers as they are in teaching older children. A simple, one-dimensional drawing displaying the parts/whole relations of major human body parts can be used to teach preschoolers about the human body. Simple maps are also used by preschool teachers to display relationships among geographical locations. In the study by Lawton and Fowell (1978) (summarized at the end of this chapter), pictures on flannel boards, posters, and bulletin boards were used to convey relationships among main ideas of stories and procedural relationships for accomplishing assigned tasks. Subject matter unifiers have many uses in effective preschool instruction.

CLARIFYING COMMUNICATION

Every educator knows that clarity of communication is essential for effective teaching. Clear communication is more difficult when teaching preschoolers because of their very limited knowledge of language and low tolerance for ambiguity. A special effort needs to be made by teachers to speak distinctly, to use simple words and transitional terms, and to avoid vagueness and irrelevant interjections. These practices apply to all forms of effective communication.

Effective instructional communication has its own special requirements. Question-and-answer instruction is used to clarify communication, and so are many of the effective instructional strategies previously discussed. Communication is clarified when instructional expectations are defined and repetition, contiguity, subject matter unifiers, corrective instruction, and ample teaching time are provided.

The following studies (summarized at the end of this chapter) illustrate how communication can be clarified in effective preschool instruction: Carnine (1977); Hong (1996); Perlmutter and Meyers (1975); Rickel and Fields (1983); Stipek et al. (1995); Toyama, Lee, and Muto (1997); Wolff (1972).

The following instructional strategies detailed earlier in the book have been reviewed and applied to preschool education so far in this chapter: (1) reducing student/teacher ratio, (2) defining instructional expectations, (3) taking student readiness into account, (4) providing effective instructional evaluation, (5) providing effective corrective instruction, (6) providing ample teaching time, (7) keeping students on task, (8) utilizing repetition effectively, (9) providing contiguity, (10) providing subject matter unifiers, and (11) clarifying communication. From 50 to over 200 research studies established the effectiveness of these instructional strategies in increasing academic achievement from elementary school through college. However, their effectiveness had not been previously established at the preschool level. The review of research at the preschool level in this chapter shows that they are effective in enhancing the academic achievement of preschoolers as well. The review also suggests how to adapt the strategies to the teaching of preschoolers.

Five instructional strategies shown to be effective in increasing academic achievement above the preschool level were not confirmed to be effective at the preschool level: (1) providing transfer of learning instruction, (2) providing decision-making instruction, (3) utilizing reminders, (4) providing teamwork instruction, and (5) providing ample learning time. These strategies warrant discussion.

In transfer of learning instruction students are taught how to enhance their effectiveness in transferring learning to perform tasks they need or want to perform. Obviously preschoolers are not ready to master this challenge. They are too young to understand the concept of transfer of learning, and it will be a while before they are ready to learn how to facilitate transfer of learning on their own. However, they are not too young to transfer learning to perform an assigned task when the learning prescribes procedures for performing similar tasks. Although the ability to transfer learning becomes more proficient with learning and maturation over time, some ability to transfer learning appears to be innate, and this endowment is essential to adaptation. Without being able to transfer learning to perform new tasks, learning would be useless.

Rickel and Fields (1983) take advantage of preschoolers' ability to transfer learning. First, they gave preschoolers a simple problem to solve. Then they exposed the preschoolers to a story, quite similar to the situation confronting them, that describes how to solve the problem. Preschoolers were able to transfer the solution depicted in the story to solve their immediate problem. (See the summary of their study at the end of this chapter.)

It is also obvious that decision-making instruction is too advanced for preschoolers. Decision-making instruction is more advanced than transfer of learning instruction because decision-making know-how presupposes and incorporates transfer of learning know-how.

Utilizing reminders is an interesting instructional strategy. It is evident that preschoolers are too young to be taught how to create their own reminders, but it appears that certain kinds of reminders can be and are used to help preschoolers commit things to memory. Although no research could be found validating the effective use of reminders at the preschool level, there is abundant research confirming the effective use of reminders by teachers in higher grade levels (for example, the use by teachers of the acronym HOMES to help students remember the names of the Great Lakes). And preschool teachers can be observed using reminders to help preschoolers remember such things as the letters of the alphabet. For instance, teachers have preschoolers sing little ditties as they recite the alphabet to help them remember the letters. Research should be conducted to test the hypothesis that preschool teachers can effectively use simple reminders to help preschoolers remember such rudiments as words, letters, and numbers.

Providing teamwork instruction is another curious instructional strategy. Middle school and older students can be taught how to work together to maximize achievement of group goals, an asset they can use in most walks of life. Although preschoolers are not yet able to work together with the competency required to maximize achievement, they can be and are taught underlying fundamentals. They are taught the basics of cooperation while having fun playing simple group games.

Finally, providing ample learning time does not seem to be as much of an issue at the preschool level as it is at higher grade levels. At higher grade levels teachers need to provide ample time to complete extended seatwork, homework, and project and term paper assignments, something preschoolers will need to accomplish a few years hence. Providing ample learning time is an issue at all levels during spontaneous teaching when students are asked to perform a task. Under these conditions teachers must make certain they give students ample time to perform the assigned task, perhaps with some teacher guidance and cueing, as necessary, to help them succeed. Spontaneous teaching occurs, for example, during question-and-answer instruction. A major difference between preschoolers and older students is that preschoolers typically have a shorter attention span and should only be required to perform tasks that they can perform immediately or in a short span of time. In addition, they need more teacher guidance.

The two promising instructional strategies described in Chapter 5 are also too advanced for preschoolers. With respect to "Providing Prediction and Problem-Solving Instruction," students are not ready to learn a problem-solving system until after they learn how to make decisions. Decision-making is incorporated in problem solving. With respect to "Enlisting the Control Motive," preschoolers are too young to understand and cope with motivation.

The following instructional strategy is not one of the instructional strategies shown to be generally effective above the preschool level. However, it was shown to be effective at the preschool level.

PROVIDING SENSORY CONTACT

Although providing sensory contact is not an effective instructional strategy that is generalizable above the preschool level, it appears to be very important in the instruction of young children. This is because, in general, over the years learning proceeds from the concrete to the abstract, and learning the characteristics of concrete objects in the early years occurs through sensory contact with the objects. Thus, when preschool learning involves concrete objects, as it most often does, sensory contact with the objects needs to be provided. It is also the case that when preschoolers are being taught basic abstractions, such as categories, they need to be able to distinguish examples from nonexamples of the categories. This requires that they have sensory contact with the examples and the nonexamples.

Rather than become involved in arguments that favor one type of sensory exposure over another, it is more advantageous to point out that whenever students are assigned to learn about concrete objects, whatever age they may be, sensory contact with the objects is advantageous, the more senses involved the better. When "Utilizing Repetition Effectively" was being explained, an example of using repetition to learn about a concrete object such as a peach was given. In using repetition to learn about a peach, it was advised that students be given the opportunity to see, taste, feel, and smell a peach and to hear the sound made when a peach is being eaten.

Wolff (1972) used sensory contact successfully when teaching preschoolers to associate one toy with another. Preschoolers who had sensory contact with the toys were better able to associate paired toys. Toyama, Lee, and Muto (1997) showed that sensory contact with animals improved preschoolers' knowledge of biology and their predictive ability. (The above two studies are summarized at the end of this chapter.)

Summaries of Exemplary Preschool Research on Instructional Strategies

The following are summaries of exemplary preschool research studies on effective instructional strategies. They meet the selection criteria presented at the end of this chapter. The studies are exemplary for two reasons. First, they are examples of competent preschool research, which is in short supply. In addition, they clearly describe instructional strategies that are effective in increasing academic achievement in a particular area. The references at the end of the chapter enable the reader to read about each study in greater detail.

Author: Carnine (1977)

Student Beneficiaries: Four- and five-year-old preschool children

Learning: Vocabulary

Instructional Tactics:

Phonics

- Each child was taught and tested individually by the teacher.

- Eight letters of the alphabet were presented to the child one at a time. As a letter was presented the child was asked, "What sound is this?" If the child answered correctly they were told, "That is correct" or "Good." If the child answered incorrectly the teacher said, "No, this sound is . . . What sound is this?" The child was not permitted to proceed to the next letter until they had mastered the sound for the current letter.

- After the child mastered the sounds for all of the letters, they were presented a word containing some of the letters they had mastered the sounds for. The children were instructed to sound out the word slowly by making the sound for each individual letter following a teacher prompt, "Follow my finger and say each sound when I touch it. Keep saying the sound until I touch the next letter." (Example: Sam became Sssaaammm). If the student responded incorrectly, the teacher corrected the student by saying, "Watch and listen. I can do it." The teacher would model the correct response. Next the teacher would repeat the instruction and answer with the child. Finally, the child was required to answer alone. The procedure was repeated until the child's response was correct.

- The teacher then verbally presented the individual words to the children slowly. The children were then required to look at the individual words and say them at a normal rate. (Example: Sssaaammm became Sam). If the child's response was incorrect the teacher said, "No, that word is . . ." This was repeated until the child correctly identified each word.

- The students were then tested on the individual letter sound, words phonetically similar to words studied, and novel words.

Look-Say

- Each child was taught and tested individually by the teacher.

- The teacher then verbally presented the individual words to the children slowly. The children were then required to look at the individual words and say them at a normal rate. (Example: Sssaaammm became Sam). If the child's response was incorrect the teacher said, "No, that word is . . ." This was repeated until the child correctly identified each word.

- The students were then tested on the individual letter sound, words phonetically similar to words studied, and novel words.

Findings: Children who received the Phonics instruction correctly verbalized significantly more phonetically similar words, novel words, and letter sounds than did children who received the Look-Say instruction.

Effective Instructional Strategies Employed: Providing Contiguity, Defining Instructional Expectations, Utilizing Repetition Effectively, Providing Effective Evaluation, Providing Effective Corrective Instruction, Reducing Student/Teacher Ratio, Clarifying Communication.

Cautions and Comments: This appeared to be a well-designed study of children in a preschool setting.

Author: Hong (1996)

Student Beneficiaries: Preschool children ages 4 years, 2 months to 6 years, 4 months

Learning: Mathematics (classifications, number combinations, shape construction, spatial sense)

Instructional Tactics:

- The teacher leads the children in a storybook reading activity related to a weekly theme and related mathematics. Examples provided were for the weekly theme of family, with the related mathematics appearing in parentheses: *Goldilocks and the Three Bears* (size, seriation), *Ten Brave Brothers* (measure), *A Wolf and Seven Little Goats* (spatial position), and *Good Brothers* (number combinations).

- Children were assigned to follow-up activities related to the story, such as acting out the story situation or extending the story situation to the children's real situation via the story's mathematical content.

- During free play time children were allowed to practice the mathematics, if they wished to, with play materials in a learning corner.

Findings: Children taught with the above instructional tactics performed significantly better than children who did not have the benefit of the tactics on classification, number combination, and shape construction tasks. There was no significant difference in performance on spatial sense tasks. No significant difference was found for the Early Mathematics Achievement Test used as a posttest.

Effective Instructional Strategies Employed: Providing Contiguity, Providing Ample Teaching Time, Clarifying Communication, Utilizing Repetition Effectively.

Cautions and Comments: This appears to be a well-designed, quasi-experimental study conducted on Korean children.

Authors: Lawton and Fowell (1978)

Student Beneficiaries: Preschool children ages 3 years, 7 months to 5 years, 9 months

Learning: Math Concepts (organizing objects and events, matching sets by shape, matching sets by color and size, matching sets by weight and function, matching like pairs, matching associated pairs, counting and sequencing sets of 1–5, matching sets by number priority)

Instructional Tactics:

• Children were told what they would be learning.

• Using objects and pictures on flannel boards, posters, and bulletin boards, the teacher demonstrated for the children the main ideas being taught and how the children were to accomplish their assigned tasks.

• The examples provided by the teacher were maintained in the room for the students to review while practicing the tasks.

• The children's progress was evaluated on a daily basis.

• Pacing of instruction was based on daily evaluation results.

• Individual children requiring additional help were provided one-on-one instruction.

Findings: Children taught using the preceding instructional tactics performed significantly better on math concept attainment tasks than children who were not taught using the instructional tactics.

Effective Instructional Strategies Employed: Providing Contiguity, Defining Instructional Expectations, Providing Subject Matter Unifiers, Utilizing Repetition Effectively, Providing Effective Evaluation, Providing Effective Corrective Instruction, Reducing Student/Teacher Ratio, Taking Student Readiness into Account.

Cautions and Comments: The groups of children for this study were intact groups in two different preschool settings. Additionally, the groups were unequal in size at 24 and 12 respectively.

Authors: Perlmutter and Myers (1975)

Student Beneficiaries: Preschool children aged 3 years, 6 months to 4 years, 11 months

Learning: Word recall/recognition

Instructional Tactics:

Research Procedures

Items that could be labeled with a single word, such as dog, cat, spoon, and pen, were placed in a box. Children were then either told verbally what items were in the box, allowed to visually see the items in the box, or told verbally and shown the items in the box.

Tactics

- The children were told they would be playing a remembering game.
- The children were told to either carefully look at each item in a box or listen to the word description presented by the teacher for each item in the box.
- The children were told to watch or listen carefully and try to remember everything that is in the box.
- The children were told that after they had been shown or told about everything in the box they would be asked whether or not some other items are like the ones in the box.
- The children were told to answer "yes" if they thought the items were like any of the items in the box, and "no" if they were not.

Findings: Children who were only told what the items were in the box performed significantly worse on the word recall/recognition tasks than did children who saw the items in the box and children who saw and were told what items were in the box.

Effective Instructional Strategies Employed: Defining Instructional Expectations, Providing Contiguity, Clarifying Communication, Providing Sensory Contact.

Cautions and Comments: In their concluding remarks, researchers indicated that children who had seen the objects in the box were able to spontaneously verbalize word labels for the items in the box, whereas children who had been given a word label description of items in the box seemed unable to attach visual labels to the items in the box.

Authors: Rickel and Fields (1983) Experiment II

Student Beneficiaries: 46- to 60-month-old preschool children

Learning: Problem solving

Instructional Tactics:

Research Procedures

Experiment I results had findings of no significant difference for task performance after a story was read to the children once. However, it was found that children who had greater recall of the story events were significantly more likely to be successful in performance of the required task. Therefore, Experiment II was conducted with a new sample of children and incorporating repetition in the reading of the story. Children in the experimental condition were exposed to a story about a circus ball that was stuck under a bridge and blocking traffic, for which the solution to the problem was to let some air out of the ball to remove it from under the bridge. The child story characters were varied (depending on gender) as either Penny or Patrick. For the control condition the story children were exposed to was an illustrated presentation on the life of baby farm animals.

The performance task involved the child finding the proper way to remove an 11-inch diameter inflated beach ball from a bird cage through a 4" × 4" opening.

Tactics

- Use of a story analogous to the problem (task performance).
- Students were read the story on three separate occasions while in small groups.
- During each of the three small group readings, children were encouraged to discuss specific occurrences in the story.
- Immediately prior to the performance, task children individually were read the story again.

Findings: Children in the experimental condition were significantly more likely to perform the task successfully than were the children in the control condition. There was no significant difference for degree of persistence in task performance, gender of the child, gender of the story character, or the child gender by character gender interaction.

Effective Instructional Strategies Employed: Clarifying Communication, Utilizing Repetition Effectively, Reducing Student/Teacher Ratio, Providing Contiguity.

Cautions and Comments: Although ability to solve a problem during task performance was the learning formally assessed, it would appear that reading comprehension and recall were also assessed.

Authors: Stipek et al. (1995)

Student Beneficiaries: Preschool children aged 45 to 76 months; kindergarten children aged 59 to 84 months

Learning: Numbers (number recognition, counting skills, simple addition and subtraction, telling time, concepts of length and size, monetary values); Reading (letter recognition, word recognition, symbol association)

Instructional Tactics:

Child-Centered Programs

- Emphasis is placed on social climate and development of social skills.
- Children are given a choice of diverse sets of activities and materials in a play-like environment.

- Peer interaction is encouraged.

Didactic Programs

- Children spend the majority of their time on academic topics.
- Emphasis is on direct instruction of basic skills.
- Subject matter areas are clearly differentiated.

Findings: Children in didactic programs performed better on reading achievement measures than children in child-centered programs. There was no significant difference for number achievement measures.

Effective Instructional Strategies Employed: Providing Contiguity, Defining Instructional Expectations, Utilizing Repetition Effectively, Providing Effective Evaluation, Providing Effective Corrective Instruction, Clarifying Communication, Keeping Students on Task.

Cautions and Comments: The purpose of this study was to compare program types on a number of variables. Only those associated directly with academic achievement were reviewed. Little information was provided on specific instructional tactics utilized by the two program types. However, references are provided describing the instructional approaches for direct instruction and child-centered instruction. No p value was provided in the text of the study to support the finding of a significant difference between didactic and child-centered programs for letters/reading achievement. However, there does appear to be a substantial difference between means for reading, but not for numbers.

Authors: Toyama, Lee, and Muto (1997)

Student Beneficiaries: Five-year-old preschool children

Learning: Biology/Predictive ability

Instructional Tactics:

Research Procedures

- Children were identified as active or nonactive participants in animal care.
- Both groups were given instruction on animal care.
- The active participant group actually cared for animals. The inactive group did not.
- Children were tested by researchers on the biological meaning for the care procedures they were following.
- Children were further tested by researchers to assess their ability to predict the consequences for not following the procedures properly and to predict what should be done for similar but unfamiliar animals.

Findings: Children who participated in the care of the animals were significantly more aware of biological meanings and provided better predictions than did children who did not participate in the care of the animals. Children who participated in the care of the animals were significantly more likely to give accurate biological explanations for nonbiological procedures than were children who did not participate in the care of the animals.

Effective Instructional Strategies Employed: Clarifying Communication, Defining Instructional Expectations, Utilizing Repetition Effectively, Providing Ample Teaching Time, Providing Sensory Contact.

Cautions and Comments: The children that participated in this study were Japanese children in Japanese preschool settings.

Author: Wolff (1972)

Student Beneficiaries: Kindergarten

Learning: Recognition and recall/association

Instructional Tactics:

Research Procedures
- The children were placed in eight groups: a manipulate (the child causes paired toys to interact together) and a control (the child imagines paired toys interacting) for each of the following additional conditions.
    1. Visual–Tactual: The child held and looked at the toys, followed by tactual manipulation or control.
    2. No Visual–Tactual: The child was allowed to hold the toys but tactually manipulated them without seeing them or control.
    3. Visual–No Tactual: The child was allowed to see the toys but was not allowed to touch them, followed by the child pantomiming an interaction (manipulation) or control.
    4. No Visual–No Tactual: The children were briefly allowed to see the toys, followed by manipulation without seeing the toys or control.

Tactics
- Children in each of the groups were provided instructions on what they were supposed to do.
- The experimenters provided an example using pairs of toys for each part of the instructions.
- The first example was followed up with a second example.
- All possible interactions for the paired toys in each example were demonstrated to the children.

- Children in the manipulate condition were told to "make the two toys do something together and at the same time try to make up a picture in your head of what the toys are doing together."
- Children in the control condition were told to "make up a picture in your head of the two toys doing something together."
- Evaluation: After the experimental procedures were employed, the children were tested on their ability to select the second toy in a pair after being shown the first toy. Explicitly, there was no feedback on the child's correctness.

Findings: The children's task performance was significantly better when they had visual or tactual contact with the toys. Manipulation instruction was found to significantly improve task performance as compared to imagery instruction (control) alone. Manipulation instruction was found to be more facilitative of correct task performance when there was tactual contact.

Effective Instructional Strategies Employed: Clarifying Communication, Defining Instructional Expectations, Utilizing Repetition Effectively, Providing Sensory Contact.

Cautions and Comments: This study was conducted on the effects of sensory contact on recognition, recall, and association. It appears to be applicable to teaching students to recall and associate various items.

SELECTION CRITERIA FOR RESEARCH STUDIES

Population: Children up to 6 years old

Learning: An overall improvement in academic achievement associated with an instructional treatment needs to be reported. *The main interest is overall gain in learning generated by instruction.* Interaction effects among subgroups in a study are not sufficient.

Instruction: Effects of at least one instructional treatment must be studied. Instructional tactics must be distinct and sufficiently detailed so that they can be replicated. If instructional tactics are being compared the contrast must be clear. However, comparison groups are not required.

Statistics: The magnitude of relationships reported must be of importance. Correlations need to be .50 or higher. Effect sizes need to be .50 or larger. Importance of frequencies and percentages need to be estimated and discussed. When tests of significance are applied, the significance level reported would need to be .05 or beyond.

The studies described previously in this chapter met the above criteria.

DISCUSSION

To provide preschoolers with a head start in school, they need to be given more academic instruction than is presently offered in most preschool programs. Research shows that they are able to learn academic subjects such as language, math, and science, even problem solving. Moreover, research has identified instructional strategies that are effective in teaching academic subjects to preschoolers. Now we need to provide more time in preschool programs to teach academics, and we need to teach those responsible for the education of preschoolers how to use the effective instructional strategies. The strategies are generic and can be used to teach nonacademic subjects as well as academic subjects.

Since some of the packaged instructional programs described in Chapter 3 are designed to teach beginning math and language starting at the kindergarten level, some of the instructional materials used in those programs may prove to be useful in teaching math and language to preschoolers. On the other hand, they may not. The learning capabilities of preschoolers are more limited than kindergarten and older children. The methods and materials used in those packaged programs should be pilot tested before being adopted for use.

One-on-one tutoring should be maximized in teaching preschoolers. The evidence reported in Chapter 3 shows that one-on-one tutoring is much more effective than any kind of group instruction, and students who receive one-on-one tutoring require less corrective instruction. However, preschoolers should be given all the corrective instruction they need to remediate misconceptions and to keep them from falling behind preschoolers in their group.

Taking these suggestions and cautions into account, it is probably best to design a preschool program to meet your needs and constraints, provided that all those engaged to educate preschoolers are trained to use the 12 effective instructional strategies described earlier in this chapter. Even caretakers involved in teaching basic self-care and hygiene procedures can profit from knowing how to apply the 12 strategies in their teaching. Should they be of value to you, most of the studies reviewed are listed in the following references, even though they may not have been mentioned in the chapter.

REFERENCES

Altom, M. W., & Weil, J. (1977). Young children's use of temporal and spatial order information in short-term memory. *Journal of Experimental Child Psychology*, 24, 147–163.

Amundsen, J. et al. (1985). *Bringing Out Head Start Talents (BOHST). Trainer's Guide.* Washington, DC: Administration for Children, Youth, and Families. ERIC Document Reproduction Service No. ED 279 110.

Barchlay, K. D., & Walwer, L. (1992). Linking lyrics and literacy through song and picture books. *Young Children*, 47(4), 76–85.

Barnett, W. S. (1995). Long-term effects of early childhood programs on cognitive and school outcomes. *The Future of Children*, 5(3), 25–36.

Baumeister, A. A., & Maisto, A. A. (1977). Memory scanning by children: Meanfulness and mediation. *Journal of Experimental Child Psychology*, 24, 97–107.

Becher, R. M. (1980). Teacher behaviors related to the mathematical achievement of young children. *Journal of Educational Research*, 73(6), 336–340.

Becker, W. C. (1977). Teaching reading and language to the disadvantaged—What we have learned from field research. *Harvard Educational Review*, 47(4), 518–543.

Berg, L. et al. (1985). *Bringing Out Head Start Talents (BOHST)*. Washington, DC: Administration for Children, Youth, and Families. ERIC Document Reproduction Service No. ED 279 111.

Bloom, B. S. (1964). *Strategy and change in human characteristics*. New York: Wiley.

Boggs, Stephen T. (1983). *Discourse analysis of classroom narrative and speech play of island children*. Final report. Washington, DC: National Institute of Education. ERIC Document Reproduction Service No. ED 228 851.

Bredekamp, S. (1996). 25 years of educating young children: The high/scope approach to preschool education. *Young Children*, 51(4), 57–61.

Bryant, D. M., Clifford, T. M., & Peisner, E. S. (1991). Best practice for beginners: Developmental appropriateness in kindergarten. *American Educational Research Journal*, 28(4), 783–803.

Burchinal, M. R. (1999). Child care experiences and developmental outcomes. *The Annals of the American Academy of Political and Social Science*, 563(2), 73.

Burgess, S. R., & Lonigan, C. J. (1998). Bidirectional relations of phonological sensitivity and prereading abilities: Evidence from a preschool sample. *Journal of Experimental Child Psychology*, 70, 117–141.

Butler, A. L. (1972). *Headstart for every child*. New York: The Associated Press. ERIC Document Reproduction Service No. ED 068 178.

Campbell, F. A., & Taylor, K. (1996). Early childhood programs that work for children from economically disadvantaged families. *Young Children*, 51(4), 74–80.

Carnine, D. W. (1977). Phonics versus Look-Say: Transfer to new words. *The Reading Teacher*, 30, 636–639.

Cohen, M. F. (1971). *Effects of cueing and overt responding in films designed for preschool children*. ERIC Document Reproduction Service No. ED 067 160.

Cole, K. N., & Dale, P. S. (1986). Direct language instruction and interactive language instruction with language delayed preschool children: A comparison study. *Journal of Speech and Hearing Research*, 29, 206–217.

Cole, K. N., Dale, P. S., & Mills, P. E. (1991). Individual differences in language-delayed children's responses to direct and interactive preschool instruction. *Topics in Early Childhood Special Education*, 11(1), 99–124.

Datta, L. et al. (1971). *A comparison sample of full year and summer Head Start programs operated by community action agencies and local education agencies*. Washington, DC: Office of Child Development. ERIC Document Reproduction Service No. ED 067 154.

Davis-Dorsey, J., Ross, S. M., & Morrison, G. R. (1991). The role of rewording and context personalization in the solving of mathematical word problems. *Journal of Educational Psychology*, 83(1), 61–68.

Denny, N. W., Zeytinoglu, S., & Selzer, C. (1977). Conservation training in four-year-old children. *Journal of Experimental Child Psychology*, 24, 129–146.

Durkin, D. (1970). A language arts program for pre-first-grade children: Two-year achievement report. *Reading Research Quarterly*, 5, 534–565.

Gersten, R., Woodward, J., & Darch, C. (1986). Direct instruction: A research-based approach to curriculum design and teaching. *Exceptional Children*, 53(1), 17–31.

Gollin, E. S., & Schadler, M. (1972). Relational learning and transfer by young children. *Journal of Experimental Child Psychology*, 14, 219–232.

Gordan, C. H. (1984, April). *Rolling Terrace: An effective school under adverse conditions.* Paper presented at the annual meeting of the American Educational Research Association, New Orleans. ERIC Document Reproduction Service No. ED 310 524.

Graham, M. J. (1991, November). *Integrating preschool programs and preschool children.* Paper presented at the Conference on Appalachia, Lexington, KY. ERIC Document Reproduction Service No. ED 336 236.

Greenberg, P. (1994). How and why to teach all aspects of preschool and kindergarten math naturally, democratically, and effectively (for teachers who don't believe in academic programs, who do believe in educational excellence, and who find math boring to the max)—Part 2. *Young Children*, 49(2), 12–19.

Gross, T. F. (1977). The effect of mode of encoding on children's problem-solving efficiency. *Developmental Psychology*, 13(5), 521–522.

Hale, M. (1990, November). *Building a constituency for children.* Paper presented at the Conference on Appalachia, Lexington, KY. ERIC Document Reproduction Service No. ED 336 235.

Hansen, S. (1975). *Getting a headstart on speech and language problems: A guide for preschool teachers.* Washington, DC: Office of Child Development. ERIC Document Reproduction Service No. ED 119 398.

Harrison, P. R., & Soderstrom, E. J. (1977). Sequential analysis of visual habituation in preschool children. *Journal of Experimental Child Psychology*, 24, 495–504.

Haskins, R., Walden, T., & Ramey, C. T. (1983). Teacher and student behavior in high- and low-ability groups. *Journal of Educational Psychology*, 75(6), 865–876.

Hong, H. (1996). Effects of mathematics learning through children's literature on math achievement and dispositional outcomes. *Early Childhood Research Quarterly*, 11, 477–494.

Horak, V. M. (1981). A meta-analysis of research findings on individualized instruction in mathematics. *Journal of Educational Research*, 74(4), 249–254.

Howard, S., Shaughnessy, A., Sanger, D., & Hux, K. (1998). Let's talk! Facilitating language in early elementary classrooms. *Young Children*, 53(3), 34–39.

Jenkins, J. R., Bausell, R. B., & Jenkins, L. M. (1972). Comparison of letter name and letter sound training as transfer variables. *American Educational Research Journal*, 9, 75–86.

Lawton, J. T. (1977). The use of advance organizers in the learning and retention of logical operations and social studies concepts. *American Educational Research Journal*, 14(1), 25–43.

Lawton, J. T., & Fowell, N. (1978). Effects of advance organizers on preschool children's learning of mathematics concepts. *Journal of Experimental Education*, 47, 76–81.

Lawton, J. T., & Fowell, N. (1989). A description of teacher and child language in two preschool programs. *Early Childhood Research Quarterly*, 4, 407–432.

Lowenstein, L. F. (1977). *An empirical study concerning the incidence, the diagnosis and the treatment and follow-up of academically underachieving children.* ERIC Document Reproduction Service No. ED 166 921.

Maclean, M., Bryant, P., & Bradley, L. (1987). Rhymes, nursery rhymes, and reading in early childhood. *Merrill-Palmer Quarterly, 33*(3), 255–281.

Marcon, R. A. (1992). Differential effects of three preschool models on inner-city four-year-olds. *Early Childhood Research Quarterly, 7,* 517–530.

Mason, J. M. (1980). When do children begin to read: An exploration of four-year-old children's letter and word reading competencies. *Reading Research Quarterly, 15*(2), 203–227.

McArthur, L. Z., & Eisen, S. V. (1976). Achievements of male and female storybook characters as determinants of achievement behavior by boys and girls. *Journal of Personality and Social Psychology, 33*(4), 467–473.

McCormick, C., & Mason, J. M. (1986). *Use of little books at home: A minimal intervention strategy that fosters early reading.* Technical Report No. 388. Cambridge, MA: Bolt, Beranek, and Newman, Inc.; Urbana: Illinois University. ERIC Document Reproduction Service No. ED 314 742.

Miller, P. S. (1998). Blended interdisciplinary teacher preparation in early education and intervention: A national study. *Topics in Early Childhood Special Education, 18*(1), 49–58.

Monaghan, A. D. (1973). *An exploratory study of the match between classroom practice and educational theory: Models in Headstart planned variation.* Washington, DC: Office of Child Development. ERIC Document Reproduction Service No. ED 113 012.

Morrongiello, B. A., Trehub, S. E., Thorpe, L. A., & Capodilupo, S. (1985). Children's perception of melodies: The role of contour, frequency, and rate of presentation. *Journal of Experimental Child Psychology, 40,* 279–292.

Nielsen, D. C., & Monson, D. L. (1996). Effects of literacy environment on literacy development of kindergarten children. *Journal of Educational Research, 89*(5), 259–271.

Perlmutter, M., & Meyers, N. A. (1975). Young children's coding and storage of visual and verbal material. *Child Development, 66,* 209–223.

Peterson, P. L., Swing, S. R., Stark, K. D., & Waas, G. A. (1984). Students' cognition and time on task during mathematics instruction. *American Educational Research Journal, 21*(3), 487–515.

Quintero, E. (1984). *Preschool literacy: The effect of sociocultural context.* ERIC Document Reproduction Service No. ED 282 181.

Rawls, R. K., & O'Tuel, F. S. (1982). A comparison of three prereading approaches for kindergarten students. *Reading Improvement, 19,* 205–211.

Read, C. (1971). Pre-school children's knowledge of English phonology. *Harvard Educational Review, 41*(1), 1–14.

Rickel, A. U., & Fields, R. B. (1983). Storybook models and achievement behavior of preschool children. *Psychology in the Schools, 20,* 105–112.

Saltz, E., Soller, E., & Sigel, I. E. (1972). The development of natural language concepts. *Child Development, 43,* 1191–1202.

Samuels, S. J. (1972). The effect of letter-name knowledge on learning to read. *American Educational Research Journal, 9*(1), 65–74.

Scandura, J. M., & Wells, J. M. (1967). Advance organizers in learning abstract mathematics. *American Educational Research Journal*, 4, 295–301.

Scandura, J. M., Woodward, E., & Lee, M. (1967). Rule generality and consistency in mathematics learning. *American Educational Research Journal*, 4, 303–320.

Scherzer, C. E., & Goldstein, D. M. (1982). Children's first reading lesson: Variables influencing within lesson emotional behavior and postlesson achievement. *Journal of Educational Psychology*, 74(3), 382–392.

Sheehan, R. (1992). Connecting classroom practice and research. *Journal of Research in Childhood Education*, 6(2), 142–143.

Smith, M. L. (1976, October). *The effects of preschool experiences on achievement in reading.* Paper presented at the annual meeting of the College Reading Association, Miami. ERIC Document Reproduction Service No. ED 130 256.

Smith, T. D. (1972). Development of tokens as secondary reinforcers. *Journal of Experimental Child Psychology*, 14, 133–138.

Southard, N. A., & May, D. C. (1996). The effects of pre-first-grade programs on student reading and mathematics achievement. *Psychology in the Schools*, 33, 132–142.

Stipek, D. et al. (1995). Effects of different instructional approaches on young children's achievement and motivation. *Child Development*, 66, 209–223.

Toyama, N., Lee, Y. M., & Muto, T. (1997). Japanese preschoolers' understanding of biological concepts related to procedures for animal care. *Early Childhood Research Quarterly*, 12, 347–360.

Walls, R. T., & Rude, S. H. (1972). *Exploration and learning-to-learn in disadvantaged preschoolers.* Washington, DC: Social and Rehabilitation Service. ERIC Document Reproduction Service No. ED 073 847.

Walter, E. L. (1994). *A longitudinal study of literacy acquisition in a Native American community: Observation of the 4-year-old classes at Lummi Headstart.* Lummi Tribal Council. ERIC Document Reproduction Service No. ED 366 479.

Werden, D., & Ross, L. E. (1972). A comparison of the trace and delay classical conditioning performance of normal children. *Journal of Experimental Child Psychology*, 14, 126–132.

Whiten, D. J. (1994). Literature and mathematics in preschool and primary: The right connection. *Young Children*, 49(2), 4–11.

Wolff, P. (1972). The role of stimulus-correlated activity in children's recognition of nonsense forms. *Journal of Experimental Child Psychology*, 14, 427–441.

Wolff, P., Levin, J. R., & Longobardt, E. T. (1972). Motoric mediation in children's paired-associate learning: Effects of visual and tactual contact. *Journal of Experimental Child Psychology*, 14, 176–183.

Yagi, K. (1987). *ECIA, Chapter I early childhood education program in the Portland public schools. 1986–1987 evaluation.* Portland, OR: Portland Public Schools. ERIC Document Reproduction Service No. ED 291 763.

Young, G. L., & Robicheaux, L. (1985). *The language of flowcharting.* Urbana, IL: National Council of Teachers of English. ERIC Document Reproduction Service No. ED 264 576.

9

Teaching Students to Innovate

Chapter 1 stressed the importance of achieving high school learning objectives in order to perpetuate society and the personal interests of its citizens. However, although a high school education may be a necessary standard to set, it can hardly be considered an optimum standard. A high school education instills little more than the basic skills required in a modern society. People are capable of learning much more than they do in high school, and many do in higher education. Furthermore, a high school education does not prepare people to advance themselves to the highest status and salaried positions or to make significant contributions to the advancement of society.

Most people understand that basic math, science, social studies, and language skills are needed to perpetuate society and the people in it. On the other hand, there is no common understanding of the skills needed to advance the status of society or its people. Before we can prepare to teach these skills, it is necessary to determine what they are. And to determine what the skills are in America, it is necessary to identify America's superior achievements. The challenge is to identify the skills responsible for American superiority and to teach them to our youth. First, let us attempt to identify American superiority; then we can attempt to determine the skills needed to attain it and design an instructional program to teach the skills.

Contrary to popular belief and national chauvinism, research shows that the United States is not superior to other nations on most desirable attributes. Quality-of-life indicators were used to study the quality of life in nations (Slottje et al., 1991). These indicators show how the United States ranks among 126 nations on each of the indicators (see Table 9.1). Despite the leadership role of the United States among nations, it does not rank consistently high on important quality-of-life attributes.

Table 9.1 provides an example of a study of the relative strengths and weaknesses of the quality of life in the United States. In contrast, Table 9.2 provides a comparative example of the quality of life in different societies. The rankings of 40 nations on the same societal quality-of-life indicators combined are shown.

Table 9.1
U.S. Ranking Among 126 Nations on 20 Quality-of-Life Indicators

U.S. Ranking	Indicators
14th	Political rights (e.g., legitimate election of government officials, campaigning opportunities, minority self-determination)
10th	Civil liberty (e.g., freedom of press, speech, assembly, religion)
2nd	Average household size
108th	Soldiers per 1,000 civilians
3rd	Energy consumption per capita
37th	Percent of women in the labor force
30th	Percent of children in the labor force
27th	Length of roads per square kilometer of territory
1st	Telephones per capita
19th	Male life expectancy
9th	Female life expectancy
17th	Infant mortality rate per 1,000 births
32nd	Population per hospital bed
20th	Population per physician
4th	Daily calorie consumption
13th	Male literacy rate
11th	Female literacy rate
1st	Radio receivers per 1,000 people
2nd	Number of daily newspapers
1st	Real gross domestic product (adjusted gross national product)

Note: Higher ranking indicates higher quality of life.
Source: Slottje et al. (1991).

   The inclusion of countries like Switzerland, the United Kingdom, New Zealand, Sweden, Canada, the United States, and Japan in the top 20 is not much of a surprise. The presence of countries like New Guinea, Jamaica, Barbados, and Gambia is somewhat more surprising. Had the rankings relied solely on one dimension, like real gross domestic product (RGDP), for example, none of these countries would be in the top 30. The other criteria give a different dimension to the rankings. By incorporating liberty indicators into the analysis, countries known for political repression finish at the bottom of the rankings, even though some of them have relatively higher RGDP and physical quality-of-life attributes, such as life expectancy.

Table 9.2
Quality-of-Life Rankings of Nations on the 20 Quality of-Life Indicators (in Table 9.1) Combined

1. Switzerland	15. Japan	29. Norway
2. United Kingdom	16. Gambia	30. Dominican Republic
3. New Zealand	17. Costa Rica	31. Bolivia
4. Jamaica	18. Portugal	32. Italy
5. New Guinea	19. Ireland	33. Fiji
6. Canada	20. Ghana	34. Kenya
7. Austria	21. Denmark	35. Trinidad & Tobago
8. Luxembourg	22. Botswana	36. Belgium
9. Australia	23. Hong Kong	37. Spain
10. Sweden	24. Senegal	38. Uganda
11. Mauritius	25. Honduras	39. Argentina
12. Barbados	26. Uruguay	40. Colombia
13. United States	27. Netherlands	
14. Iceland	28. Finland	

Source: Slottje et al. (1991).

It may also be surprising to find that the United States ranks thirteenth on the combination of quality-of-life attributes.

The United States is a pluralist melting pot. Clashes among social factions and haves and have-nots are commonplace and seem to generate continuing upheaval, legal battles, and violence. The civil liberties guaranteed in the Constitution are far from being realized in daily life. Moreover, the United States has developed the most technically advanced war machines to protect itself from foreign enemies and to lend muscle to United Nations edicts when the United States agrees with them, while internally crime runs rampant. In addition, although the United States has developed more advanced medical procedures, available medical treatment is not delivered to as large a percentage of the total population as in other countries. As a result, the United States does not rank at the top on indicators such as infant mortality or hospital beds and physicians per population. It is no wonder that crime, warfare, and health care hang heavy on the minds of the public.

In December 1994, the World Bank reported that the United States is the seventh richest nation, as measured by the economic output per person. The top eight rankings were as follows:

1. Switzerland	$36,410
2. Luxembourg	$35,850
3. Japan	$31,450
4. Denmark	$26,510
5. Norway	$26,340
6. Sweden	$24,830
7. United States	$24,750
8. Iceland	$23,620

Although other research studies are available on quality-of-life factors, they are not markedly different from the ones reported. The results show that U.S. superiority does not lie in the areas of civil liberty, health care, riches, life expectancy, political rights, literacy, and other desirable areas, so we need to look for American superiority elsewhere.

America does appear to be superior in one attribute not measured in the studies reported or any other study that could be found—the development and introduction of innovations. Although this assertion is an hypothesis at this time, it is worth testing, because it is through innovation that quality of life can be improved. The fact that other nations are often more successful in providing their citizens with the benefits of innovations than we are is beside the point. The fact that other nations deliver the medications we invent to a higher percentage of their needy citizens than we do does not denigrate the importance of the innovations. If we did not invent new medications, they could not be disseminated to anyone.

Unfortunately, we have not yet addressed or appreciated the scope of America's innovativeness, our investment in innovation, or the contribution of innovation to America's superiority. American business and industry invest a substantial percentage of their profits in research and development to innovate better products and services to sell. Our federal government invests huge sums of money in R&D for innovations to improve public health and welfare in areas that are not profitable to private enterprise, and many charitable gifts are earmarked for research to find cures for debilitating and fatal diseases and to improve education.

We have yet to fully understand the extent to which innovation is an inevitable by-product of free thought, free choice, free expression, and free enterprise. We are most cognizant of our innovation of material goods, such as tools, machinery, medicines, and electronics. We also are aware of innovations in services, such as improved delivery of mail and packages, improved emergency services, improved repair services, and more convenient access to information and products. But there is more to be understood about American innovativeness than Americans are commonly aware of.

Because Americans are almost assured of enough money to survive and typically are obliged to work only 40 hours a week, they have time to explore and test alternatives before making a choice. And if they are not satisfied with available alternatives, they have time to innovate additional options. Free personal expression breeds innovation.

Freedom of choice creates a greater demand for alternatives, not only material alternatives but spiritual alternatives as well. Even though Americans may join a church or temple to practice an organized religion, many introduce their own innovative interpretations and practice the religion in their own way, exercising their right to freedom of thought and choice. Moreover, in the United States there are more organized religions to choose from. Almost every organized religion in the world is represented in the United States, and new organized religions have been invented here. Some Americans prefer not to join an organized religion and innovate their own personal way of worshipping God. Other nations are more homogeneous in their beliefs and provide the option of joining fewer houses of worship than Americans. In some cases there is only one national church or temple to join.

Freedom of spiritual choice is also honored and nurtured in our public educational institutions, where students are taught that they have free choice and how to exercise it, and no particular religion is advocated. Moreover, if they are not imprinted with a religion before they enter school they can find out about their spiritual options in their association with schoolmates and in the courses that are available. Classes are offered in "values clarification," in which students are encouraged to think about alternative values before they adopt or innovate their own set of values. They are also taught about the importance of subscribing to personal values to give meaning and foundation to their lives. In addition, they can take courses in "comparative religion" if they choose. In short, Americans have free choice and exposure to alternatives, enabling them to innovate their own lifestyle, which almost always includes a spiritual component.

Within the American culture innovators are more likely to succeed in our free enterprise system. People who understand that "there is more than one way to skin a cat" and find new ways to solve problems when standard operating procedures are not effective typically receive greater rewards from free enterprise employers. They tend to be more successful in business for themselves and attain more of their personal aspirations.

It is important to realize that innovation is encouraged more in the private sector than it is by government employers. In government the watchword is "don't rock the boat"; people keep their jobs by playing by the rules. Innovators are catalysts of change; innovation by its very nature rocks the boat. Government employees who follow the rules seldom lose their jobs. It is the innovators who are considered agitators and troublemakers that are fired—when firing does not rock the boat too much. So as the number of government employees grows in proportion to the number of employees in the private sector, we can expect less innovation and less productivity.

Education is primarily a government enterprise, and like other government enterprises it has been resistant to change, which is a reason public education has not been more successful. The purpose of all education enterprises is clear: to produce desired learning. It is difficult to fire an educator, and when one is discharged, more often than not it is for rocking the boat. Conversely, educators are seldom rewarded for measured increases in the academic achievement of the students they teach.

It is interesting to note that when innovative enterprises compete with government institutions, the government institutions improve and the public benefits. For example, the success of United Parcel Service and Federal Express in introducing innovations resulted in improvements being introduced in the U.S. Postal Service, such as faster delivery and improved delivery confirmation options. This suggests that if public funds were spent to subsidize private schools that competed with the public schools, the public would benefit and public schools would be prodded to improve by adopting the innovative practices that research has proven increase academic achievement. Although there is concerted opposition to this, a few charter schools have been approved and operated on public funds. A few have introduced innovations and have proven success records. Some have succeeded with students who failed in public school.

For a long time America has been the world leader in developing and introducing innovative products in great demand the world over, some of which are computer, automotive, aeronautic, medical, and food processing innovations. However, in recent years we have been losing the competitive edge. Many of our innovations can be produced less expensively elsewhere, and often quality control is better elsewhere. We are often slower in getting new products to market, and our price is not as competitive as it once was. Our leadership in producing cars, television sets, duplicators, cameras, and telephones is being seriously challenged. Most important, a smaller percentage of our citizens benefit from health care innovations than other nations' citizens. In short, although America leads in the number of innovations developed, our ability to produce, apply, and benefit from the innovations leaves a great deal to be desired.

Innovation extends far beyond the production of new goods and services. In the arts, outstanding musicians such as Bach, Beethoven, and Mozart are innovators. Outstanding painters such as Van Gogh, Rembrandt, Monet, and Dali are innovators. Great social scientists such as Freud, Emile Durkheim, and Karl Marx are innovators. Renowned mathematicians such as Euclid, Newton, and Pythagoras are innovators, and famous physical scientists such as Einstein are innovators. The icons in every field, including philosophy, religion, architecture, and so on, are innovators. Whatever subject we teach in school, a great deal of time is spent discussing the contributions of innovators in the field.

Innovation is in fact a means of improving the quality of life—all aspects of life. Enacting a new law, designing a new educational program, developing a new psychotherapy procedure, formulating a new diet are innovations that can benefit humankind. Innovation serves selfish as well as altruistic ends. Employees that find a way to increase the profits of their employers are more likely to receive a raise, as are coaches who find new ways to win games. People who improve their household budgets have more money to spend. Part of the American dream is to improve one's lot in life, and innovation is quite often a means to that end. Being innovative is less threatening when we realize that all of our actions are idiosyncratic—a current action may be similar to a previous one but will not be identical. With a little thought we can attempt to improve our efforts, and we can all reap the benefits of innovation more often. Then we will be stymied less often in pursuit of our own goals and will be more apt to make social contributions.

It is time to realize the importance of innovation to American superiority, our way of life, and the success of our citizens and to formally establish the development of innovations as a national priority. It would follow then that teaching students to innovate would become a major goal of American education. Methods of innovating, such as the scientific method, are already taught in school in science classes, but teaching students how to innovate should extend beyond science to all subjects taught in school. The study of innovators and their innovations in all subject areas is common school practice in social studies, language arts, and math as well as science. Once students learn about innovators and their innovations in a particular subject area, they can be required to produce their own innovation in the subject area. They can be taught general standard operating procedures that will enable them to become innovators in any subject area and in their daily life. The following suggestions for teaching students how to innovate are for your consideration. Innovation is not difficult to teach or learn.

HOW TO TEACH STUDENTS TO INNOVATE

In the section "Enlisting the Control Motive" in Chapter 5, purposeful behavior was defined as behavior directed toward an outcome and symbolized as behavior → outcome. It was stated further that teaching students to perform assigned tasks could be simplified by translating assigned tasks into behavior → outcome units. This shows students how their behavior can control the achievement of outcomes. Examples were given illustrating how almost all tasks, from long division to writing a composition, can be broken down into behavior → outcome units.

Using the behavior → outcome unit innovation can be defined for students as generating a new behavior → outcome relationship. Students can innovate by (1) innovating a new behavior to achieve a known outcome: for example, conceiving of a new way to manufacture (new behavior) cars (known outcome) or creating a new recipe (new behavior) for roasted chicken (known outcome); (2) innovating a new outcome using a known behavior: for example, legislatures following established procedures (known behavior) to enact new laws (new outcome); (3) innovating new behaviors to achieve new outcomes. The invention of the airplane provides an example. Although individual features of an airplane, such as propellers, wings, and engines were perceived before, nothing had been perceived that possessed the combination of features of the airplane (new outcome). And the combination of behaviors required to manufacture an airplane had not been executed before (new behavior). Although individual behaviors may have been performed before, the new combination of behaviors had not.

It is important to understand that innovations are fashioned from existing knowledge. Innovative behaviors and innovative outcomes have known components. The challenge in innovating is to extrapolate from the known to the unknown.

The innovative process can produce things new to all humankind or just the uninformed, including the innovator. However, it is the production of innovations new to all humankind that is primarily responsible for humans' superior control of the environment. Environmental control increases as each succeeding generation produces new innovations and passes them on the next. Moreover, the nation that leads in the production and application of innovations gains greater superiority and control over other nations.

A suggested format for innovating is as follows:

INNOVATING DESIRED OUTCOMES

To innovate desired outcomes, (1) the attributes of the desired outcome to be achieved are specified and (2) constraints enumerating limitations that must be taken into account and side effects to be avoided in achieving the desired outcome are specified.

Innovating Behavior

To innovate behavior to achieve outcomes, (1) factors that must be controlled to achieve the outcome are enumerated, (2) constraints that need to be dealt with when controlling the factors are specified, (3) means of controlling the factors are determined from memory and through research, and (4) prescribed innovative behavior is derived from the information gleaned from steps (1), (2), and (3).

It should be mentioned that the means of innovating behavior was taken from Stage 1 and Stage 2 of the Prediction and Problem-Solving Cycle in Chapter 5. Also, constraints are taken into account whether one is innovating outcomes or behavior. The following simplified examples show how the proposed format is applied to produce the three types of innovations mentioned previously.

Innovating New Outcomes Using Known Behavior

The problem addressed is: Too many people die of cancer (existing state). There is a need to reduce the number of deaths caused by cancer (desired state).

- Desired innovative outcome: A cure for cancer

  Attributes of the desired outcome:

     1. Cancer growth is reduced.

     2. Patients stop suffering.

3. Patients return to their daily routines.

4. There are no remissions.

Constraint(s):

5. Patients must be able to tolerate side effects.

- Known behavior: Scientific method

The effectiveness of potential cancer cures is tested by means of the scientific method.

Consider a second example, in which the problem addressed is to increase the revenue of a state by establishing a lottery (desired state) in a state where there is no lottery (existing state).

- Desired innovative outcome: Enacting a state lottery

Attributes of the desired outcome:

1. The lottery must make a profit for the state.

2. Out-of-state residents can participate.

3. Personnel, space, and equipment to conduct a lottery must be provided.

4. There must be guards against cheating.

Constraint(s):

5. Profits are to be invested in education.

6. Minors are to be prohibited from participating.

- Known behavior: Follow existing state legislative procedures for enacting laws.

Innovating New Behavior to Achieve a Known Outcome

The problem being addressed is the weight of a person weighing 180 pounds (existing state) who wants to weigh 160 pounds (desired state).

- Desired known outcome: Weight loss

Attributes of the outcome:

1. Loss of 20 pounds

2. Smaller clothes fit

Constraint(s):

3. Within six months

- Innovative behavior: Developing a new personalized diet regimen.

Research is conducted to obtain the following data.

Factors to be controlled:

Relevant research might reveal that the factors necessary to control are:

1. Calorie intake

2. Calorie expenditure

Constraint(s):

Maintenance of health

Means of controlling the factors:

1. Calorie intake: reduced nutrients

2. Calorie expenditure: increased exercise

3. Maintenance of health: intake of nutritious food and drink, plus avoidance of overly strenuous exercise

Prescribed innovative behavior:

Research might suggest the following somewhat innovative strategy. The strategy is innovative in that, although means of controlling the factors are already known, it provides for a different means of controlling them.

1. Calorie intake: a reduced calorie and low-fat, high-fiber diet.

2. Calorie expenditure: an hour of exercise each day.

3. Maintenance of health: providing for a balanced diet with a vitamin supplement as well as provision for prolonged rather than stressful exercise. A doctor might also monitor the person during the regimen.

Having derived the ingredients of a weight-loss regimen, specific procedures for administering the regimen would be developed.

Consider another example in which a class of students innovates behavior to achieve a known outcome. The problem being addressed is: 20% of a class completes their homework on time (existing state). The teacher wants all of the students to complete their homework on time (desired state).

• Desired known outcome: Class to improve its record of completing homework on time.

Attributes of the outcome:

1. An 80% improvement in the number of students who complete their homework on time.

2. All students are to be able to complete assigned homework in the allotted time.

Constraint(s): Improvement is to be achieved by midterm.

• Innovative behavior: Developing new class rules to improve the time it takes the class to complete homework assignments.

Factors to be controlled:

1. The amount of time students are allowed to complete assignments.

2. Readiness of students to complete assignments.

3. Penalties for homework completed late.

Constraint(s):

Homework must be assigned to help students achieve each learning objective.

Means of controlling the factors:

Formulate rules that control the three factors.

Prescribed innovative behavior:

It was determined that innovative rules would be formulated to:

1. Allow more time for completion of homework.

2. Provide tutoring for students who are not academically ready to complete an assignment.

3. Provide for penalties for late homework assignments.

4. Specify the number of homework assignments required to help students achieve each learning objective.

These innovations were predicted to achieve the objective.

After students are taught procedures for innovating outcomes and behaviors, they might be assigned the task of innovating outcomes and behaviors on their own for practice. Table 9.3 provides examples of innovations students might create.

Innovating New Behaviors to Achieve Innovative Outcomes

To illustrate how new behaviors are innovated to achieve new outcomes, we can continue with the example introduced earlier. The problem to be addressed is: Air transportation is inefficient (existing state). Air transportation needs to be more efficient (desired state).

- Desired innovative outcome: A better aircraft for transporting humans.

  Attributes of the desired outcome:

    1. Flies faster

    2. Is more maneuverable

  Constraint(s): The safety of passengers must be provided for.

- Innovative behavior: Developing specifications, plans, and procedures for building the aircraft and executing the procedures.

  Factors to be controlled:

Table 9.3
Innovations

Innovative Behaviors (Procedures)	Innovative Outcomes (Products)
1. New recipe	1. New toy
2. New pattern to make a dress	2. New game
3. New formula for a perfume	3. New song
4. New plan or blueprint for a house or a car	4. New sculpture
5. New route to work or school	5. New painting
6. New manufacturing methods to produce products	6. New story
7. New arrangement of a song	7. New poem
8. New research method	8. New model airplane or car
9. New rules to enact laws	9. New exercise equipment
10. New art process	10. New knowledge
11. New law enforcement procedures	11. New plant
12. New communication method	12. New animal
13. New transportation method	13. New cloth
14. New routine for organizing gear	14. New clothing
15. New diet	15. New container (e.g., bookbag)
16. New academic sanctions for failing students	16. New organizer
17. New grading system (for meats, for school)	17. New principle (e.g., cause–effect relationship)
18. New testing method	18. New rainwear
19. New dance routine	19. New fastener (e.g., pins, clips)
20. New filing system	20. New musical instrument
21. New planning system	21. New hat
22. New computer program	22. New swimming and beach accessories (e.g., flippers, raft, water wings)
23. New display system	23. New playpen or car seat for children
24. New car washing system	24. New advertisement
25. New entertainment system	25. New package
26. New study method	26. New chalkboard, cleaner
	27. New test

It was known to the Wright brothers that particular factors needed to be controlled to enable humans to fly: (1) lift, (2) thrust, and (3) maneuverability—an aircraft must be able to (1) lift humans off the ground, (2) thrust them through the air, and (3) be maneuvered.

Constraint(s):

A budgetary limitation

Means of controlling each factor:

Factor 1, lift: fixed wings, rotor, gas lighter than air.

Factor 2, thrust: wind, propeller, jet, rocket.

Factor 3, maneuverability: rudder, ailerons.

Research would indicate that lift can be created by using gas lighter than air, rotors, and fixed wings. Thrust can be created by the wind, engine-driven propellers, jet engines, and rockets. Maneuverability can be attained through the use of rudders and ailerons. Balloons, rockets, and toy aircraft had been invented before the Wright brothers invented the airplane. They were aware of the means of controlling the factors that were required.

Prescribing innovative behavior:

The Wright brothers had reason to believe that their innovative conception of the airplane would provide for improved control of the factors. The airplane provides for greater control over lift, thrust, and maneuverability by using an engine-driven propeller to create thrust, fixed wings to create lift, and a rudder and ailerons to obtain maneuverability. Although their airplane was of no practical value at the time it was invented, when compared to the balloon, it was possible to predict that the airplane would become a superior form of human air travel. This was because the airplane provided for greater control of lift, thrust, and maneuverability. The engine-driven propeller was superior to the wind in providing thrust, the fixed wing provided superior lift, and the ailerons in addition to the rudder provided greater maneuverability. Also the airplane provided potentially greater safety than the hydrogen balloons used at the time. So the Wright brothers had reason to predict that producing their conception of the airplane could improve human air travel.

Having derived a way to improve control of the factors that needed to be controlled, procedures would be developed and implemented to produce an example of the innovative aircraft as conceived.

After students practice innovating new behaviors to achieve known outcomes and innovating new outcomes using known behaviors, it may be advisable for them to practice the more difficult task of innovating new behavior to achieve new outcomes.

This concludes our suggestions for teaching students how to innovate. The prescribed format for innovating can be incorporated in the prediction and problem-solving process described in Chapter 5, once students have learned the process. The advantage of doing this is that the prediction and problem-solving process prescribes how to produce innovations by successive approximation when students fail to produce an innovation on their first attempt—and most often students do not succeed in producing an innovation on their first attempt.

Hopefully, from the presentation in this chapter you have come to appreciate the importance of innovation to American leadership in the world and the importance of teaching students to innovate. Even the most conservative people desire to be creative and to learn how to create new products and procedures, even though the innovations they generate are not earth-shaking. In everyday life, when people are stymied and standard operating procedures they know do not work, they are challenged to innovate a solution. Their innovation may be as mundane as a new recipe, a slight improvement in their household budget, fixing the leg of a lopsided table, designing a new sweater to knit, writing a poem, essay, short story, novel, or new lyrics to a well-known tune, or drawing a caricature of an amusing person. People quite naturally seek novelty and challenge when they are bored and often engage in innovative expression, if only in the form of doodling.

Students welcome opportunities to be innovative, if only to counterbalance the conformist, ritualistic behavior they are required to learn in acquiring the basic social skills they are taught in school. But desire to be innovative extends beyond the need to escape from monotonous, rote learning when students are required to memorize the alphabet or multiplication tables. People find their own innovative expression enjoyable in itself. Even two-year-olds are elated with the stool they create when they see it in the toilet. And as people mature and their innovative capacity increases, they take pleasure in all forms of innovative expression.

In addition to stressing the importance of innovation to American superiority, the desire of people to innovate, and the need to teach people to innovate, an attempt was made to design a program to teach students how to innovate. The program is admittedly rudimentary and designed to be improved with application and experience. Refinements and elaborations are needed.

In closing, we need to focus on the challenge to education, that is, to teach students how to innovate in all subject areas and in their daily living. In teaching academic subjects students can first be taught about the innovators and their innovative contributions in the subject area; then they can be taught to generate their own innovations in the subject area, as simple as they may be at first.

REFERENCE

Slottje, D. J., Scully, G. W., Hirschberg, J. G., & Hayes, K. J. (1991). *Measuring quality of life across countries*. Boulder, CO: Westview Press.

Appendix:
Statistical Data Supporting
Conclusions of Preschool Research

The following summaries of statistical findings of research studies on instructional strategies described in Chapter 8 are reported in alphabetical order.

Carnine (1977)
Table 1
Mean Correct Responses for the Sounds and Word Treatments on the Transfer Test

Treatment Group	Test Type		
	Regular Words	**Novel Words**	**Letter Sounds**
Phonics	5.5	0.6	8.0
Look-Say	1.7	0.0	4.7

Total number of test words = 6; total number of letters = 8.

Comparisons:			
t value	5.59	3.24	5.08
df	19	19	19
p	< .001	< .01	< .001

Notes: p = level of significance; df = degrees of freedom.

Hong (1996)
Table 2
Assessments of Mathematics Achievement for Experimental and Control Groups

	Experimental Group[a]		Control Group[b]			
Measure	M	SD	M	SD	t	p
Pretest	30.03	7.97	29.96	7.81	1.47	.15
Posttest	31.68	6.55	31.00	6.91	0.37	.71
Classification	25.47	13.86	14.90	8.17	2.16	.041
Number	2.83	0.37	1.99	0.79	4.34	.000
Shape	11.91	3.86	8.29	2.23	3.15	.004
Spatial Sense	9.70	2.36	10.02	2.01	−0.45	.65

Notes: [a]n = 29; [b]n = 28; M = mean; SD = standard deviation; t = t value; p = level of significance.

Lawton & Fowell (1978)
Table 3
Mean Scores on Math Concept Attainment Tasks

Treatment Group	n	Pretest[a]	SD	Posttest[a]	SD
Experimental	24	8.13	6.57	15.70	6.16
Control	12	7.00	6.63	9.92	7.02

Notes: [a]Total possible score = 24; n = the number of children in each group; SD = standard deviation.

Table 4
T-test Scores for Pre- and Posttests

	Pretest			Posttest		
Treatment Group	t	df	p	t	df	p
Experimental vs. control	.53	35	n.s.	2.98	35	.01

Notes: t = t value; df = degrees of freedom; p = level of significance; n.s. = not significant.

Stipek et al. (1995)
Table 5
Mean Scores by Grade and Program Type

Achievement	Didactic			Child-Centered		
	P[a]	K[b]	Total	P[c]	K[d]	Total
Letters/Reading	24.55	29.95	27.13	19.07	27.32	21.89
Numbers	24.42	33.45	28.93	24.46	34.64	27.94

Notes: P = Preschool; K = Kindergarten; [a]n = 60; [b]n = 61; [c]n = 61; [d]n = 30.
No p value was provided in the text of the study to support the finding of a significant difference between Didactic and Child-Centered programs for letters/reading achievement.

Toyama, Lee, and Muto (1997)
Table 6
Percentage of Children Who Gave Correct, Incorrect, and Non-Explanations for Meaning and Prediction Questions About "Separating" and "Cutting" Procedures

	Meaning		Prediction	
	P (n = 20)	N (n = 21)	P (n = 20)	N (n = 21)
Separating a duck and a rabbit				
Correct	65	5	55	5
Incorrect	35	57	35	62
No response	0	38	10	35
Cutting a whole carrot				
Correct	80	9	75	19
Incorrect	20	71	25	57
No response	0	19	0	24

Notes: P = Participant group; N = Non-Participant group; n = the number of subjects in a group. "Separating Species" Meaning: Chi-Square(1) = 16.5, p < .01. Prediction: Chi-Square(1) = 12.5, p < .01. "Cutting Foods" Meaning: Chi-Square(1) = 20.7, p < .01. Prediction: Chi-Square(1) = 12.9, p < .01.

Appendix

Table 7
Percentage of Children Who Gave Biological, Other, and Non-Explanations for Meaning Questions About "Covering" and "Taking Out" Procedures

	Covering		Taking Out	
	P **(n = 20)**	**N** **(n = 21)**	**P** **(n = 20)**	**N** **(n = 21)**
Biological	40	0	55	9
Other	55	71	45	71
No response	5	29	0	19

Notes: P = Participant group; N = Non-Participant group; n = the number of subjects in a group. "Covering": Chi-Square(1) = 9.0, p < .01. "Taking Out": Chi-Square(1) = 9.8, p < .01.

Index of Researchers

Note: Because some index entries pertain to summarized topics, in some cases the author's name may not appear on the page(s) listed below.

Subject Index

About the Author

MYLES I. FRIEDMAN is Distinguished Professor Emeritus of Education at the University of South Carolina. A renowned educator and author, Dr. Friedman's books include *Rational Behavior, Teaching Reading and Thinking Skills, Improving Teacher Education: Resources and Recommendations, Teaching Higher Order Thinking Skills to Gifted Students, Taking Control: Vitalizing Education*, and, with Steven P. Fisher, *Handbook on Effective Instructional Strategies: Evidence for Decision-Making*. He has spent more than 20 years conducting and applying research to improve education.